Leviticus

INTERPRETATION

A Bible Commentary for Teaching and Preaching

INTERPRETATION

A BIBLE COMMENTARY FOR TEACHING AND PREACHING

James Luther Mays, *Series Editor*
Patrick D. Miller, *Old Testament Editor*
Paul J. Achtemeier, *New Testament Editor*

SAMUEL E. BALENTINE

Leviticus

INTERPRETATION

A Bible Commentary
for Teaching and Preaching

John Knox Press
LOUISVILLE

Scripture quotations from the New Revised Standard Version of the Bible are copyright © 1989 by the Division of Christian Education of the National Council of the Churches of Christ in the U.S.A. and are used by permission.

Excerpt from *The Torah's Vision of Worship* by Samuel E. Balentine, copyright © 1999 Augsburg Fortress. Used by permission.

Submitted excerpt from "Just As the Winged Energy of Delight" from *Selected Poems of Rainer Maria Rilke,* Edited and Translated by Robert Bly, Copyright © 1981 by Robert Bly. Reprinted by permission of HarperCollins Publishers Inc.

Excerpt from Poem 1958 "Who is it seeks my pillow nights" is reprinted by permission of the publishers and the Trustees of Amherst College from *The Poems of Emily Dickinson,* Thomas H. Johnson, ed., Cambridge, Mass.: The Belknap Press of Harvard University Press, Copyright © 1951, 1955, 1979 by the President and Fellows of Harvard College.

Excerpt from R. S. Thomas's "The Kingdom" is reprinted by permission of the University of Arkansas Press. Copyright 1972 by R. S. Thomas.

A catalog record for this book is available from the Library of Congress.
0-8042-3103-6

© Copyright Samuel E. Balentine 2002
This book is printed on acid-free paper that meets the American National Standards Institute Z39.48 standard. ♾
02 03 04 05 06 07 08 09 10 11 — 10 9 8 7 6 5 4 3 2 1
Printed in the United States of America
John Knox Press
Louisville, Kentucky

SERIES PREFACE

This series of commentaries offers an interpretation of the books of the Bible. It is designed to meet the need of students, teachers, ministers, and priests for a contemporary expository commentary. These volumes will not replace the historical critical commentary or homiletical aids to preaching. The purpose of this series is rather to provide a third kind of resource, a commentary which presents the integrated result of historical and theological work with the biblical text.

An interpretation in the full sense of the term involves a text, an interpreter, and someone for whom the interpretation is made. Here, the text is what stands written in the Bible in its full identity as literature from the time of "the prophets and apostles," the literature which is read to inform, inspire, and guide the life of faith. The interpreters are scholars who seek to create an interpretation which is both faithful to the text and useful to the church. The series is written for those who teach, preach, and study the Bible in the community of faith.

The comment generally takes the form of expository essays. It is planned and written in the light of the needs and questions which arise in the use of the Bible as Holy Scripture. The insights and results of contemporary scholarly research are used for the sake of the exposition. The commentators write as exegetes and theologians. The task which they undertake is both to deal with what the texts say and to discern their meaning for faith and life. The exposition is the unified work of one interpreter.

The text on which the comment is based is the Revised Standard Version of the Bible and, since its appearance, the New Revised Standard Version. The general availability of these translations makes the printing of a text in the commentary unnecessary. The commentators have also had other current versions in view as they worked and refer to their readings where it is helpful. The text is divided into sections appropriate to the particular book; comment deals with passages as a whole, rather than proceeding word by word, or verse by verse.

Writers have planned their volumes in light of the requirements set by the exposition of the book assigned to them. Biblical books differ in character, content, and arrangement. They also differ in the way they have been and are used in the liturgy, thought, and devotion of the church. The distinctiveness and use of particular books have been taken into account in decisions about the approach, emphasis, and use of space in the commentaries. The goal has been to allow writers to develop the format which provides for the best presentation of their interpretation.

The result, writers and editors hope, is a commentary which both explains and applies, an interpretation which deals with both the meaning and the significance of biblical texts. Each commentary reflects, of course, the writer's own approach and perception of the church and world. It could and should not be otherwise. Every interpretation of any kind is individual in that sense; it is one reading of the text. But all who work at the interpretation of Scripture in the church need the help and stimulation of a colleague's reading and understanding of the text. If these volumes serve and encourage interpretation in that way, their preparation and publication will realize their purpose.

The Editors

PREFACE

I am deeply grateful to James L. Mays for the invitation to contribute this volume to such a distinguished series as *Interpretation* and to the staff of John Knox Press for the care with which they prepared the manuscript for publication. I wish also to express appreciation to Baptist Theological Seminary at Richmond (BTSR) for supporting my work with a sabbatical leave, to my students at BTSR who joined me in serious conversation about Leviticus, and especially to my faithful student assistant, Woody Jenkins, who offered enormous help in tracking down and retrieving bibliographical materials. As always, my wife, Betty, and my children, Graham and Lauren, have blessed and sustained my work by their unflagging patience and love. Without them, I would not know where to begin, let alone how to complete, anything I do.

This work is dedicated to David Nelson Duke, my best friend and most faithful conversation partner for more than twenty years. In his living and in his dying, David taught me more than anyone in this world about the importance of the rituals of faith that bind us so resolutely to each other and to God. Among the last words we shared together as he embarked on his ascent into "life forevermore" were those of Psalm 133. With these words, he was and remains anointed, grieved, and blessed. Surely the Talmud is right to remind us that "when the dead are quoted, their lips move." In the assurance of this discernment, I take comfort from the abiding vision of David's smile.

Hanukkah 5762
December 18, 2001

For David (1950–2000)

A Song of Ascents
How very good and pleasant it is
   when [brothers] live together in unity!
It is like the precious oil on the head,
   running down upon the beard of Aaron,
   running down upon the collar of his robes.
It is like the dew of Hermon,
   which falls on the mountains of Zion.
For there the LORD ordained his blessing,
   life forevermore.
               —Psalm 133

CONTENTS

Introduction

Of the many challenges that come with the commission to write a commentary on Leviticus, perhaps the biggest is the introduction. How is one to introduce a book such as this, especially if the goal of an introduction is to invite a durable relationship between readers and text? The challenge is more formidable, not less, because of the stated objective of this series, which is to provide commentaries "for those who teach, preach, and study the Bible in the community of faith," commentaries that both "explain" the meaning and "apply" the significance of biblical texts. How best to accomplish this when the book to be introduced is Leviticus? To put a sharp edge on this question, how does one "explain" and "apply" a book that devotes seven chapters to the bewildering, if not seemingly bizarre, requirements of ancient Israel's sacrificial system and five chapters to details of ritual impurity, including such indelicate matters as menstrual blood and semen?

An anecdotal experience provides one, but by no means the only, clue to the challenge. At the beginning of the research for writing this book, I went to a large bookstore in Richmond, Virginia, to purchase a commentary on Leviticus by a distinguished scholar, a volume in a highly regarded series that I did not have in my personal library. When I did not find the book on the shelves, I asked a clerk to check the inventory, only to learn that the store had sold but one copy in eight years. That copy had been the one shipped automatically because of the store's standing subscription to the series. Apparently, once that copy had been sold, there had not been a single request for this commentary, hence no need to replace it on the shelves, until I appeared.

I recount this incident not to call attention to some new trend in the marketability of biblical commentaries. It is not news to report that commentaries—on any biblical book—seldom appear on the *New York Times Book Review* "Best Sellers" list. The incident is telling, nevertheless, because it strengthens a strong suspicion, which resurfaces each time I see the curious expression on the faces of persons to whom I've just reported that I was writing a book on Leviticus. Despite many earnestly glib responses from pastors, such as "I really do need to beef up my sermon file on Leviticus," my strong impression is that even in the depressed market for biblical commentaries, this particular book is a leading candidate for a not-so-distinguished recognition: It is perhaps the most neglected of the neglected biblical books. Whatever our best intentions, all the evidence indicates that the book of Leviticus has made little dent in the way we "teach, preach, and study the Bible in the community of faith." We might appropriate one of the "imperfect sympathies" of Charles Lamb, the English essayist and literary critic who helped introduce to the world such important contemporaries as Coleridge and Wordsworth: "I have been trying all my life to like Scotchmen, and am obliged to desist from the experiment in despair" (Lamb, p. 152). To be charitable, were we to substitute "Leviticus" for "Scotchmen," the judgment might still be only half right.

How, then, should an introduction to Leviticus proceed? Will the challenge of inviting the audience for this series into a reading and thinking relationship with this book be addressed by confirming that the Hebrew text of Leviticus has been very well preserved (cf. Hartley, pp. xxix–xxx; Levine, *Leviticus*, pp. xix–xxi; Wenham, pp. 13–15)? That the variations in the versions, for example, the Septuagint and the Samaritan Pentateuch, and in the fragments preserved from Qumran (4QLev and 11QLev), are interesting but mostly insignificant? Will the incentive for recognizing the authority of the commandments in Leviticus be enhanced by making a case, along the lines so vigorously argued by J. Milgrom, that the Priestly tradents of this book should be located in the pre-exilic period (*Leviticus 1–16*, pp. 3–35)? That Wellhausen's conventional and largely negative assessment of the Priestly tradition as representative of Judaism's deterioration into a ritualistic religion that is no more than a lingering "ghost of a life which is closed"—for more than a century so dominant in biblical studies—must now be turned on its head (Wellhausen, p. 405)? If readers are shown from a survey of the history of interpretation that Leviticus has remained a staple for both Jewish and Christian commentators, albeit for different reasons, from the second century B.C.E. to the twenty-first century, will they be persuaded not to abandon the book soon after they wade into its first chapters (cf. Hartley, pp. xliii–lvi; Milgrom, *Leviticus 1–16*, pp. 63–66; Levine, *Leviticus*, pp. 215–38)? Judging by the clerk's report and the responses to my work from friends and colleagues, I am inclined to believe the answer to these questions is "No, probably not."

Perhaps another approach is in order. Toward this end, the introduction that follows singles out three broad matters that provide a beginning point for reading this commentary. It is important to acknowledge at the outset that these issues are not offered as a substitute for the important and still instructive introductory information found in other commentaries. Indeed, what is highlighted here is in many respects not only dependent on but also culled from the disciplined and creative scholarship of those who have been my teachers in reading Leviticus. In the wake of their work, what follows may be described with the analogy of simply rearranging the furniture in a house already long occupied. Even so, as every potential home owner knows, envisioning how to rearrange what you see to make it more hospitable for your own dwelling is often an important part of deciding whether to make the purchase or not.

Reading and Appropriating Ritual Texts

It may defy caution to lead with a discussion of ritual, for much of modern biblical study, especially as practiced by Protestants, has long been characterized by a negative, often hostile attitude toward this subject (Gorman, "Ritual Studies and Biblical Studies"). And yet, the opening chapters of Leviticus (1–7), with their detailed instructions on sacrifices, immediately demand the reader's attention to just these matters. In truth, these demands only escalate as the book continues its invitation into the rituals of ordination (chaps. 8–10), the rituals of purity/impurity (chaps. 11–15), and the rituals of purification or atonement (chap. 16). It is therefore with good reason that J. Milgrom notes that the theology of Leviticus is not expressed in the biblically conventional form of pronouncements; it is instead embedded in rituals. In his words, "every act, whether movement, manipulation, or gesticulation, is pregnant with meaning" (Milgrom, *Leviticus 1–16*, p. 42). In the modern world, where the very word *ritual* conveys to many the notion of something old, ceremonial, and likely superstitious—such as stepping over a crack in the sidewalk or refusing to walk under a ladder—how are we to find a positive place in our religious sensibilities for immersion into a book like Leviticus?

F. Gorman has shown that Leviticus requires a different approach than we bring to other biblical texts, where narrative rather than ritual laws typically conveys the message. For ritual texts like Leviticus, the interpreter must broaden the exegetical task beyond traditional historical-critical preoccupations with questions of authorship, setting, form, and transmission of *texts* in order to focus on the meaning of the *ritual* the text conveys. Because all ritual is a form of social drama, ritual analysis requires that interpreters seek to "discover the worldview that stands behind the ritual, that gives rise to the rituals, that is enacted and made real in the rituals" (Gorman, *Ideology of Ritual*, p. 15). What is required is an imaginative construal of both the rituals described in the text—their gestural acts and symbolic words—and how their enactment has meaning within a specific understanding of the world.

3

With Gorman and others we may understand that the worldview underlying priestly rituals rests on two crucial beliefs (Gorman, *Ideology of Ritual*, pp. 39–60; *Divine Presence and Community*, pp. 4–5, 14–16). The first is the conviction that God has created the world and purposefully designed the rhythmic orders that keep it tuned to its capacity to be "very good." Carefully differentiated categories and boundaries, for example, earth/heaven, day/night, land/water, animals/humans, provide for harmonious relationships between God and all parts of God's creation. As long as this order is actualized and sustained, the world and everything in it prospers. When this order is neglected or violated, creation succumbs to chaos, and the harmony between God and world is fractured.

The second priestly conviction is that God's *creational order* is generative of and sustained by human observance of an imaging *ritual order*. This ritual order is manifest in the litany of the primordial week, when through *seven* commands God speaks into being a cosmic order that finds its culmination in the observance of the Sabbath day (Gen.1:1–2:4a). This primordial design provides the foundation for the liturgy of covenant making, when God's *seven* commands (Exodus 25–31) and Israel's *seven* acts of compliance (Exod. 40:17–33) bring into existence a cultic order centered in the tabernacle, which provides God's holy residence in the midst of a fragile world. Leviticus sustains the liturgy of covenant, and with it the abiding vision of creation's purposeful design, by repeatedly tying its rituals to the same founding heptadic pattern (see below). In sum, the ritual order, like the cosmic order, establishes the boundaries and categories that enable a holy God to dwell in the midst of a world vulnerable to sin and defilement. When these rituals are faithfully enacted, God's presence is palpably available; when they are ignored or breached, God's sacred space on earth is compromised, and the harmony between God and the world is subverted. As Gorman puts it, because rituals are grounded in creation theology, they have the capacity to become a "means of world construction" (*Ideology of Ritual*, p. 59).

Rituals are, however, more than ways for *thinking* about the world. They are fundamentally concerned with concrete ways to conceptualize and thus to *enact* or *body forth* the world *as it is* or *as it should be*. Priestly rituals, therefore, seek not only to reinforce existing assumptions about the world's order and structure. They seek also to critique status quo ways of seeing and living in the world and to alter them, in accordance with God's abiding vision, by embodying different models of behavior that bring *what is* into conformity with God's hopes and expectations for *what should be*.

4

In this connection, it is instructive to consider the work of C. Geertz, who has argued that the sacred rituals of religion provide models both *of* and *for* reality (Geertz, "Religion as a Cultural System," pp. 90–94). For example, building a house enacts a plan that has already been established in the blueprint; the house is a *model of* the preconceived plan, which its construction now makes apprehensible. But the blueprint is also a symbol, and in its own way it provides a *model for* conceptualizing and thus bringing into existence a house that does not yet exist. We may appropriate this analogy with respect to the priestly understanding of the tabernacle. On the one hand, the tabernacle, which, according to Exodus, Moses "finished" just as "God finished the work" of creation (Exod. 40:33; cf. Gen. 2:2), is envisioned as a completion of God's primordial blueprint of the world. On the other hand, when the tabernacle is defiled by the sins of Israel, the rituals of the annual Day of Purification (Leviticus 16) body forth behavior that symbolically, yet tangibly, becomes a model for re-creating a vision that is yet to be fully realized but still *should be* and, more important, *can be*.

Finally, rituals are a principal means by which communities of faith engage in a distinctive kind of theological reflection. Gorman has called attention to the important contribution rituals make to traditional, especially Protestant, ways of doing theology. He notes that although "human existence is marked as much by enactment as by thought and reflection," much of Protestant theology has typically privileged the latter rather than the former (Gorman, "Ritual Studies and Biblical Studies," p. 24). By inculcating worship patterns that emphasize mind over body, word over deed, and rational thought over "merely" reflexive sacramental systems, all legacies of the Protestant Reformation, religious communities learn to be at home in the cognitive, typically abstract world of theological ideas. Ritual invites something different: the active participation in "embodied" theological reflection. Both the knowing and the learning of theology come from performing the ritual act itself. Through rituals, persons engage in very specific flesh-and-blood acts. They engage mind and body. They take a stand in the world by acting upon what they believe and what they aspire to believe. In so doing, they enact theological exegesis in a way that moves them from cognitive apprehension to concrete execution of God's design for the world.

"Speak to the People of Israel"

Introductions typically note that the Hebrew name for this book, "and he called" (*wayyiqra*ʾ), comes from the ancient practice of calling a book by its first word. The English title "Leviticus" comes from the Vulgate, *Levitikon*, which in turn reflects the Septuagint understanding that the book is addressed to "Levites" or, more generally speaking, to priests. The translators' choice of words invites an unfortunate, if unintentional, false impression of what this book is all about. On the one hand, the term *Levites* appears only once in the book, and this in a brief passage (25:32–34) that has little to do with their priestly responsibilities. On the other, the suggestion that the book addresses Levitical or priestly concerns becomes too easily ensnared in the web of negative presuppositions common among some Christians about anything to do with priests, Levites, or, still more broadly, Sadducees and Pharisees, presuppositions tied at least in part, it must be admitted, to the New Testament (see, for example, the Gospel of Matthew's frequent equation of Sadducees and Pharisees with "hypocrites"). E. Gerstenberger has pointedly described the long and sad reach of such presuppositions in the Christian tradition as follows:

> Christian tradition has often arrogantly distanced itself from the sacrificial practices of the Old Testament, and has strictly rejected the ceremonial legislation of the Jews. It has rendered suspicious and disparaged the Jews' entire practice of worship as well as their devotion, and through such religious slander has prepared the ground for discrimination and persecution. Perhaps the annihilation camps of the Nazi period would not have been so easily possible without this centuries-long poisoning of the religious climate and the destruction of the religious soul of the Jewish people. (Gerstenberger, p. 15)

Gerstenberger's remarks may well strike readers as both extreme and unjustified. He does not suggest, nor do I, that a causal line of connection can be drawn between the ancient translators' choice of words for the title of this book and the Nazi death camps. The reasons for the church's attitudes toward Leviticus and Judaism more generally are complex and involve a wide range of issues, a good many of them falling under the umbrella of the general antipathy toward anything having to do with ritual, as has been mentioned above. Even so, there is no denying that once this book became primarily associated with the priests, a way was opened for its neglect, misreading, and, at worst, abuse within the Christian tradition.

One particularly instructive example of the church's disparagement of things associated with ancient Israel's priests is J. Colenso's *Lectures on the Pentateuch and the Moabite Stone*. (I have referenced this work in another context, and it remains to my mind one of the more revealing illustrations of what the label "priestly" has meant in some circles of biblical scholarship and thus derivatively in the church; see Balentine, pp. 70–76.) As the bishop of Natal, Colenso's stated objective in writing about the Pentateuch was to offer guidance to those in the church "who desire to impart to their children an intelligent knowledge of the real nature of these books, which have filled all along, and still fill, so prominent a part in the religious education of the race" (Colenso, p. vii.). The most important result of biblical scholarship he wished to impart was the "death blow" struck by Pentateuchal criticism to the whole sacerdotal system presented in the books of Exodus, Leviticus, and Numbers. This ritualistic system, Colenso argues, which J. Wellhausen had claimed was not of Mosaic origin, contains nothing more than late, fictitious "pretensions of the very numerous body of priests, lording it over the consciences of the comparatively small number of devoted laity" (Colenso, p. 373). This priestly "fraud," which Colenso characterizes with the words of Zech. 13:3 as "lies" spoken in the name of God, has far-reaching and evil consequences for Christianity. In his judgment, once the priestly yoke was fastened upon the neck of the people,

> true spiritual life became at last deadened in them, and so, when the Great Prophet came, they blinded their eyes and stopped their ears, that the Truth might not reach them, and the multitude *urged on by the priests* cried, "Crucify him! Crucify him!" and "the voices of them and of the chief priests prevailed." (Colenso, p. 346; emphasis added)

By any measure, Colenso's sharply negative characterization of the priestly legacy—"pretensions," "fraud," "lies"—and his easy connection between the priests who killed Israel's religion and those who instigated the crucifixion of Jesus are a sad witness to the church's relationship with Judaism and its Scriptures. As unsettling as Gerstenberger's assessment may be, perhaps the time is long overdue for Christians to heed his counsel and acknowledge that we

> have been horribly ungrateful sons and daughters of our ancestors in faith (or are still). We have been glad to serve as the heirs of our parents in faith—without admitting it either to ourselves or to the world—while delivering them over to constables and henchmen. . . . Only with a composed and anxiety-free consideration of our own dependency on Jewish ceremonial law can we come to appreciate that *every community of faith develops rites and customs functionally comparable to those priestly-congregational regulations* from the sixth and fifth centuries B.C.E. (Gerstenberger, p. 16; emphasis added)

Gerstenberger's summons to the church to engage in an "anxiety-free consideration" of its dependency on the "priestly-congregational regulations" that comprise God's address in Leviticus to the "people of Israel" offers a useful way to return to the point I wish to make here. For all its concern with things priestly, Leviticus is in fact a book addressed to all the people of Israel; its objective is to emphasize the abiding

7

importance of the priestly-congregational partnership that keeps the community of faith, and the world it serves, in the center of God's will.

Toward this end, the first half of Leviticus (chaps. 1–16) provides ten *tôrôt,* or "commandments" (Milgrom, *Leviticus 1–16,* p. 2). The first five offer instructions concerning sacrifice: the burnt offering (6:2–6); the cereal offering (6:7–16); the purification offering (6:17–23); the reparation offering (7:1–7); and the well-being offering (7:11–21). The second five *tôrôt* provide instructions concerning impurity: animal carcasses (11:1–23, 41–42); childbirth (12:1–8); skin disease (13:1–59); purification from skin disease (14:1–57); and genital discharges (15:1–32). These ten *tôrôt* clearly have to do with priestly matters; indeed, it is fair to say that the first half of Leviticus is primarily addressed to the priests. But on close inspection, it is also apparent that they deal with the laity's responsibilities to be active participants, alongside the priests, in the maintenance of Israel's worship. The sacrifices must be offered at the holy sanctuary, where rituals at the altar require the special administration of the priests. But as the instructions in chapters 1–5 make abundantly clear, even the sacrificial system depends on the laity's faithful enactment of a range of requisite preparatory rites, including the selection and presentation of animals, hand-laying, slaughtering, and washing. If the priest serves as the laity's divinely commissioned agent at the altar, the laity also serve as the priest's divinely appointed partners in the preparation and execution of the sacrificial rituals, a point underscored by the repeated inclusion of the laity in God's address (e.g., "Speak to the people of Israel" in 1:2; 4:2; 7:22). The impurity *tôrôt* depend on the priests, who are charged with the responsibility to teach the people how to distinguish "between the holy and the common, and between the unclean and the clean" (10:10–11). But by the same token, these *tôrôt* address not the rituals of the sanctuary but instead the customs and practices of everyday life in the home and at the table, and in these domains, both laity and priests are charged with the responsibility of obedience. Without priests to teach them the *tôrôt,* the people cannot become the *priestly* kingdom God envisions (cf. Exod.19:6). And without obedience to the *tôrôt,* both inside and outside the sanctuary, neither the priests nor the laity can become the *holy* people that the commandments summon them to be.

The second half of the book extends the priestly-congregational emphasis, but in reverse proportions. Whereas chapters 1–16 address primarily the priests, the Holiness Code set forth in chapters 17–27 addresses primarily the laity. Apart from a block of instructions in Leviticus 21–22, very few of God's commands are addressed directly to the priests. The clarion summons to holiness set forth in these chap-

8

ters—"Be holy, for I the Lord your God am holy" (19:2)—calls each and every person in Israel to know that fidelity to God always requires more than priestly ritual. The command to be holy as God is holy necessarily means that neither priests nor laity may leave any aspect of life unexamined. Neither the "common" matters of everyday life outside the sanctuary—dietary concerns (17:1–16), sexual behavior (18:1–30), social ethics (19:1–37), family relations (20:10–21), and land ownership (25:1–55)—nor the "sacred" matters of worship (20:1–8), sacrifice (22:17–33), and the observance of holy days (23:1–44) can be neglected. In sum, what Leviticus envisions, as Milgrom discerns, is a *"partnership of trust* between the priest and the layman" (*Leviticus 1–16*, p. 56; emphasis added). Should either partner be unfaithful to the responsibilities God gives, the partnership fractures, and with it God's hopes and expectations for all the people. Colenso's assessment of priests "lording" their elitist position over the vulnerable consciences of the laity is more than a caricature of Leviticus. It is an interpretation that is representative of the "pretensions," the "frauds," and the "lies" he himself decries so vigorously.

Embedded in the priestly-congregational emphases of Leviticus is an additional and perhaps still more important understanding. Milgrom has helpfully contrasted priestly theology with basic religious understandings in other ancient cultures. Three premises undergird the practice of everyday religion in what he calls "pagan societies": (1) their deities are themselves dependent on and influenced by a metadivine realm; (2) this realm is the domain for the competition of numerous autonomous powers, some benevolent, some pernicious; and (3) if humans can tap into this realm, they can acquire the magical power to persuade the gods to do good rather than evil to them (Milgrom, *Leviticus 1–16*, p. 42). Priestly theology counters these premises with the conviction that there is one supreme God in whose divine realm there are no competing peers. Further, priestly theology abolishes the idea of a world full of demonic entities that must either be appeased or defended against through the exercise of magical powers. The only real power for evil is that which belongs to human beings. Milgrom makes the point as follows: "The forces pitted against each other in a cosmic struggle are no longer the benevolent and demonic deities who populate the mythologies of Israel's neighbors, but the forces of life and death set loose by man himself through his obedience to or defiance of God's commandments" (*Leviticus 1–16*, p. 47).

Ultimately, priestly theology dares to invest the full weight of its convictions on the firm belief that God was not wrong to create human beings in the divine image. To be sure, humans have the capacity to defile the sanctuary and drive a holy God out of a world no longer fit for divine habitation. And yet, in the providence of God they also have the capacity to purge the sanctuary through rituals and to cleanse the world through moral behavior, and by so doing to create new and still larger domains in which God's will may be realized. A crucial part of the priests' investment rests on a risky but well-tested theological girder. Because human beings are created in God's image, they have the assurance that even as *God is actively sanctifying them* for the task of living holy lives in this world (21:8, 15, 23; 22:9, 16, 32), they may also *sanctify themselves and the world* through the priestly-congregational partnership with which they have been entrusted. Upon this conviction, grounded in God's initial decision to speak the words "Let there be . . ." (Gen. 1:3), sustained by God's decision to instruct Moses to speak to all the people of Israel (Lev. 1:1–2), the book of Leviticus bets all of its theological capital.

Leviticus and the Torah's Vision of Worship

Both the rituals and the priestly-congregational emphases of Leviticus are presented as an integral part of what I have elsewhere referred to as the "Torah's vision of worship." (What follows reprises my earlier presentation; for an overview, see Balentine, pp. 59–77, and with specific attention to Leviticus, pp. 148–76.) I choose the word *vision* in order to acknowledge that the Torah imparts above all else a religious perspective, not a strictly historical or social one, of God, the world, and humankind's place in the world. Alongside other ways by which meaning may be construed, the religious perspective speaks with a distinctive voice and a peculiar orientation. Its capacity to create meaning in life derives from a faith perspective that tunes human action to truths that ask to be believed before they can be known. Religious truth does not, of course, exist in a cultural vacuum. It must vie for attention in a marketplace of competing perspectives that are forcefully and almost always persuasively tied to "given" social and political realities. Even so, as Geertz has discerned, the religious perspective is distinguished from its rivals by its claims to move "beyond the realities of everyday life to wider ones which correct and complete them." The pivot on which religion rests its appeal is its claim to know the difference between the "real" and the "really real" (Geertz, "Religion as a Cultural System," p. 112).

The Torah's religious perspective, what I call its vision of God, the world, and humankind, is clearly and inevitably *shaped by* the world(s) of its various writers, redactors, and tradents, to whom we conventionally assign the alphabetical sigla J (the Yahwist source), E (the Elohist source), D (the Deuteronomic source), and P (the Priestly source). At the first level, we may single out the Priestly source, which in its various redactions is responsible for the book of Leviticus, and know that

10

it is distinctively shaped by the preexilic world of the eighth century and, in its final form, by the world of the exile. At the second level, we may take it that the final form of the Pentateuch is shaped by the Persian period (539–333 B.C.E.), during which a relatively insignificant colony called Yehud carved out an existence within the given political realities of Persian hegemony. At both levels—the micro level of Leviticus and the macro level that defines its place within the Pentateuch—the Torah's vision makes the bold claim that its message reflects a wider reality, a transcendent ("really real") truth that corrects and completes the given ("real") historical and political realities. In the Torah's vision, this truth about God's ultimate intentions for the cosmos and for humankind is generated, sustained, and actualized through Israel's worship. Moreover, this worship, the Torah asserts, summons the community of faith into a distinctive way of living that has the capacity to *shape* the given world, thus to bring it ultimately into conformity with God's own vision of the world's potential to be "very good."

The Torah's vision of worship consists of three principal affirmations: (1) The invitation to worship is encoded in the liturgy of creation; (2) worship is itself a primary means of honoring, nurturing, and, when necessary, restoring God's creational design for the world; and (3) for a people called into relationship with God, worship is at the heart of community building and world construction. Each of these affirmations requires further exposition.

The invitation to worship is encoded in the liturgy of creation. In the Torah's vision, the creation of the world is part of a grand, cosmic liturgical celebration. The liturgy culminates on the seventh day (Gen. 2:1–3), which provides the primordial foundation for the Sabbath day (cf. Exod. 31:12–17). This day marks the intersection between the six days of God's creative work in purposefully shaping the world (Gen. 1:1–31) and the eighth and following days that define God's creative hopes for humankind on earth. In between the creation God has completed and the "creaturely creativity" (Fretheim, "Creator, Creature, and Co-Creation," p. 18) that God awaits, the seventh day is a day of celebration. The music that sustains the celebration beats to the established and lingering tune set by God's pronouncement: Everything is (and can remain) "very good" (Gen. 1:31).

The liturgy of creation is, however, too candid to suggest that worship joins God and humankind in perfect harmony. God's "very good" world is open to both the best and the worst that humans contribute; it is vulnerable to both human distortion and divine anguish (Gen. 6:5–7). And yet, even when God determines that the world no longer merits the affirmation "very good," God is ever responsive to acts of worship that hold the possibility for new beginnings. According to the Torah's

11

vision, it is Noah's altar, the first mentioned in Genesis, that marks the recession of the floodwaters and the uncovering of a cleansed earth (Gen. 8:20). It is Noah's ritual of speechless thanks that marks the change in God's heart from pain to promise. On the other side of this ritual, a new world emerges, this one anchored to a cosmic covenant that announces God's relentless intentions to stay in relationship with a fragile but ever-hopeful created order (Gen. 9:8–11). From this point onward, the world's abiding potential to be "very good," ever conflicted by the shifting balances between the human capacity for both good and evil, will be sustained by a new, often inexplicable, promise from God: "never again . . . never again" (Gen. 8:21; 9:11, 15).

Worship is itself a primary means of honoring, nurturing, and, when necessary, restoring God's creational design for the world. As the Torah understands creation to be the context in which God summons forth a primordial liturgy of worship, its concomitant focus on the tabernacle and its attendant rituals (Exodus 19–Numbers 10) envisions worship itself to be a constitutive act that sustains and reclaims God's intentions for the world. Inside the tabernacle and encoded in the rituals associated with it, Israel is empowered to sanctify time, space, objects, and persons in ways that reflect and honor God's own sanctification of creation.

One measure of this sanctification, as has been mentioned above, is the tabernacle's reflection of the heptadic foundation for creation itself. The theophany in which the instructions for building the tabernacle are revealed to Moses begins on the *seventh* day, following six days of preparation for entering the cloud of divine presence on Mount Sinai (Exod. 24:16); *seven* speeches from God provide the blueprint for building the tabernacle, each one distinguished by the introductory formula "The Lord spoke/said to Moses" (Exod. 25:1; 30:11, 17, 22, 34; 31:1, 12); the *seventh* speech (Exod. 31:12–17) culminates with instructions for observing the *Sabbath* day, which echoes the climax of the creational account of Gen. 1:1–2:4a. The building of the tabernacle begins with instructions concerning the *Sabbath* day (Exod. 35:2), then continues in successive chapters with repeating references to work completed "as the Lord commanded Moses," a phrase that occurs *seven* times in Exod. 40:17–33. Leviticus sustains and builds upon the same pattern: *Seven* speeches convey God's instructions for sacrifices (chaps. 1–7); *seven* acts comprise the ordination to the priesthood (chap. 8); a *seven*-day period is prescribed for bodily impurities (12:2; 15:19, 24); *seven*-plus-*one*-day purification rituals are prescribed for persons recovered from a skin disease (chap. 14); a *seven*fold aspersion ritual cleanses the sanctuary on the Day of Purification (16:11–19); *seven*-day festivals, *seven* "holy

12

days," the *seventh* month, and the *seventh* or sabbatical year (the jubilee year) comprise the ritual calendar (chaps. 23, 25).

The second and equally important measure of Israel's capacity to sanctify the world is the Torah's vision of a requisite commitment to justice, to which the rituals of worship remain inextricably connected. The Sinai pericope, Exodus 19–Numbers 10, envisions an eleven-month pause in Israel's journey toward Canaan, during which God invites the people into a liturgy of covenant making that spells out the laws and commandments that define the summons to be "a priestly kingdom and a holy nation" (Exod. 19:6). The Decalogue commands Israel both to love God absolutely (Exod. 20:3–7) and to live in the world with absolute fidelity to the nature and purposes of God (20:12–17). The center on which all the Decalogue's commandments converge is the commandment to keep the Sabbath day holy, for in doing so Israel images God's own sanctification of the world (20:11). The Book of the Covenant (Exod. 20:22–23:33) continues the emphasis on the centrality of worship for Israel's commitment to justice by rhetorically inverting the Decalogue's presentation. Whereas the Decalogue places the concern for worship at the center of its commandments, the Book of the Covenant begins and ends with basic stipulations regarding worship (20:22–26; 23:10–19), which in turn provide the context for the intervening laws governing the ethical, social, and moral requirements of communal behavior (21:1–23:9). From this point forward, once Israel declares its intentions—"All the words that the Lord has spoken we will do" (Exod. 24:3)—and the covenant with God is enacted, there can be no separation between the community's worship of God and its commitment to be stewards of justice in the world. Faithfulness to God must be enacted as faithful living in the world. In all aspects of life—in social issues of slavery, capital offenses, personal injury, property loss (Exod. 21:1–22:20), and in ethical and moral issues that impact on the disadvantaged in society (widows, orphans, the impoverished; Exod. 22:21–23:9)—Israel's love of God must be exemplified by its commitment to live in consonance with God's expectations for justice in the world.

Leviticus sustains this worship-justice nexus by coupling to it commandments summoning Israel to behavior that exemplifies covenantal holiness. The fulcrum on which this summons rests is the Holiness Code (chaps. 17–27), at the center of which stands the commandment to "love your neighbor as yourself" (19:18). This commandment is, in turn, explicated by repeating exhortations to work for justice and righteousness in and for the sake of the land, which Israel holds in trust as a gift from God (18:24–30; 20:22–26; 25:18–24; 26:3–45; cf. Blenkinsopp, *The Pentateuch*, pp. 224–25). To cite but one clear witness to this

13

emphasis, the complex of commandments in Leviticus 25–26 admonishes Israel to define justice as the basic and God-given right for persons to be free from permanent enslavement to debt. Toward this end, economic principles must be governed by sabbatical cycles that guarantee remission of debt, the redemption of property, and the restoration to full, unindentured freedom of those who have become destitute. Not surprisingly, the rationale for obedience is tied once again to God's commandment to "keep my sabbaths and reverence my sanctuary" (26:1–2). Indeed, with remarkable and revealing candor, the Holiness Code concludes by suggesting that God *not only establishes* the jubilee law of redemption (chap. 25) but *also respects and obeys* it (chap. 27; cf. Douglas, *Leviticus as Literature*, p. 244). In the end, God's own model for justice provides the explication of what may be regarded as the preeminent commandment of the Holiness Code: "You shall be holy, *for I the Lord your God am holy*" (19:2).

It is not just that the tabernacle and its rituals honor God's creational design for the world. In the Torah's vision, they are also divinely endowed with the capacity to sustain and, where necessary, restore God's creational intentions. The prescriptions for daily, monthly, and annual offerings in Leviticus 23, for example, not only reflect the natural rhythm encoded in creation; they also actualize this order in everyday life. The rituals for the Day of Purification in Leviticus 16 not only recognize sin's defilement of the sanctuary, and by extension, the world; they also seek to repair the damage by cleansing the sanctuary and restoring it to its role as the central place on earth for the residence of God. The redemption of the land in the jubilee year (Leviticus 25) not only acknowledges economic structures that leave some impoverished; it also provides concrete measures that have the potential to correct systemic abuses. In sum, the Torah's summons to worship is a summons to justice. And worship that issues forth in justice makes of covenantal partnership a flesh-and-blood commitment to join with God in creating and re-creating a world that by God's decree remains ever vulnerable to what G. Steiner has so evocatively described as the "anarchic shock of excellence" (Steiner, p. 292).

Worship is at the heart of community building and world formation. When Israel leaves Sinai for the land of Canaan, it is commissioned as both a covenant community and a worshiping community. This commission, however, carries with it the summons to depart from the sacred mountain, where obedience to God's commands might enjoy unthreatened fulfillment, and to journey toward the land of Canaan, where the obstacles to obedience will be concrete and significant. In tracking this journey, the book of Numbers reports that the community prepared for

14

its journey by organizing itself into concentric circles. At their center was the tabernacle, the central symbol of the presence of God. Encircling the tabernacle was the tribe of the Levites, special custodians of the tabernacle and its sancta. Surrounding the Levites, in expanding circles, were the remaining tribes of Israel, with their respective tents facing toward the tabernacle (Num. 1:50–53). Such a picture, for all its impracticality, envisions a community on the march that aspires to be centered by its summons to worship God.

But as in its portrait of the liturgy of creation, the Torah's vision of Israel's constitution as people of God in the real world of Canaan is quite candid. Both the world that lies before Israel and the vision of community that beckons them are vulnerable to collapse. On the journey to Canaan, a number of crises develop (Numbers 11–14) that are no less threatening to God's creational designs than those that provoked an anguished God to send the flood in primeval days. Once again the Torah reports the death of an old generation and the cleansing of a sinful community (Numbers 21–25). Once again God summons forth a new generation of people to carry forward the divine commission (Numbers 26–36). And once again God announces that the Torah's vision, now recapitulated by Moses in Deuteronomy, remains critically important if a new generation is to realize its destiny as a "priestly kingdom and holy nation."

Deuteronomy provides the charter for Israel's journey from Sinai to Canaan. Moses begins to unfold the map by recalling the Sinai experience and the vital role that worship will play in Israel's constitution as a people of God. He reviews the religious imperatives of the "decrees," that is, the Decalogue (Deut. 5:6–21), then outlines the "statutes and ordinances" (Deuteronomy 12–26) that must inform the constitutional structures of society. Both the religious imperatives that define Israel's piety and the social constitution that will govern the body politic are tied to the commandment for exclusive loyalty to God. Toward this goal, both the "decrees" and the "statutes and ordinances" begin with First Commandment imperatives: "You shall have no other gods before me" (Deut. 5:7; 12:1–13:8).

The "decrees" and the "statutes and ordinances" in Deuteronomy reprise in several respects their counterpart legislation in the Sinai pericope, the Decalogue and the Book of Covenant. There are, however, important variations. The sequence and the substance of the Ten Commandments in Exodus and Deuteronomy are very similar. Both books move from commandments to love God (commandments 1–3) to commandments to live in community with others in ways that enact this love (commandments 5–10). Both books present the Sabbath command as the center on which all the commandments converge; in

15

effect, it is the bridge between love of God and love of neighbor. Deuteronomy's version of the Sabbath commandment, however, begins differently: "Observe (*šāmôr*; cf. Exod. 20:8: "Remember" [*zākôr*]) the sabbath day and keep it holy" (Deut. 5:12). P. Miller elucidates the distinction as follows: "In the case of Exodus, the community is called to remember and to live out of that memory; in the Deuteronomic form, the community obeys to keep alive the memory of redemption and to bring about the provision of rest for all members of the community" (Miller, *Deuteronomy*, p. 80).

This emphasis on obedience, on specific and concrete enactment of the Commandments, also characterizes Deuteronomy's "statutes and ordinances." Like the book of the covenant, the statutes and ordinances in Deuteronomy frame social justice concerns in the context of the summons to worship (Deut. 12:1–13:18; 26:1–15). Within this frame, however, Deuteronomy broadens the book of the covenant's admonitions and tunes the summons to justice explicitly to a "sabbatical principle" that extends even beyond what the Holiness Code in Leviticus envisions. The prime exemplars of this are the redemption laws in Deut. 15:1–18. Debtors are to be released from their financial burdens "every seventh year" (15:1–6). Slaves are to be released from their bondage "in the seventh year" (15:12–18). But the poor and the needy are to be released not every seven years but instead on a calendar that schedules perpetual generosity and compassion. *Whenever* and *wherever* Israel encounters the poor, it is to respond with a warm heart and an open hand (15:7–11). This is not an appeal for optional charity; it is instead a requirement backed up with the force of law. When it comes to economic justice for the poor and the disadvantaged of society, sporadic or even extraordinary, but random, acts of compassion do not meet God's expectations. Once more the Torah's vision affirms that justice, no less than worship, must be part of the sacred rhythms that define the community of faith.

In short, Deuteronomy understands Moses to have summoned forth a new community. On the other side of the plains of Moab, this new community will set its compass by the Torah's vision of the new and ever-renewing covenant that binds together God, humankind, and the cosmos (Deut. 27:1–30:20). Just as in the primeval days, so forever after the community of faith must decide whether to live in harmony with this vision or in opposition to it. And just as it was "in the beginning," the choice remains a critical one. It is the choice between "life and death, blessings and curses." Then as now, the Torah's vision hangs on God's abiding hope that the decision will be to "choose life so that you and your descendants may live" (Deut. 30:19).

16

Figure 1
The Centrality of the Sinai Pericope in the Torah's Vision*

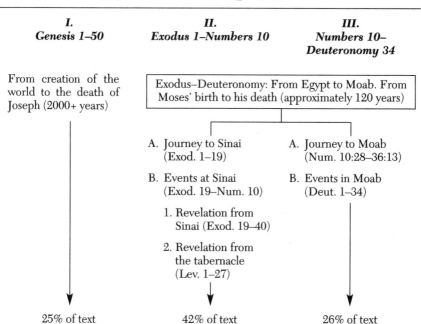

I. *Genesis 1–50*	II. *Exodus 1–Numbers 10*	III. *Numbers 10– Deuteronomy 34*

From creation of the world to the death of Joseph (2000+ years)

Exodus–Deuteronomy: From Egypt to Moab. From Moses' birth to his death (approximately 120 years)

A. Journey to Sinai (Exod. 1–19)

A. Journey to Moab (Num. 10:28–36:13)

B. Events at Sinai (Exod. 19–Num. 10)

B. Events in Moab (Deut. 1–34)

1. Revelation from Sinai (Exod. 19–40)

2. Revelation from the tabernacle (Lev. 1–27)

25% of text   42% of text   26% of text

*For this outline of the literary units of the Pentateuch, see Knierim, "Composition of the Pentateuch," 395–415. I have modified slightly Knierim's proposal.

The importance of Leviticus for the Torah's vision as outlined above may be conceptualized by charting the pride of place accorded the Sinai pericope in the Pentateuch's final form.

According to the Pentateuch's own chronology, the time span for the events recorded between the creation of the world and the death of Moses in the plains of Moab is 2,706 years (Blenkinsopp, *The Pentateuch*, p. 33). Within this time framework, the events that transpire at Sinai comprise less than one year of the total. By any reasonable definition of a proportional account of Israel's story, the year at Sinai might have been given little more than the space of a footnote. And yet, in what must be judged to be one of the most important theological anomalies of the Pentateuch's composite account, Israel's story allots fifty-eight chapters, Exodus 19–Numbers 10—more than 40 percent of the space—to the Sinai pericope. According to the Torah's vision, the year

17

at Sinai is *the* constitutive experience in the formation of Israel as a "priestly kingdom and holy nation" (Exod. 19:6).

As Figure 1 illustrates, the Sinai pericope records two revelations to Israel. The first is God's revelation from the mountain of Sinai (Exodus 19–40); the second, God's revelation from the tabernacle (Leviticus 1–27). From the Torah's perspective, the revelation from the mountain is foundational and anchors Israel's past; the revelation from the tabernacle belongs to the present and future, and as such it is decisive for the ongoing life of Israel (cf. Knierim, p. 405). In the Pentateuch's final arrangement into five books, therefore, it is the third book, Leviticus, that centers the community of faith on the most important part of God's revelation. That revelation, conveyed through Moses to all Israel, announces that the worship of God, with its unyielding summons to righteousness and justice "on earth as it is in heaven," is the ultimate goal of creation (cf. Blenkinsopp, *The Pentateuch*, p. 221).

A final *introductory*, and perhaps *inviting*, observation may be in order. The first words of Leviticus in Hebrew, *wayyiqra*ʾ, may be literally translated as "and God *continued calling*." That call reached first from God to Moses, then through Moses to the people of Israel, priests and laypersons alike. Although Leviticus records no direct response, no specific verbal reply, to God from either Moses or Israel, its abiding assumption is that God's commands will be heard, heeded, and obeyed. To be sure, even in Leviticus there is a place for narratives that are mindful of the potential for disobedience (10:1–20; 24:10–23), narratives reinforced by the accounts of Israel's flawed efforts that appear so frequently and so candidly in the story that precedes and follows this one. Nevertheless, within this one pregnant pause in the larger story, it is not Israel's potential for failure but God's unabashed confidence in its capacity for fidelity that takes center stage. As God continues calling, and as Israel continues listening, the future remains open, full, and incalculably promising. Perhaps it is just here, in these seemingly tedious, often peculiar instructions about worship and justice, that a community of faith, even a contemporary one, may find its bearings. Who among us does not yearn for that one place, however small and difficult to find, that invites us to believe the "very good" world God created and the world in which we scratch out our frail existence are in fact one and the same? To all of us who hear our names in this question, the book of Leviticus offers these words:

> These are the commandments that the LORD gave to Moses for the people of Israel on Mount Sinai. (27:34)

PART ONE

The Gift of Sacrifice

LEVITICUS 1–7

Leviticus 1–7 introduces the *gifts* of sacrifice. Two series of instructions identify the gifts and outline how they are to be brought to God. The first (1:3–6:7; MT: 1:3–5:26) deals with five major offerings, each presented from the perspective of the donor: burnt offerings, cereal offerings, well-being offerings, purification offerings, and reparation offerings. The first three of these are voluntary offerings; the last two are required. The second series (6:8–7:36; MT: 6:1–7:36) addresses the same offerings, this time from the perspective of the priests. The two sets of instructions are framed by an introduction (1:1–2) and a conclusion (7:37–38) that tie all the offerings to the revelation from God to Moses at the tent of meeting that was erected at Sinai (cf. Exodus 25–31, 35–40).

Leviticus 1:1–17
Burnt Offerings

The instructions concerning burnt offerings move from the general to the specific. An introductory statement (vv. 1–2) addresses the general category of animal "gifts" (*qorbān*: NRSV: "offering") that anyone may bring to God. Three subunits define these gifts as burnt offerings "from the herd" (vv. 3–9), "from the flock" (vv. 10–13), and "of birds" (vv. 14–16). The instructions concerning these gifts are given in considerable detail, first in the section dealing with offerings from the herd, then a second and third time, with some variations, in the sections dealing with the flock and the birds. Readers may be tempted to rush past the details in order to find more quickly the theology they convey. The search for theological meaning is clearly important. It is prudent to remember, however, that here and throughout Leviticus, the journey toward understanding necessarily runs *through*, not *around*, the specifics of the text. To recast a popular saying, readers of Leviticus will find that "God is in the details."

Introduction (1:1–2)

The first words of Leviticus are designed to introduce a special revelatory experience in the history of Israel. According to the final arrangement of the Pentateuch, God has "summoned (*yiqrā*ʾ) Moses" on three previous occasions. In Exod. 3:4, God summons Moses from the burning bush in order to disclose the name YHWH that would mark God's special relationship with Israel. In Exod. 19:3, God summons Moses a second time, on this occasion from Mount Sinai, and gives to him the Ten Commandments. On the third occasion, Exod. 24:16, God summons Moses from the cloud that has covered Mount Sinai; what follows are God's instructions for building the tabernacle (Exodus 25–31). Leviticus 1:1 announces that God summons Moses from the newly erected "tent of meeting" (see Exodus 35–40), also called the "tabernacle" (cf. Lev. 8:10; 15:31; 17:4; 26:11), which has now become the only specific place in all creation that is described as being filled with the "glory of the Lord" (Exod. 40:35; Fretheim, *Exodus*, p. 315). Leviticus presents what God now says to Moses, and what Moses must now speak to the whole community of Israel, as the most immediate and intimate revelation from God available in the cosmos.

This is surely an astonishing claim. The closest parallel in Christian Scripture is the assertion that God is fully present in Jesus (John 1:14–16). The Christian community will typically hear and embrace the latter claim as a requisite part of its credo. For many Christians, however, the revelation from Leviticus is passively ignored or actively shunned. The introductory verse serves notice that Leviticus, with all its instructions and rituals, claims to be an essential part of the ongoing revelation from God to humanity. To hear and respond to its disclosures is to draw near to the very presence of God.

The term *tent of meeting* designates the structure built at Sinai as the place where God and people "meet" or "come together." In the priestly traditions of Exodus, the construction and purpose of the tent/tabernacle explicate creation theology. The theophany in which God discloses to Moses the instructions for the tabernacle begins on the seventh day (Exod. 24:16). The instructions are then conveyed through seven speeches, each distinguished by the introductory formula "The Lord said/spoke to Moses" (Exod. 25:1; 30:11, 17, 22, 34; 31:1, 12). The seventh speech (31:12–17) concludes the instructions by specifying God's plans for the Sabbath day, thus echoing the seventh-day celebration in the creational account of Gen. 2:1–4. The construction of the tabernacle begins by returning to the instructions concerning the Sabbath day (Exod. 35:2–3), following which the work is done "just as the Lord had commanded Moses," a phrase that repeats seven times in Exod. 40:17–33. The conclusion formula in Exod. 40:33—"So Moses finished the work"—recalls the similar notice in Gen. 2:2—"God finished the work" (on these and other parallels, see Balentine, pp. 136–41). Such parallels suggest that the construction of the tabernacle completes the work God began in creating the world. A necessary part of creation's completion, Leviticus insists, are these instructions enabling ordinary people to come into the presence of a holy God.

Toward this end, Lev. 1:2 addresses the "people of Israel" as *ʾādām* (NRSV: "any [of you]"), the same term that Gen. 1:26–27 uses to describe the creation of human beings (*ʾādām*) in the image of God. The term is all-inclusive and signals that all persons, regardless of gender, race, or economic station, are summoned and enabled to respond to these first divine words from the tent. Elsewhere Leviticus uses *ʾādām*, or the equivalent term *nepeš*, "person" (2:1; 4:2; 5:1, 2; etc.; NRSV: "anyone"; "any of you"), in ways that suggest the invitation extends to resident aliens and foreigners as well as Israelites (Milgrom, *Leviticus 1–16*, pp. 144–45). The response that is invited is to "bring" (*yaqrîb*) an "offering" (*qorbān*). The verb, which specifies the performative act, has the sense of "drawing near" and in a cultic setting means to approach God for the purpose of making a presentation or offering. The noun, which derives from the verb, specifies the object that is presented to God. The term *qorbān*, which is unique to the Priestly tradition, is inclusive of a variety of offerings and sacrifices. Common to all is the basic sense of "gift," that is, a presentation intended to please, satisfy, delight the recipient.

"If the Offering Is a Burnt Offering from the Herd" (1:3–9)

Under the general category of gifts offered to God, the instructions now proceed to describe three subtypes of the specific offering known as the "burnt offering." The burnt offering (*ʿōlâ*) is the most frequently mentioned and likely the most ancient of the offerings used in Israel. Although its history is complicated (for a full discussion, see Milgrom, *Leviticus 1–16*, pp. 172–76), the burnt offering appears to have served a wide variety of emotional, psychological, and religious purposes,

21

including entreaty (1 Sam. 13:12), appeasement (1 Sam. 7:9; 2 Sam. 24:21–25), thanksgiving (Lev. 22:17–19; Num. 15:3), and expiation, which is the purpose singled out in Lev. 1:4 (cf. Lev. 9:7; 14:20; 16:24). The distinguishing feature of the ʿōlâ (literally, "that which ascends") is that the entire animal (with the exception of the skin; cf. Lev. 7:8) is burned on the altar. According to the Hebrew expression in verse 9, the whole animal is "turned into smoke," thus producing a pleasing aroma that *ascends* toward heaven and pleases God. The designation of the burnt offering as the first of the offerings conforms to the practice in other lists, where it consistently precedes other types of sacrifices. This practice may have signaled nothing more than a practical, perhaps administrative way of arranging the offerings (Milgrom, *Leviticus 1–16*, p. 146). It is instructive to speculate whether the burnt offering may also have served as the "inviting offering," that is, the initial gift designed to attract God's attention, thereby inviting a gracious response to those who desire to approach God's presence (Kaiser, p. 1010).

Each of the subtypes is introduced with a conditional clause beginning with "if" (vv. 3, 10, 14), which is followed by prescriptions for the offering. Three types of animals—an unblemished male from the herd (e.g., bull or ox; vv. 3–9), an unblemished male from the flock (sheep or goat; vv. 10–13), or birds (doves or pigeons; vv. 14–17)—may be selected for the burnt offering. The choices are arranged on a sliding scale of cost to the donor. The most costly gift is the bull, which only the wealthy could afford to sacrifice. The least costly is the offering of birds, which are more plentiful and thus more obtainable, even by the poor, who may not have or be able to afford to spare anything from the herd or the flock. There is no suggestion that God values the choices differently, just as there is no suggestion that God regards the offerings of the wealthy as more desirable or efficacious than those of the poor. In each case the legitimate hope and expectation of every donor is that the gift will be "an offering . . . of pleasing odor to the Lord" (vv. 9, 13, 17).

"If the offering is a burnt offering from the herd" (v. 3), the following seven general prescriptions obtain:

- *Presentation (v. 3).* The donor brings an unblemished male to the sacrificial altar located at the entrance of the tent of meeting. In a spatial sense, the sacrificial altar is located in the outer court between the entrance to the entire tabernacle complex and the Holy Place. In a theological sense, the "entrance of the tent" is the place for the ritual enactment of the

22

intersection between God and people, between the holy and the common. As Gorman puts it, "God and humans come together in the actualization of the story they share. In ritual, God and people . . . construct, enact, and actualize a community that is identified not only in, by, and through its story but also in, by, and through its ritual" (Gorman, *Divine Presence and Community*, 25).

- *Laying a hand on the animal's head (v. 4).* The purpose of this symbolic act is not entirely clear. It certainly conveys the idea of ownership; that is, donors indicate by this gesture that the animal belongs to them and that they desire that it be acceptable on their behalf. Beyond this, some commentators reference the hand-laying rite in Lev. 16:21–22, which suggests a symbolic transference of sin from the donor to the animal (e.g., Kaiser, p. 1011; Gerstenberger, p. 28). Because the offering described here is *voluntary* and spontaneously motivated, one *not required* by sin or guilt, it is questionable whether transference of sin is the primary idea.

- *Slaughter (v. 5).* Having presented and claimed ownership of the animal, the donor ritually slaughters it by cutting its throat. The ritual is enacted "before the Lord," which indicates that to this point the process continues to take place in the outer court. The rabbis add that both the animal and the donor must face west, toward the sanctuary, which further indicates that the sacrifice is intentionally and specifically directed to God (Milgrom, *Leviticus 1–16*, p. 155).

- *Presentation of the blood (v. 5b).* From this point forward the responsibility for presenting the offering shifts from the donor to the priests, since only the priests can ascend to the altar (1 Sam. 2:28). The priests "dash" or "throw" the blood against the sides of the altar, a ritual reminder that in priestly theology, "the life of the flesh is in the blood" (Lev. 17:11). Priestly sensitivity to bloodshed is based on the understanding that the taking of a life, whether animal or human, is a dangerous act. God alone sets the boundaries that mark where life begins and ends.

The rationale for this theology may be traced to the Priestly account of the proscriptions regarding blood in Genesis 9. In the postflood world, God reissues the creational commission for humans to be fruitful, multiply, and fill the earth (Gen. 9:1, 7; cf. Gen. 1:28). Within this summons to life there is, however, a pointed, thrice-repeated warning that God will "require a reckoning" (v. 5) for the shedding of blood. The warning applies to eating the blood of animals and to shedding human blood. Both cases serve as a reminder that the taking of life, carelessly, needlessly, even sacrificially, moves one into the area of God's domain. With this proscription in place, God reissues a covenantal promise that now extends to all creation (vv. 9–10, 12–13, 15–17). The promise is God's unilateral commitment to life. Humans are summoned to participate in this promise and sustain its claim, because they have been created in the image of God (v. 6; cf. Gen. 1:27). Leviticus enjoins such imaging of God by instructing that the killing of an animal be enacted ritually and in a sacred place where blood/life is returned to God.

• *Flaying the animal (vv. 6–8)*. The donor skins and quarters the animal. The priest stokes the fire, arranges the wood, and places the animal parts on the fire. Special attention is given to the head and the suet, the fat that surrounds the internal organs. There appears to be a careful ordering in the placement of the items on the altar—meat quarters, head, suet, then entrails and legs (see v. 9)—although the significance of the arrangement is not clear. One suggestive proposal is that body parts are stacked in a hierarchy that corresponds to the hierarchical gradations of holiness in the tabernacle (Douglas, *Leviticus as Literature*, pp. 66–86). Thus the head and meat quarters correspond to the tabernacle's outer court area, the first level of holiness; the suet, which may be viewed anatomically as the middle area that separates the upper body (head) from the lower abdomen (entrails), correspond to the middle area of the tabernacle complex, the Holy Place, which constitutes the second level of holiness; the entrails (including the genital organs?) correspond to the Holy of Holies, the most sacred part of the tabernacle. In other words, at the apex of the burnt offering, the place where the sacrifice begins the last step in the ascent to God, the priest places the most holy part of the animal's anatomy: the entrails, the innermost being of the body, the place from which life itself—human or animal—is generated.

- *Washing the entrails and legs (v. 9a).* The donor washes the entrails to remove the dung, and the legs presumably to remove any uncleanness caused by contact with semen, urine, or contaminations from the ground. The ritual of washing reflects the priestly concern to avoid defiling the holy by having it come into contact with anything unclean. Distinguishing between the clean and the unclean, particularly with reference to food, body fluids, and skin diseases, is the principal concern of Leviticus 11–15. Readers will find further discussion of the issues in the commentary on these chapters.
- *Burning (v. 9b).* The priest burns the whole offering on the altar. The verb, *hiqtîr*, literally "turn into smoke," is instructive for two reasons. First, it is not the normal word for "burn" (*śārap*), which is used for nonsacrificial incineration; it is rather a distinctive term for offerings to God on the altar (e.g., 3:11: suet; 6:8: cereal; 8:20–21: meat). Second, the root *qtr* has to do with "smoke." In this verbal form the precise meaning is "to turn something into smoke." The primary sense is that the burnt offering goes up *as smoke*. From a theological perspective, one may say that the act of burning is more concerned with transformation than with incineration (Milgrom, *Leviticus 1–16*, pp. 160–61). What has been placed on the altar is literally an animal. The ritual has transformed the animal into something else—smoke—and this smoke now requires a new name. It now ascends as a "gift" (*ʾiššēh*; NRSV: "offering"), a food offering specifically and intentionally given to God. More important, this gift is purposeful. Its express purpose is to provide a "pleasing odor to the Lord" (cf. vv. 13, 17). The donor desires and expects that the gift will

25

give pleasure to God. In other words, the primary purpose of the burnt offering, its expiatory function notwithstanding (cf. v. 4), is to *give something to God*, not to *get something from God*.

"If Your Gift . . . Is from the Flock" (1:10–13)

If the donor cannot afford an animal from the herd, one from the flock—a lamb or a goat—is acceptable. The sheep is the animal most frequently used for burnt offerings in the public cult (cf. 9:3; 12:6; 14:10; 23:12, 18). By contrast, goats are always brought as voluntary sacrifices of the individual (22:19; Num. 15:11). The sacrificial procedure is essentially the same as that described in Lev. 1:3–9, although some details are omitted. One detail is added: The animal is slaughtered on the "north side of the altar" (cf. v. 5). The reason for the different location is not clear. Perhaps there are practical considerations: The bull is more difficult to control than the sheep, hence its management requires the larger area of the outer court. Perhaps the issue is the allocation of space around the outer altar. To the east of the altar is the ash heap (v. 16); to the west is the washbasin (Exod. 40:30); to the south are the stairs leading up to the altar. Given this arrangement, the north side of the altar may have been the only adequate space remaining (Milgrom, *Leviticus 1–16*, p. 163).

"If Your Offering Is . . . a Burnt Offering of Birds" (1:14–17)

If donors cannot afford either a bull or a lamb, they may bring a gift of doves or pigeons. The midrash supplies a rationale by appealing to Psalm 22:24: "For he [God] has not despised or abhorred the affliction of the afflicted, and he has not hid his face from him but has heard, when he cried to him" (*Leviticus Rabbah* 3:1). This scriptural base-verse is then amplified with the report of a poor man who comes to the priest saying that he catches four birds every day; two to sustain himself and two to give as offering to God. He successfully implores the priest to accept the offering, lest his living be cut in half (*Leviticus Rabbah* 3:5).

The anatomy of the bird requires a slightly different sacrificial procedure. The priest pinches off the bird's head, squeezes out its blood against the altar, removes its crop along with the intestinal contents, and cast these parts on the refuse of ashes at the east of the altar. The priest then tears open the bird by its wings, without severing them, and turns the whole into smoke. Although the smallest and least costly of the burnt offerings, the bird actualizes the same hopes and expectations as the bull and the lamb. The donor presents it wholly, voluntarily, as a gift that will be pleasing to God.

Theological Reflections

Any book that leads with detailed discussion of bulls, lambs, and birds, whether it claims to be Holy Scripture or not, invites disregard by modern readers. The neglect of Leviticus, at least as far as the Bible goes, is perhaps the example that proves the point. As T. Mann has observed, "Many a pious vow to read straight through the Bible from cover to cover has foundered on the shoals of Leviticus" (Mann, p. 113). If we are read to beyond the shoreline of Leviticus 1, we must find a way to believe that bulls, lambs, and birds are more than "merely corroborative detail; intended to give artistic verisimilitude to an otherwise bald and unconvincing narrative" (*The Mikado*, act 2). The following reflections lay a foundation for launching the journey.

1. *Leviticus invites readers to "meet" God.* The first clue is the assertion that Leviticus offers words that come from the "tent of meeting." The biblical narrative that introduces this tent is hardly "bald and unconvincing." According to the story line in Exodus, the children of Israel were slaves in Egypt when God heard their cries of misery and came down to deliver them. Through Moses, God brought them out of Egypt, led them to Sinai, commissioned them to become "a priestly kingdom and a holy nation" (Exod. 19:6), and gave them commandments that issued forth in a covenant partnership based on reciprocal love and devotion. Their destination was the promised land, where the terms *kingdom* and *nation* would find new meaning. But their commission was also to become "priestly" and "holy," and for the realization of this objective God instructed them to build a sanctuary, a place that would approximate God's holiness and make it both accessible and dispersible on earth. Leviticus is the word from this sanctuary and the instruction for this commission. It insists that the journey toward the promised land can neither begin nor succeed without its revelation. To go with God, people must meet God, be imbued with the vision of God's holiness, and concretize this vision by the way they live. Bulls and lambs and birds are one part of the journey toward obedience.

2. *The "gift" of sacrifice.* In today's world, sacrifice usually means giving up something of value, something we would rather keep unless forced to let go. Leviticus offers a different place to begin our thinking about sacrifice. Before the first instruction about sacrifice is given,

27

Leviticus inserts the word *gift* (1:2: *qorbān*). The word applies generally to any offering presented in the sanctuary. As indicated in Leviticus 1, the offerings may come in different sizes and shapes. They may be large and costly or small and ordinary. The critical criterion is that they are brought voluntarily and spontaneously. They are indeed *sacrificed*, as we moderns would say, but Leviticus understands this more as a giving *to* (or *for*) than a giving *up*. The donors do not grudgingly give up something they prefer to withhold; they happily offer something that they know to be worth more as a gift to God than as a personal possession. The gift is *qorbān* because it enables an ordinary person to "draw near" (*qārab*) to the inestimably holy God. The gift is spontaneous because it is the happy response to the God who has graciously drawn near to the person.

It is true that even gifts may sometimes be viewed more as duty than devotion. It appears that this gradually happened with the *qorbān*. Josephus, the first-century Jewish historian, links the *qorbān* with vows and oaths that become so burdensome that procedures are prescribed for gaining release from them (e.g., *Ant.* 4.73). A similar situation seems to be reflected in Mark 7:11, where Jesus rebukes the Pharisees for arguing that because their gifts were *korban*, that is, dedicated to God, they did not have adequate provisions to support their parents. The possibility for misappropriation is not what Leviticus addresses. The focus instead is on the positive. Bulls and lambs and birds are gifts, not burdens. They make possible a proximity to God that relativizes every calculation of cost. Of course, the gift is only a symbol, but symbols do matter. Kathleen Norris offers a case in point. A lapsed Protestant, she became a Benedictine oblate, and through the disciplined observance of the monastic rituals she rediscovered her faith. She pens this new discernment concerning Judas's rebuke of the woman who "wasted" precious nard by anointing Jesus' feet:

> Maybe monks and poets know, as Jesus did when a friend, in an extravagant, loving gesture, bathed his feet in nard, an expensive, fragrant oil, and wiped them with her hair, that the symbolic act *matters*; that those who know the exact price of things, as Judas did, often don't know the true cost of anything. (Norris, p. 147)

3. *Gift as analogy.* Leviticus teaches by using analogies (Douglas, *Leviticus as Literature*, pp. 13–40). In this approach it is different, and therefore requires a different reading strategy, from the books that precede and follow it in the Pentateuch. Exodus teaches by narrating the story of God's deliverance of the Israelites. Deuteronomy teaches by retelling this story in a sermonic style that exhorts hearing and obedi-

ence. Leviticus, by contrast, contains but one narrative-like story (chaps. 8–10) and little or no sermonic appeal. Instead, it offers instructions that invite readers to compare *this to that*. The comparison encodes a larger truth that includes literal meaning but moves beyond it. The first clue to this analogical mode of instruction is the phrase "turn the whole into smoke," which repeats three times in chapter 1 (vv. 9, 13, 17).

The bull, the lamb, and the bird are literally animals. The ritual of sacrifice turns each one into something else: smoke. The account of the theophany on Sinai correlates smoke (and cloud) with the top of the mountain where God comes to meet with Moses (Exod. 19:18; 24:15–18). The smoke marks the most holy zone of the mountain, the place where God is most palpably present. Leviticus extends the correlation between smoke and God's presence a step further. Animals offered to God on the altar are turned into smoke, which then rises from the summit of the pile to intersect with the holy presence of God, symbolized by the glory of the Lord in the cloud that accompanies the tent wherever it goes (Exod. 40:34–38). At the point of intersection, the offering is transformative. The offerings are no longer merely animals; they are gifts. The offerers are no longer distant from God; they have drawn near to the most tangible presence of God that is available on earth.

The transformation remains essentially a mystery. No explanations are provided. No rationale is spelled out. The donors are instructed simply how to give a gift to God. The presumption is that in the act of giving the analogy takes hold, and donors find that they have mysteriously moved from concept to concrete experience, from ritual to worship, from living in the world of their own possessions to participating in a world where offerings to God connect them with the greatest possession they can never manufacture or control: the gift of the presence of God.

Leviticus 2:1–16
Cereal Offerings

The instructions concerning the cereal offering (*minḥâ*) comprise three major sections, each corresponding to a different type of grain: uncooked wheat (vv. 1–3), cooked wheat (vv. 4–10), and natural barley (vv. 14–16). Verses 11–13 provide special instructions concerning the

29

use of leaven, honey, and salt. The ritual procedure, which is only vaguely described, includes the following steps: preparation (vv. 1, 6), presentation (vv. 2a, 8a), and burning or "turning into smoke" (vv. 2b, 9, 16) a token part of the offering. The donor is responsible for the first two steps; the priest completes the ritual by placing the cereal offering on the altar (see the commentary on 1:3–9).

Uncooked Wheat (2:1–3)

The instructions begin by juxtaposing the general term for animal gifts (*qorbān*; cf.1:2) with a second term—*minhâ* (2:1)—which is an equally broad term for "gift" (Anderson, pp. 27–34). In nonpriestly texts, *minhâ* frequently denotes the "tribute" or "homage" that signifies personal friendship (e.g., Gen. 32:14, 19; 43:11) or political submission (e.g., 2 Sam. 8:2, 6; 1 Kgs. 4:21 [MT: 5:1]). In priestly texts, *minhâ* always refers to the broad category of cereal or grain offerings, which may be presented independently, as envisioned in Leviticus 2, or in association with other sacrifices (e.g., with the burnt offering, as in Numbers 28). The placement of the cereal offering immediately after the least costly burnt offerings of birds (Lev. 1:14–16) suggests that it provides a further option for the poor. If persons cannot afford even a bird, they may offer a gift of grain, which has the same capacity to become a "pleasing odor to the Lord" (vv. 2, 9) as the "more expensive" gifts. Further confirmation that the cereal offering was regarded as the "poor man's burnt offering" (Milgrom, *Leviticus 1–16*, p. 195) comes from rabbinic tradition, which amplifies the sacrificial instructions as follows:

> R. Joshua of Siknin said in the name of R. Levi: come and see how the Holy One, blessed be he, tried to spare the Israelite expense, for he said to them: "Whoever is obligated to bring a sacrifice, let him bring from the herd . . . if he cannot afford from the herd, let him bring a lamb . . . if he cannot afford to bring an offering from the lambs, let him bring one from the goats . . . if he cannot afford to bring from the goats, let him bring from the birds . . . if he cannot afford to bring from the birds, let him bring some cereal, as it is said 'His offering shall be of cereal' (Lev. 2:1)." (*Leviticus Rabbah* 8:4)

The first subtype of the cereal offering is the offering of semolina or grits, which is the portion of the wheat that remains after the fine floor has been sifted. The donor adds to the semolina two ingredients: oil and frankincense. Both ingredients are considered precious, the former because of the labor required to produce it (pressing and grinding), the latter because of the cost of purchasing it through spice trade with southern Arabia and Somaliland. The priest takes a "token portion"

30

(ʾ*azkārâ*) of the offering and "turns it into smoke" (cf. 1:9, 13, 17) on the altar. The precise meaning of the term ʾ*azkārâ* is uncertain. The verbal root, *zākar*, means "remember" and thus may convey the notion that the representative portion enables the donor to call to mind God's gracious provisions of daily food. A noun derivative of the same root, *zeker*, means "remembrance," which may suggest that the "token portion" is a "commemorative" portion, in itself "a pleasing odor to the Lord," that takes the place of the whole offering. The remainder of the cereal offering, which is designated "the most sacred portion," belongs to the priests; it is one main source of their income (cf. 6:14–18 [MT: 6:7–11]).

Cooked Wheat (2:4–10)

Three types of cooked grain may be offered as a cereal offering: oven-baked cakes or wafers, griddle-toasted cakes, and pan-fried cakes (vv. 4–7). The three types reflect not only different modes of cooking but also different venues for the preparation (cf. Gerstenberger, p. 40). The oven, a large clay pot, was conventionally embedded partially or wholly in the ground outside the home. The griddle, a clay or iron plate without a top, and the pan, a shallow utensil with a top, were cooking items normally used in the home. All cooked grain offerings required unleavened semolina; none required frankincense.

When the cooked offering had been prepared in one of these ways, the donor brought it to the priest for presentation on the altar. The priest removed the token portion, presumably a small amount roughly equivalent to a handful (cf. v. 2), and turned it into the smoke that provides a "pleasing odor to the Lord." The remainder of the offering, once again designated as "the most holy part," was reserved for the priests.

Special Instructions (2:11–13)

In the penultimate paragraph of the chapter, the instructions focus specifically on the use of three ingredients: leaven, honey, and salt. The verbs in this section are plural, not singular as in the preceding paragraphs, which suggests that the priests, not the donor, are the addressees. The priests are to make certain that no cereal offering contains either leaven or honey. The rationale for these prohibitions is nowhere clearly given. The conventional explanation associates both leaven (as yeast) and honey (as sugar) with fermentation, which rabbinic, Christian (e.g., Mark 8:15; Luke 12:1; 1 Cor. 5:8), and Hellenistic sources seem to have regarded as a metaphor for corruption and decay and, by extension, death (Milgrom, *Leviticus 1–16*, p. 189). To

31

the extent that information from these later sources accurately reflects the practice in ancient Israel, we may assume that the priests were concerned to keep anything associated with corruption away from the altar.

There is, however, an irony in the proscriptions concerning leaven and honey that the conventional rationale does not address. As agents of fermentation, leaven and honey are materially associated with *life*, not *death*. Leaven activates the dough, thus causing it to rise. Sugar is a sweetening agent; it increases rather than decreases the taste of food. It seems clear that in and of themselves leaven and honey are not negative ingredients, a fact further born out by the recognition that they "were not unsuitable for all offerings, only for those burned on the altar" (Levine, *Leviticus*, p. 12). What is it, then, about these agents of life that makes them off limits for offerings on the altar? One suggestion is that leaven and honey, along with semen and blood, are agents of natural generation, that is, they fall within the domain of life that humans may control on their own. Offerings on the altar, by contrast, become agents of divine generation, that is, they acknowledge that all life is a gift from God. Perhaps the proscriptions concerning leaven and honey are meant to reinforce the truth that there is an important difference between what God creates and humans make (cf. Douglas, *Leviticus as Literature*, pp. 163–66).

Whereas leaven and honey were prohibited, salt was required with all the offerings. Salt is a preservative, hence its use in the sacrificial offerings conveys a certain literality: The offerings have a perpetual place in the economy of the ritual. Beyond this, the phrase "salt of the covenant" (cf. Num. 18:19; 2 Chron. 13:5) extends the literal application to a wider sphere. In the ancient world, covenant making often involved sharing a meal in which the partners partook of salt (for examples, see Milgrom, *Leviticus 1–16*, pp. 191–92). The idea is also applied to God's covenant with Israel, which is perpetually binding and, as the priestly tradition is concerned to reiterate, perpetually sustained by God's commitment (cf. Gen. 9:16; 17:7, 13, 18, 19; Exod. 31:16).

Natural Barley (2:14–16)

A third type of cereal offering is the first-ripened grain. The reference may be to either wheat (cf. Num. 28:26) or barley (cf. 2 Kgs. 4:42). Because the instructions for wheat have already been addressed, it is likely that barley is the concern here. The same basic ritual applies to this offering as to those previously described. The donor prepares the grain by roasting it and adding oil and frankincense. The priest then turns the token portion into smoke as a gift to the Lord (cf. 1:9, 13, 17).

Leviticus 3:1–17
Well-Being Offerings

Chapter 3 brings the list of voluntary gifts to a close with a description of the well-being offering. Three paragraphs specify the animals that may be offered: a male or female animal from the herd (vv. 1–5); a male or female sheep from the flock (vv. 6–11); a goat from the flock (vv. 12–16a). Each unit begins with the same general introduction—"If the offering is . . ." (vv. 1, 6, 12)—and ends with a general statement, although differently worded, that the offering is acceptable to God (v. 5: "an offering by fire of pleasing odor to the Lord"; v. 11: "a food offering by fire to the Lord"; v. 16: "a food offering by fire for a pleasing odor"). Verses 16b–17 provide a concluding statement on the prohibition of eating fat and blood.

The ritual procedure for each animal is essentially the same as that for the burnt offering: presentation, hand-laying, slaughter, and presentation of the blood (see the discussion at 1:3–9). There are, however, two distinct differences. First, only specific parts of the animal are burned in the well-being offering. Second, although the present text does not mention it specifically, the well-being offering is generally understood to have provided a meal that was shared by both the priest and the donor (note especially Lev. 7:11–18, 28–36).

"If You Offer an Animal from the Herd" (3:1–5)

Two issues complicate understanding the well-being offering. First, the phrase *zebaḥ šelāmîm* combines two words that may be used independently to refer to sacrifice. Some scholars have argued (Rendtorff, 1967, pp. 119–68) that the two terms originally designated different types of sacrifice: the *zebaḥ*, an occasional private or family-oriented sacrifice, and the *šelāmîm*, a public royal sacrifice offered at the conclusion of a festive occasion. Others have argued (especially Milgrom, *Leviticus 1–16*, pp. 217–25) that the two terms are virtually synonymous. The first, *zebaḥ*, from the Hebrew root meaning "slaughter," refers generally to any slain animal on the altar (*mizbeaḥ*) whose meat is eaten by its offerer. The second, *šelāmîm*, from the Hebrew root *šlm*, which may be rendered in different ways depending on its particular form (see below), refers to the specific motivation or occasion that prompts the sacrifice. The evidence that may be cited in support of the first argument is both difficult to reconstruct and open to conflicting interpretations. Based on the biblical evidence, it is likely that the second argument has the greater

33

weight. Support for this position comes from Lev. 7:11–16, which specifies three motivations for offering the *šelāmîm* variety of the *zebaḥ*: thanksgiving, the successful fulfillment of a vow, and freewill. The common thread that ties these three motivations together is joy (cf. Deut. 27:7). The *zebaḥ šelāmîm*, whenever and however it is offered to God, is an occasion of great rejoicing. It is a ritual that enacts and concretizes the donor's delight in being able to draw near to the presence of God.

The second difficulty is the meaning of the word *šelāmîm*. The root *šlm* occurs in a variety of forms with different meanings. Modern translations reflect the range of possible renderings: *"peace* offering" (NAB; from *šālôm*, "peace"); "shared offering" (REB); "fellowship offering" (NIV); "communion sacrifice" (JB; from *šelem*, "alliance," "friendship," conventionally understood to have involved a shared meal); "sacrifice of well-being" (NRSV; from *šālēm*, "whole," "complete," "harmonious"). Because the etymology of *šlm* is uncertain, all translations are, as Milgrom notes, "at best, educated guesses" (Milgrom, *Leviticus 1–16*, p. 220). Commentators have tended toward either a maximalist or a minimalist view. W. Kaiser, for example, has argued that the basic idea of "peace" (*šālôm*) informs all presentations of this offering. He construes this broadly to mean that the main purpose of the offering is "to express friendship, fellowship, and peace with God" (Kaiser, p. 1024). Milgrom, in contrast, argues for the meaning "well-being" (*šālēm*), and he applies this strictly to the offerer. The main purpose of the offering, in his view, is "to provide meat for the table" (*Leviticus 1–16*, p. 221). Given the complexities of the issue, it is probably best to hold these different possibilities in tension. In this connection, it is worth noting that Leviticus 3 places the emphasis on presenting the offering as a "food gift *to the Lord*" (vv. 11, 14; cf. v. 16). Leviticus 7:11–18, which provides further discussion of this offering, goes beyond Leviticus 3 to describe a presentation "to the Lord" that also involves a meal shared by the priest and the donor.

If the donor offers an animal from the herd, it may be male or female; in either case the animal must be unblemished. Initially, the ritual of presentation follows the same steps as the burnt offering. The donor's responsibility is to lay a hand on the animal, slaughter it at the entrance to the tent of meeting, and make a presentation to the priest of the parts to be burned on the altar. The priest's responsibility is to dash the blood against the sides of the altar and to turn the presentation into smoke (vv. 1–2).

34 The ritual departs from what has been previously described by providing instructions concerning the specific parts that are to be removed from the animal and offered to God on the altar: the fat, the kidneys,

and the small lobe that extends from the liver (vv. 3–4). Three kinds of fat (*ḥēleb*) are mentioned: "the fat that *covers* the entrails," that is, the thick, apron-like membrane that covers the intestines and internal organs; "the fat that is *around* the entrails," that is, the supporting membrane that enfolds the individual organs; and "the fat that is on them [the kidneys] at the sinews." The amount of attention given to removing the fat makes clear that special care must be taken to reserve it exclusively for God (see v. 16b), although the reason for the proscription is nowhere provided. Two explanations merit consideration. On philological grounds, *ḥēleb* represents "the best" part (cf. Num. 18:12; Pss. 81:16 [MT: 81:17]; 147:14), and by theological extension, it is therefore the part that is most valuable as a gift to God. Viewed anatomically, the fat is located in the middle zone of the body, between the outer skin and the internal organs. As such it may correspond to the middle zone of the tabernacle, which is restricted to the priests, and thus, by theological extension, to the careful ordering of the cosmos that reflects the boundaries God has established in the created order (see Douglas, *Leviticus as Literature*, pp. 71–76).

"If Your Offering . . . Is from the Flock" (3:6–16a)

The offering from the flock may be either a sheep (vv. 6–11) or a goat (vv. 7–16a). The procedure is essentially the same as that described for the cattle (vv. 1–5). One detail is added concerning the broad-tailed sheep that is found in the Near East. The tail of this species is unusually long and may weigh fifteen or more pounds. This tail is to be removed completely, from tip to sacrum, and offered on the altar along with the fat, the kidneys, and the liver lobe. The priest then turns these parts into smoke, which becomes a "food offering" (vv. 6, 16) and a "pleasing odor" (v. 16; cf. v. 5) that God accepts as a worthy gift.

"All Fat Is the Lord's" (3:16b–17)

The concluding sentence forms an inclusio with 1:2 (Rendtorff, p. 25). Both use second-person plural language, an indication that chapters 1–3 form a discrete set of instructions concerning voluntary offerings that is addressed primarily to the *laity*. The proscription against eating fat and blood brings together the two forbidden items that have been of principal concern in chapters 1 and 3. All fat and all blood belong to the Lord; neither is to be consumed, under any circumstances, by people. At the heart of this prohibition is the priestly concern with the loss of life, animal or human. To guard against violating

35

God's "everlasting covenant" (Gen. 9:16) with all of creation, priestly theology insists that there must be no profane or nonsacrificial slaughter. The proscription, like the covenant it sustains, has the force of a "perpetual statute." It applies across time ("throughout your generations") and space ("in all your settlements").

Further Reflections on Voluntary Offerings

The concluding sentence of Leviticus 3 provides a transition point between the instructions for *voluntary* gifts—burnt offerings, cereal offerings, well-being offerings—and the instructions concerning offerings *required* for expiation—purification (4:1–5:13) and reparation (5:14–6:7 [MT: 5:14–26]). The transition invites reflection on where the journey into Leviticus has taken us thus far (see further "Theological Reflections," Leviticus 1, above).

1. *The encounter with God begins with voluntary gifts.* It is instructive that the first words from the tent of meeting envision a voluntary and spontaneous movement toward God. The motivation for coming into God's presence is joy, not obligation. The catalyst for the gift is happiness in search of celebration, not duty in fulfillment of mandate or guilt in need of nullification. In its own way, Leviticus begins with a word from God that provides an answer to the psalmist's question: "What shall I return to the Lord for all his bounty to me?" (Ps. 116:12). The "bounty" of which the psalmist speaks is God's beneficent response to the cries of people in need. In Leviticus, the bounty of God that invites celebration is anchored to the story line of Exodus, which begins with the affirmation that God heard the groanings of a beleaguered group of hopeless slaves and ends with a free people standing in the presence of the God whose glory has transformed their world. How does one respond to the gift of life that opens up unlimited possibilities? Leviticus begins its answer to this question by providing instructions that channel joy into tangible acts of celebration.

The psalmists convey their glad response to God in evocative poetry that recruits the reader into an imaginative interplay with their lyrics. Leviticus is different. Its instructions are measured and seemingly atonal. They require a more patient reading and another level of imagination. Nevertheless, the instructions concerning burnt offerings, cereal offerings, and well-being offerings have their own inviting lyricism (Damrosch, p. 67). Each of these three kinds of offerings is divided into three "stanzas" that play out variations on a common theme. The animal offerings in chapters 1 and 3 comprise three options that donors may select: gifts from the herd, from the flock

36

(sheep or goats), and from the birds. The cereal offerings in chapter 2 comprise three types of grain: uncooked wheat, cooked wheat, and natural barley. Each stanza is linked to the others by a repeating refrain that keeps both ancient donors and modern readers mindful of the motivation behind the gift: to provide "a pleasing odor to the Lord" (1:9, 13, 17; 2:2, 9, 12; 3:5, 16). The effect of this lyrical structure is not unlike that achieved by Psalm 136, where the "story" of what God has done for the community of faith is constantly "interrupted" by the repetition, no fewer than twenty-six times, of the refrain that motivates this song's joyful offering of thanks: "because his steadfast love endures forever." In Leviticus 1–3 the glad response to what God has done follows a different score, but the song resonates with a similar harmony. If we allow ourselves to imagine that those who stand before the "glory of the Lord" are asking the question "What shall we return to the Lord for all his bounty to us?" then Leviticus 1–3 invites us to hear this response: You may bring a gift from the herd, *because this is pleasing to God*; you may bring a gift from the flock, *because this is pleasing to God*; you may bring a gift of grain, *because this, too, is pleasing to God*.

2. *Leviticus 1–3 not only invites joyful response to God; it anticipates and enacts it*. The canonical arrangement of the Pentateuch places Leviticus inside the instructions from God to Israel during an eleven-month stay at Sinai (Exodus 19–Numbers 10). Inside this story line, Leviticus gives instructions concerning the worship Israel may offer to God *in advance* of the actualization of this worship. This proleptic view need not be uncoupled from the likelihood that Leviticus also looks back to and accurately reflects, at least in general ways, Israel's actual practice of worship. Nevertheless, the canonical story line of the Pentateuch shifts the focus of Leviticus from historical retrospective to a future envisioned but not yet realized. The covenant with God has been formalized, but its implementation in the promised land of Canaan lies in the future. The tabernacle has been built, but its role in Israel's religious, social, and political configuration will not be fully realized until those encamped at Sinai cross over into the land to which God is leading them. Similarly, the worship Leviticus enjoins looks forward to a time when a settled community will have opportunity to raise herds and flocks, to plant and cultivate grain, and to offer gifts to God of what they possess and produce.

Inside this story line, Leviticus anticipates and invites joy as the first motivation that brings Israel into God's presence. This proleptic view is important, not least because there is already sufficient evidence to confirm that Israel's journey toward becoming the people God desires has been fraught with disobedience and rebellion. From the priestly perspective, the truth that makes the point is the human sin that corrupts the world and requires that God send the cleansing waters of the flood (cf. Gen. 6:11–13). Given the demonstrable and chronic human need for forgiveness, one might well expect that Israel's instructions for approaching God would necessarily begin with the summons to bring expiatory gifts. In an evocative reversal of expectations, Leviticus begins with an emphasis not on sin and its required atonement but on joy and its spontaneous expression through voluntary gifts. From a priestly perspective, the God who covenants with such a frail and faulty people still hopes and expects that joy, not guilt, will be the primary motivation for the worship Israel will offer.

Toward this end, the instructions in Leviticus 1–3 convey more than simply the details of the gifts Israel may bring. The presentation of the gifts is envisioned as part of a large, multifaceted ritual that is both dramatic and constitutive. Priestly rituals, like all rituals, are a form of social drama that both *symbolizes* and *enacts* belief. The gift of an animal from the herd or the flock, for example, is a symbolic way of expressing the belief that God created the world and the resources it provides to sustain human life. When human beings return a gift of creation to its Creator, they acknowledge and celebrate the relationship that makes life more than simply a biological process. They exult in the belief that life itself is a gift of God. The gift is a symbol that transforms that belief, which begins as cognitive recognition, into a concrete and tangible act. But rituals do more than merely *symbolize* belief. Rituals *enact* belief. They gesture forth and embody belief that is at times more cognitive than experiential. One may *believe* that God is Creator of the world but be incapable of finding any confirming evidence that the belief is true. For such occasions, ritual acts are especially formative, because they call for an action—for example, the presentation of a gift from the herd or the flock—that creates and sustains the belief when life's experiences may threaten to eclipse it. In sum, just as belief informs and compels the ritual, so the ritual enacts and re-creates the belief, even when experience may call it into question.

Upon the death of his father, Leon Wieseltier reluctantly began observing the year-long Jewish ritual of mourning. He had little enthusiasm for the custom. He initially felt no connection with the prescribed prayers; he had no real understanding of the arcane texts he was supposed to read. He simply committed himself to the ritual, because he knew this is what his father would have wanted. After several months of going through the motions, he entered this discernment in his diary: "Ritual is the conversion of essences into acts" (Wieseltier, p. 68). About halfway through the year, he built upon a truth he had not sought but could no longer ignore:

> When I lead the prayers, I can't control my mind. It roams. Small things, small things. My thoughts and my words have nothing to do with each other. But the words keep coming, unimpeded by my abandonment of them. The triumph of rote. (Wieseltier, p. 196)

Gail Godwin explicates the same truth about rituals, but from a different perspective. Father Gower, rector of St. Cuthbert's, a small parish in rural Virginia, struggled with his faith. His salvation was the comfort he found in the sacraments, which provided "a sort of sanity filter against the onslaughts of existence." Father Adrian, his friend and colleague, recognized the wisdom in this approach to ministry and confirmed it with a personal anecdote:

> There was a Jesuit priest studying with me in Zurich, at the Institute. I once asked him, "What if you as a priest stopped believing? What would you do then?" "Make a fist in my pocket," he said, "and go on with the ritual." (Godwin, p. 274)

3. *Gifts that give and withhold.* The gifts to be offered to God are carefully described: cattle, sheep, goats, doves and pigeons, grains. Collectively, they represent the best of what humans possess and produce; hence they symbolize the happy relinquishment of the whole of one's life to God. Along with these gifts, the instructions carefully describe a number of forbidden items that humans must never possess: blood, fat, kidneys, liver lobe. These are always withheld from human consumption; they are always reserved exclusively for God. They, too, comprise the gifts that humans offer to God. The question these instructions invite but do little to answer is, why (and how) do certain forbidden items, items understood never to have been the donor's prerogative to possess, constitute a gift to God?

Two possible explanations open up avenues for further reflection. First, the forbidden items appear to be connected in some way to the essence of human life and thus by extension to the gift of life itself, which the donor affirms belongs to God. Leviticus explains the prohibition against eating blood by stating that "the life of the flesh is in the blood" (17:11). Since blood and fat are listed together in 3:17, it may be that the same rationale applies to both. A similar rationale may underlie the prohibition concerning the kidneys and the liver, for both are frequently described, along with the heart, as the seat of thoughts, emotions, and conscience (kidneys: Pss. 7:9; 26:2; Jer. 11:20; 17:10; 20:12; liver: Lam. 2:11).

39

If we take Leviticus 17:11 as a key to understanding the forbidden items, then we may consider a second and larger rationale. The words "life of the flesh" translate the Hebrew phrase *nepeš hābāśār*. The first time this collocation occurs in Priestly texts is Gen. 9:4: "You shall not eat flesh with its life (*bāśār benapšô*), that is, its blood." The term "flesh with its life" is used to introduce the *restrictions* God orders as part of the *blessing* that renews relationship in the postflood world. In the succeeding verses of Genesis 9, the words *nepeš* and *bāśār* reoccur repeatedly, in different collocations, the effect of which is to suggest that God's concern to safeguard "flesh" and "life" is to be understood in the most comprehensive way imaginable. Thus, God is concerned for "human life" (*nepeš hā'ādām*; v. 5), "all flesh" (*kol bāśār*; vv. 16, 17; cf. v. 15), and, therefore, by definition, the life of "every living creature" (*kol nepeš haḥayyâ*; vv. 10, 12, 15). Priestly theology understands this concern for the sanctity of all life, animal and human, to be the foundation for God's renewed covenant with creation (vv. 9, 11, 12, 13, 15, 17), now described for the first time in Hebrew Scriptures as an "everlasting covenant between God and every living creature of all flesh that is on the earth" (v. 16).

We may understand that in Priestly theology God's "everlasting covenant" with creation is both mirrored and sustained by "perpetual statute[s]" (Lev. 3:17; *ḥuqqat ʿōlām*; cf. the same phrase in 7:36; 10:9; 16:29, 31, 34; 17:7; 23:14, 21, 31, 41; 24:3) such as those that proscribe the consumption of blood, fat, kidneys, and liver lobe. These are reserved for God not only because they represent the best of life that humans may offer. In a larger sense, they are gifts motivated by the sheer joy of being invited to embody and ritually enact the covenant that sustains the world God has created, blessed, and endowed from the beginning of time with the capacity to be "very good" (cf. Gen. 1:31).

Leviticus 4:1–5:13
The Purification Offering

Whereas chapters 1–3 deal with voluntary gifts that are spontaneously motivated, chapters 4–5 deal with expiatory gifts that are required because of sin. Two types of offerings are described: the purification offering (4:1–5:13) and the reparation offering (5:14–6:7; MT: 5:14–26). Both offerings deal with sin that disrupts the relationship with God and therefore with the world God has created, but they do so in different ways. The purification offering addresses "unintentional" violations of "any of the Lord's commandments" (4:2). Such transgressions require not only the forgiveness of the offender but also the purification of the sanctuary. The reparation offering addresses "unintentional" violations of the "holy things of the Lord" (5:14). Such transgressions require not only the forgiveness of the offender but also reparations that restore the relationship with God and world to its proper balance.

Instructions for the purification offering begin with a brief introduction (vv. 1–2), which provides a general overview of the situation that requires this particular offering. Four successive paragraphs specify the ritual procedure, which is scaled according to the status of the offender: vv.3–12, "the anointed priest"; vv. 13–21, "the whole congregation"; vv. 22–26, "a ruler"; vv. 27–35, "anyone of the ordinary people." A concluding section, 5:1–13, addresses four specific situations that require a purification offering (vv. 1–4) and provides further instruction about what the poor may do if they cannot afford to bring what has been prescribed (vv. 5–13).

Introduction (4:1–2)

A purification offering is required whenever anyone sins "unintentionally" by violating one of God's prohibitive commandments. The focus is on sins of commission (sins of omission are addressed in 5:1–4), here broadly defined as either committing an act that is wrong without being aware that it is wrong or knowing that an act is wrong but being unaware that the act has been committed. In either case, the sin is unintentional; the offender has erred without meaning to do so. No details are provided concerning which sins are regarded as unintentional, but the cases specified in 5:1–4 indicate, for example, that inadvertently coming into contact with "any unclean thing" (5:2) is the kind of transgression that is of principal concern here. The implicit contrast is with the "intentional" sin, which Num. 15:30–31 describes as "high-handed" or premeditated acts that brazenly defy God. Unintentional sins may be expiated by the purification offering. Intentional sins that express contempt for God may not be expiated. The perpetrators of such offenses "shall be utterly cut off" and forced to live with unatoned guilt (Num. 15:31).

"If It Is the Anointed Priest Who Sins" (4:3–12)

The ritual of the purification offering begins with instructions that address the unintentional sin of the high priest (literally, "the anointed priest"). Whenever the high priest sins, he brings guilt upon the whole

41

community that he represents before God. The word for "guilt" conveys the idea of both the wrong that creates a feeling of guilt and the liability that results from incurring guilt (Milgrom, *Cult and Conscience*, pp. 3–12). Although the text does not specify how the priest might sin, it is likely that it has in mind some offense that he may have committed in the performance of his ritual duties. (See further Leviticus 16, which deals with the sin offering the priest presents "for himself.") Whatever the error, the priest's guilt is shared collectively by the people, and he is obligated on their behalf to make restitution.

The ritual for the purification offering is similar to that which has been previously described (see the discussion at 1:3–9). The priest must bring an unblemished bull to the entrance of the tent of meeting, lay his hand on the bull, slaughter it, and disperse the blood appropriately. He must remove the fat, the two kidneys, and the liver lobe in the same manner that these were removed from the bull of the well-being offering (3:3–6) and turn them into smoke on the altar. There are, however, two important elements in this ritual that distinguish it from those described in chapters 1–3.

First, the dispersal of the blood (4:5–7) is critical and varies according to the status of the offerer (see further vv. 16–18, 25, 30, 34). When the offerer is the high priest, he brings some of the blood into the tent of meeting, dips his finger into it, and sprinkles it seven times before the curtain that separates the outer sanctum from the inner sanctum, or Holy of Holies (cf. Exod. 26:31–35). Next, he places some of the blood on the horns of the incense altar inside the outer sanctum (cf. Exod. 30:1–10; 37:25–28). By daubing the extremities of the altar with the blood, the priest ritually cleanses or purifies the entire altar of the impurities that have arisen because of the sin. The rest of the blood the priest pours out at the base of the main altar outside the tent of meeting, thus ritually purifying the entire outer courtyard.

From these details we may deduce that the ritual of blood dispersion conveys a double-edged theological perspective (for further reflection, see the comments at the conclusion of 6:1–7: "The Burden of Sin, the Hope of Forgiveness, and the Gift of Ritual"). On the one hand, inadvertent sins of the high priest are very serious. They have negative consequences not only for the priest and the community he serves, because they disrupt and distort their relationship with God. They also defile the sanctuary by ritually penetrating both the outer courtyard and the inner sanctum, symbolically extending their corruption right up to the curtain that marks the entrance to the Holy of Holies, the ritual space that offers the most proximate and intimate presence of God on earth. In other words, the unintentional sins of the priest jeopardize both people and the world, for a holy God cannot and will not reside in the midst of the unholy. On the other hand, the purification offering provides a ritual way of cleansing both people and sanctuary of the sins that make them inhospitable for God. By sprinkling the blood seven times before the curtain, the priest ritually enacts God's seven-day creation of the world, which on the occasions of the purification offering becomes a ritual *re-creation* of God's primordial hopes and expectations for the world.

A second distinctive feature of the purification offering is the manner in which the remains are disposed (vv. 11–12). Apart from the portions that have been previously used in the ceremony—fat, kidneys, liver lobe, and blood—"all the rest of the bull" is taken outside the camp "to a clean place" and burned on the ash heap. The remains are specified as the hide (NRSV: "skin"), the flesh, the head, the legs, the entrails, and the dung. Two general principles undergird the instruction. First, the blood of the animal acts as a purifying agent by absorbing impurity, which is then extended to the remains of the animal. Because they have become impure, the remains of the animal are dangerous and must be disposed of outside the Holy Place to safeguard against further contamination. Second, Lev. 6:30 (MT: 6:23) proscribes the eating of any sin offering from which the blood has been brought into the tent of meeting. This instruction is based on a subtle but important distinction between sin offerings from which the blood is not taken into the tent of the meeting and those from which the blood is taken into the tent of meeting. In the case of the former, the priest must eat at least a portion of the remains on the same day of the offering (cf. 6:24–29; MT: 6:17–22; 10:16–20). In the case of the latter, when the sin offering is for the priest himself and the community he serves, the remains are not to be eaten, because the priest must not benefit or profit in any way from the ritual of personal expiation (cf. 8:14–17; 9:8–11; 16:27; for further discussion of these matters, see Milgrom, *Leviticus 1–16*, pp. 635–40).

"If the Whole Congregation of Israel Errs Unintentionally" (4:13–21)

The instructions concerning the purification offering for the community are in most respects quite similar to those for the priest. When the community unintentionally violates one of God's prohibitive commandments, the error may for a time remain unknown to them. Eventually, the liability they have incurred creates a feeling of guilt that in its own way is part of the dynamic in which the sin "becomes known" (v. 14). When this happens, the community must bring a bull from the herd to the tent of meeting for their purification offering. The "elders of the congregation," acting on behalf of the people, place their hands on the animal and slaughter it (v. 15). From this point forward, the ritual follows the same procedure as that described in vv. 5–10.

Verse 20 introduces two terms—*atonement* and *forgiveness*—that reappear in the following paragraphs (vv. 26, 31, 35; 5:10, 13). Milgrom has persuasively argued that in ritual texts the verb *kippēr*, conventionally translated "atone" or "expiate," regularly means "purge" or "purify" (*Leviticus 1–16*, pp. 253–69, 1079–84). In the context of the purification offering, *kippēr* has to do with purging or decontaminating the *object* on which it is placed, namely, the sanctuary and its sancta, not the *person* on whose behalf it is offered. This is not to say that the purification offering has only to do with purifying sacred space. Forgiveness for sins committed is also an important part of what the offering seeks to secure. In this connection, it is instructive to note that the verb *forgive* is a passive form. The implied subject is God. While the priest actualizes the purgation of the sanctuary, only God can forgive sin. The ritual purifies the place where God desires to be present. God alone decides the efficacy of the ritual, which has as its ultimate objective not only a cleansed sanctuary but, more important, a restored relationship.

"When a Ruler" or "Anyone of the Ordinary People" Sins (4:22–35)

The next two sections shift the focus to unintentional sins of an established leader or "ruler" (vv. 22–26) and of any ordinary, untitled person in the land (vv. 27–35). In a descending order of gravity, these sins are less destructive than the sins of the high priest and the entire community. The procedure for their purification offering reflects this difference. The ruler must bring an unblemished male goat (v. 23); the ordinary person must bring either an unblemished female goat or sheep. In both cases, the offering is taken from the small livestock and is less costly than the bull required of the high priest and the community at large. The priest (vv. 25, 30, 34), that is, any priest, puts some of the blood on the horns of the altar of burnt offering and pours some of the blood at the base of this altar. The restriction of the blood to the altar in the outer courtyard is a further indication that these sins have less capacity to defile the sanctuary than those previously described, which require the purification of both the outer courtyard and the inner sanctum. Finally, these instructions make no mention of the disposal of the animal's remains outside the camp. Instead, they direct the priest

44

to remove the fat, like the fat of the well-being offering (vv. 26, 31, 35), and turn it into smoke on the altar. The rest of the animal, presumably, was to be consumed by the priest (cf. 6:26; MT: 6:19).

Specific Cases and Special Concessions (5:1–13)

The instructions in this section deal with what Milgrom has described as "the graduated purification offering" (*Leviticus 1–16*, pp. 307–18). It may well be, as he suggests, that 5:1–13 is best understood as an appendix to chapter 4, which treats "borderline cases" where the transgression is more an act of omission, failing to do what is required, than commission. While these cases may not conform to the normative criterion of unintentionality (the word does not occur), they still require a purification offering, which is "graduated" or scaled according to the offerer's economic means.

Four such cases are enumerated: (1) When people hear a public call for testimony and fail to come forward with what they know concerning the matter in question, they are liable for their silence (v. 1). (2) When people touch something unclean, especially the carcass of an animal, they become unclean and incur liability for their act, whether they were conscious of it or not (v. 2). (3) When people come into contact with human impurity of any kind (for specific details, see Leviticus 12–15), they incur liability for their act, whether they were conscious of the contact or not (v. 3). (4) When people swear an oath, impulsively and without reflection, to do good or evil, thereby committing themselves to act in accordance with what they say, they incur liability for their act, whether they were careless in speaking or not (v. 4). In sum, people sin by what they say or refuse to say, for speech may advance the cause of justice or obstruct it. They sin by the way they respect or fail to respect the boundaries between the clean and the unclean, for impurities abound, and discernment must be constant if the boundaries are to be sustained.

When persons who have sinned in any of these ways become aware of their guilt, they must first confess their sin (v. 5) and then bring the required purification offering. There are but four priestly texts that explicitly stipulate confession as a required accompaniment to sacrifice (Lev. 5:5; 16:21; 26:40; Num. 5:7). Because each of these cases deals with deliberate sins, Milgrom has reasonably proposed that confession is the legal means by which deliberate sins may be converted into unintentional sins, thus making it possible for them to be expiated (*Leviticus 1–16*, pp. 301–2). The rationale for the additional requirement of confession would seem to be that deliberate sins demand more than

45

contrition. They must be not only internally acknowledged but also publicly declared. Whether intentional or not, a person's acts convert thoughts into deeds that may be destructive. Until these deeds are declared and publicly disclosed, a person has not accepted full responsibility, before God and the community, for the sin that disrupts the fullness of life God has ordained.

The purification offering required for the sins addressed in 5:1–4 is a female from the flock, either a sheep or a goat (v. 6). If persons cannot afford one of these offerings, they have two further options: They may bring two turtledoves or two pigeons (vv. 7–10). In either case, the first bird is a purification offering, the second a burnt offering (ʿōlâ). The ritual procedure is essentially the same as that described in 1:14–17. If persons cannot afford either a dove or a pigeon, they may bring a tenth of an ephah of fine flour, which is the rough equivalent of one day's provision of bread for one person. The ritual procedure is similar to that stipulated for the grain offering in chapter 2. The major difference is the omission of oil and frankincense (cf. Num.5:11), which in the grain offering produce a "pleasing odor to the Lord" and symbolize the joyous nature of the occasion. Purification is, however, a more somber occasion, for while forgiveness is the objective, the offering is itself part of the confession that joy depends on being reconciled with God and the world.

Leviticus 5:14–6:7 (MT: 5:14–26)
The Reparation Offering

The reparation offering (ʾāšām; NRSV: "guilt offering") also provides expiation for sin, but its focus is on different transgressions, and therefore different requirements, from those addressed by the purification offering. The key word is maʿal, which in cultic texts means not only "trespass" (NRSV: 5:15; 6:1 [MT: 5:21]) but also, more specifically, a "breach of faith" (Hartley, p. 75). Two speeches describe the breaches that require reparation. The first (5:14–19) addresses the violation of the "holy things of the Lord." The second (6:1–7; MT: 5:20–26) addresses the violation of other human beings, which, as these stipulations make clear, is also an act of faithlessness that fractures what God regards as holy. Both speeches stipulate that expiation is a matter not only of enacting a ritual but also of concretely replenishing something sacred that has been diminished by a "bad faith" deed.

Violation of the "Holy Things of the Lord" (5:14–19)

The first speech addresses two cases that exemplify breaking faith with God. The first case (vv. 14–16) deals with unintentional violations of the "holy things of the Lord." What constitutes the "holy things of the Lord" is not precisely clear, but the term most likely includes anything that has been dedicated to God, for example, the sacred furniture and furnishings of the tabernacle, sacrifices offered in holy places, things exclusively designated for the priests (clothing, food, land, portions of certain sacrifices).

Priestly concern for protecting the holy things of God against *maʿal*, "breaches of faith" reflects a widespread practice in the ancient Near East (for discussion, see Milgrom, *Leviticus 1–16*, pp. 345–56). A particularly revealing example is the thirteenth-century Hittite text "Instructions for Temple Officials" (Pritchard, pp. 207–10), which cites almost two dozen ways that priests and temple servants may be guilty of violating their sacred responsibilities. They are admonished, for example, not to expropriate for themselves the temple's sacrificial animals by keeping, eating, selling, or exchanging them; not to wear the temple's garments or use the temple's tools for unsanctioned purposes; not to change the set times for rituals in order to accommodate the business interests of those required to observe them. The penalty for violating each one of these proscriptions is death.

Similar strictures and punishments occur in the Hebrew Bible. Chronicles provides a number of examples, including 2 Chron. 26:16–18, which reports that Uzziah was stricken with leprosy because, in usurping the priest's prerogative to offer incense in the sanctuary, he was "false (*maʿal*) to the Lord"; and 2 Chron. 28:19, 22–25 (cf. 2 Chron. 36:14), which reports that Ahaz brought punishment on himself and all Israel by being "faithless (*maʿal*) to the Lord" in his handling of the temple utensils. Underlying all these proscriptions is the concern to avoid sacrilegious acts, that is, acts that appropriate to oneself the holy things of God. To put a sharp edge on the point, one is guilty of sacrilege, *maʿal*, a "breach of faith," whenever one *uses* God for secular, self-serving, or ulterior purposes.

Such breaches of faith make persons guilty and culpable (*ʾāšām*); to be forgiven and restored to their proper relationship with God, they must bring a reparation offering (*ʾāšām*). The details of the ritual procedure are provided in 7:1–6. The instructions in 5:14–16 focus on two particular aspects of the offering: (1) Offenders must bring an unblemished ram, "convertible into silver by the sanctuary shekel"; and (2) they must add "one-fifth" of its value as a penalty payment. The

47

phrase "convertible into silver" is obscure, but it suggests that the ram had to be of a certain value, which was determined not by human assessment but by the standards of the sanctuary. The offerer must add a penalty payment equal to 20 percent of the value of what has been violated. The penalty safeguards against the temptation to appropriate, free of cost, the things of God, as if they were simply an interest-free loan to be used for whatever purpose one chooses. Based on the instructions in Leviticus 27, one may also conclude that the penalty payment served as part of the economic system designed to fund the temple.

The second case (vv. 17–19) concerns unintentional violations of one of God's proscriptive commandments. The required reparation—an unblemished ram—is the same as that stipulated in v. 15. The language follows the wording in 4:2, 13, 22, 27, which has led some to suggest that what is envisioned here is merely a variation of the purification offering (Noth, pp. 47–48). Milgrom has countered this argument by pointing to a distinctive criterion in v. 17 (*Leviticus 1–16*, pp. 332–33). The unintentional sins addressed by the purification offering ultimately become known to the offenders (4:14, 23, 28), thus prompting them to make restitution. By contrast, the unintentional violation addressed here remains unknown (NRSV: "without knowing"). The indication is that guilt, experienced psychologically, perhaps even physically, so heightens the anxiety of persons that they suspect they have erred even though they do not know specifically how.

The theological ramification of Milgrom's suggestion is significant (see further *Leviticus 1–16*, pp. 373–78). A common assumption, especially among Protestants who take their cue from prophetic criticisms of rituals (e.g., Isa. 1:10–17; Jer. 7:1–15; Hos. 4:4–5:7; Amos 2:6–16; Mic. 3:9–12), is that the priestly system of sacrifices is largely designed to *induce* guilt, thereby coercing people into performing meaningless rites that only paper over what God truly desires. The suggestion that guilt is an existential reality, that a pained conscience may be as real an indicator of sin as an official indictment, stands the conventional assumption about priestly rituals on its head. From a priestly perspective, it is not ritual that induces guilt; it is guilt that requires the ritual, which offers comfort and enacts restoration even when all other means seem unavailable or ineffective.

Violation of Other Human Beings (6:1–7; MT: 5:20–26)

The second speech, like the first, begins with the words "The Lord spoke to Moses, saying . . ." (6:1; cf. 5:14). The focus is on "breaches of faith" that are exemplified by swearing falsely (vv. 3, 5 [MT: 5:22, 24]). Such acts not only violate other persons; they also implicate God, because in swearing an oath the guilty party has invoked God's holy name, thus making God a partner to dishonesty and fraud. Three examples are described:

- *The deception of someone in matters of a deposit, pledge, or robbery (v. 2a; MT: 5:21a).* When persons withhold a deposit that someone has entrusted to them for safekeeping, or refuse to return someone's security pledge even when the loan has been paid off, or steal someone's goods or property, and then swear by God's name that they are innocent, then they have not acted in good faith with either God or the persons they have abused.
- *Defrauding (ʿāšāq) someone by taking advantage of them in ways that may be legal but are nonetheless immoral and unethical (v. 2b; MT: 5:22b; cf. 19:13).* The Hebrew Bible preserves two clear cases of ʿāšāq (Milgrom, *Leviticus 1–16*, p. 337). Deuteronomy 24:14–15 (cf. Mal. 3:5) warns against "taking advantage" (NIV) of hired laborers by withholding the wages they are due. Even if the workers are "aliens" without legal recourse, God will hear their cry for help, and God will hold the employer accountable for failing to deal honorably with them. The second example, which is addressed in multiple contexts, is the seizure of property that is legally held as down payment on a loan. If creditors hold a debtor's only cloak, for example, they must not keep it overnight, for to do so jeopardizes the well-being of those who are most vulnerable (cf. Exod. 22:25–26; Deut. 24:10–13; Ezek. 18:7, 16). To act in such an uncaring manner is to be guilty of "extortion" (ʿāšāq; Ezek. 18:18; cf. 22:29), which, if not reversed, subjects the offender to God's wrath.
- *Finding something another has lost and lying about it (v. 3a; MT: 5:22).* To this example is added the general principle (vv. 3b, 5; MT: 5:22b, 24) that applies to each of the cases enumerated above: Whenever persons commit any of these violations, then swear by God's *"holy* name" (cf. Lev. 20:3; 22:2,

49

32; Ezek. 36:20, 21, 22) that they have not done so, they break faith not only with the people they have wronged but also with God. Because they have defrauded people in God's name, they have committed *ma'al*; they have desecrated and diminished "the holy things of the Lord" just as certainly as if they had entered the sanctuary and defiled its contents.

The reparation offering required for such violations is essentially the same as that stipulated in 5:14–16, 18. There is, however, an important sequence to the procedure that merits close attention. When offenders realize their guilt, they must *first* make restitution to the person they have wronged, adding one-fifth to their payment, *then* bring their reparation offering to the priest (vv. 5–6; MT: 5:24–25). The forgiveness they seek from God cannot be secured until they have made right the wrongs they have committed against people. We may discern here a radical qualification of the normative presumption of the sacrificial system, namely, that God must first receive the offerings at the altar before the priests or others receive their designated portions (cf. 1 Sam. 2:12–17, 29–33). Milgrom states succinctly the axiom that explains such a "startling innovation" in the priestly sensitivity to the abuse of humans: "In matters of justice man takes priority over God" (*Leviticus 1–16*, p. 370).

The Burden of Sin, the Hope of Forgiveness, and the Gift of Ritual

> Take your well-disciplined strengths
> and stretch them between two
> opposing poles. Because inside human beings
> is where God learns.
> (R. Rilke, "Just as the Winged Energy
> of Delight," in *Rag and Bone Shop
> of the Heart*, p. 236)

These closing lines of Rainer Maria Rilke's poem may invite reflection on the "two opposing poles" of the offerings reviewed thus far. Of the five major offerings in Leviticus 1–6, three are voluntary (burnt offerings, cereal offerings, well-being offerings), two are required (purification offerings, reparation offerings). The voluntary offerings are motivated by joy; they give expression to the praise-filled enthusiasm of being invited into the very presence of God. The required offerings are imperative because of what George Herbert calls "sorrow dogging sin" ("Sin," in *Complete English Poems*, p. 40); they give expression to the anguished lament that aches for a Presence no longer diminished by human frailty and failure. The "well-disciplined strengths" of the priestly sacrificial system are a bridge stretched between these two poles of the human experience, between joy and sorrow; between what cannot be contained and what cannot be denied or ignored; between an inestimable gift and an incalculable loss.

Leviticus insists that without both poles neither the human experience nor the rites and rituals in which they find expression is complete. More important, as Rilke's last line hints, until and unless human beings come into God's presence with the full range of the experiences that make and break them, neither they nor God can know with full clarity whether the world can in actuality be the "very good" world God envisioned it to be. It is fitting therefore that the instructions for sacrifice do not end with the "well-being offering," for as the first words of chapter 4 make clear, "when anyone sins" some further word from God is necessary if the journey toward "very good" is to continue.

The Burden of Sin. It is perhaps understandable, and therefore all the more regrettable, that time, distance, neglect, and frequently disdain for the Old Testament in general and the priestly in particular have conspired to reduce and thin the way we "moderns" think of sin. The title of Karl Menninger's book *Whatever Became of Sin?* (published in 1973) is but one indicator of how far removed we are from the focused concern for purification and reparation in Leviticus. On the matter of sin, as on many others that Leviticus will address, we have much work to do if we are to hear and respond to the words that God instructed Moses to speak to our ancestors in the community of faith.

The priestly understanding of sin is multifaceted. Sin operates at every level of society. No person is exempt from its reach. Rich and poor, clergy and laity, leaders and ordinary citizens, individuals and community—all are vulnerable, and everyone is accountable. The instructions in Leviticus 4–5 are therefore necessarily comprehensive, for the audience they address includes every *ʾādām* ("human being"; 1:2), every *nepeš* ("person"; 2:1; 4:2; 5:1, 2, 4, 15, 17, 21 [Eng. 6:2]). Sins may be acts of *commission* or *omission*. They may be *unintentional transgressions* that persons address without hesitation as soon as they become aware of the error, and they may be *conscious breaches of faith* that persons will deny under oath as long as they can get the consent of their consciences to do so. They may be deeds that *use God* for

51

self-serving ends, as if that which is holy can be invoked or not, depending on how it affects the balance between profit and loss. They may be deeds that *use other persons*, as if deceit, fraud, and extortion are merely legal or moral loopholes that can be cleverly circumnavigated without penalty. Whatever the sin, priestly theology insists that it disrupts relationship with God and diminishes people's capacity to be all they are created to be.

Sin leaves its mark not only on people but also on institutions. With a sensitivity that the contemporary world has largely managed to live without, the priests understand sin to be more than an abstraction. They envision it rather as a substance with physical properties. Milgrom uses the suggestive term *aerial miasma,* by which he means that sin is like a pollutant discharged into the atmosphere (*Leviticus 1–16*, p. 257). Once airborne, it targets the realm of the sacred and spreads its corruption as far as its strength will take it. At particular risk is the sanctuary, the central symbol on earth of God's holy presence. From the instructions for purification in Leviticus 4, Milgrom discerns a graduated power in sin's defilement of the sanctuary.

Sin's power to defile the sanctuary may be traced through three stages of progressing severity (Milgrom, *Leviticus 1–16*, p. 257): (1) An individual's unintentional sins pollute the outer altar and courtyard area, thus requiring the priest to cleanse the altar by daubing its sides with the blood of the purification offering (Lev. 4:25, 30). (2) Unintentional sins of the high priest or of the entire community are more serious, because they extend their reach beyond the outer courtyard to the inner sanctum. The ritual of purification requires the priest to respond by placing the blood of the offering on the inner altar of incense and to sprinkle it seven times before the curtain that separates the inner sanctum from the Holy of Holies (Lev. 4:5–7, 16–18). (3) Intentional unrepented sins are the most severe of all. They defile not only the outer altar and the inner shrine but also the Holy of Holies, which houses the very throne of God. Because intentional unrepentant sinners are barred from bringing an offering to the sanctuary (Num. 15:27–31), the defilement their sins cause can be rectified only on the annual Day of Purification, when the high priest cleanses the entire sanctuary, from the outer court to the Holy of Holies (Lev. 16:14, 16, 19).

There is a good deal of evidence to suggest that many in today's world would find the priestly understanding of sin's corrosive reach to be at most a quaint idea. It is not just that sin is an unfashionable idea or that even religious people attuned to sin seldom set their theological compass by the book of Leviticus. More telling is the fact that the bonds connecting individuals to institutional structures of any kind—

social, religious, political—have steadily eroded over the last half century. One provocative assessment of the prevailing sense of disconnectedness in American society is Robert Putnam's *Bowling Alone: The Collapse and Revival of American Community*. As the title indicates, the way we bowl is simply a cipher for Putnam's analysis of the shift in America's social commitments. Once we bowled in leagues, straining for wins and bearing the losses with a team of kindred spirits. Now we not only bowl alone, we essentially live alone. We do not join or make commitments to anything beyond ourselves. We do not connect with bridge clubs, charity leagues, Boy Scouts, YWCA, PTA, political parties, or religious denominations. We consistently tell pollsters that we value, even yearn for, a more collectively caring society, but the raw data amassed from the way we live verify only that we no longer expend the capital to be invested in any community. In sum, we succeed alone, we fail alone. To use religious terms, we are righteous alone, and to the extent that we use the language any more, we sin alone. We have come a long way from John Donne's vaguely familiar axiom that "No man is an Island," a still farther distance from the priests' notion that what we do has any bearing whatsoever on the structures of our society.

From a priestly perspective, the burden of sin is serious and consequential. To deny or ignore this burden jeopardizes both people and the world. At the personal and communal level, sin disrupts the relationship with God with bad-faith acts that obstruct God's capacity to be present in the lives of people who have been created for blessing and purpose. Absent a sense of obligation and responsibility for who we are and what we do, life without the consciousness of sin's burden is pointless narcissism posing as success and happiness. But the burden of sin is still greater than the diminishment of personal or communal well-being. In priestly theology, sin's corruption is not limited to people. It is instead like a virus released into the world that attacks and breaks down societies and institutions. The sins of government officials diminish the capacity for the political structures they serve to envision and enact policies that are just. The sins of corporate leaders or their employees skew investment in the public welfare in the interest of greater profit margins. The sins of educators infect their students; the sins of families rob children of their innocence; and the process of teaching, learning, and nurturing the skills of good citizenship is compromised, often in ways not discernible until some tragedy jolts a lazy conscience into belated concern.

More serious still, from the priestly perspective, are the sins of the faith community, for they corrupt and defile the sanctuary where God

53

would be present. Because the sanctuary symbolizes on earth God's creational plan for the entire cosmos, its defilement threatens God's departure not only from the local community but also from the whole world (see further Balentine, pp. 136–41). The sins that penetrate the outer courtyard and target the very throne of God reverberate throughout the world the sanctuary serves. The boundaries between order and chaos, good and evil, justice and injustice, are breached; the sanctuary is at best silent, at worst complicit; and the world stumbles from tragedy to tragedy without any place on earth to concretize the vision of a transcendent truth that illumines its path.

Perhaps, as T. S. Eliot suggests, we have succumbed to the modern idea that we have the capacity to dream "of systems so perfect that no one will need to be good," still less to be reminded of their shortcomings. Poets of faith, however, like Eliot, who takes his cue from Scripture, have struggled to keep us mindful of a different perspective. Eliot's concern is the church's sad neglect of its role in modeling what it means for people of faith to be citizens of heaven as well as of earth. When he looks on a broken world of shattered hopes and emptied visions, what he hears from the sanctuary, now a shell of its true self, is nothing more than senseless stammering. His question for the community of faith is one Israel's priests would embrace: "You, have you built well, have you forgotten the cornerstone?" ("Choruses from 'The Rock,'" pp. 152, 160). Indeed, Jesus, the cornerstone of the church, measures the church's mission to the world against a similar truth, which he learns from Jeremiah, son of Hilkiah the priest, his Jewish forebear in faith: "Is it not written, 'My house shall be called a house of prayer for all the nations'? But you have turned it into a den of robbers" (Mark 11:17 and parallels; cf. Jer. 7:11). The priestly legacy, passed from Sinai to Jerusalem to the church, is that sin has the capacity to turn the sanctuary into an ordinary place, a "ruined house," and, by extension, into a world "not fitly framed" for the presence of God.

The Hope of Forgiveness. Given the priestly sensitivity to the burden of sin, it is not surprising that the consistently stated objective of the required purification and reparation offerings is the promise of forgiveness (4:20, 26, 31, 35; 5:10, 13, 16, 18; 6:7 [MT: 5:26]). The passive form of the verb, "be forgiven," keeps us mindful that the agent of forgiveness is always God, never the priest or the rites the priest enacts. Only God can forgive sin. Still, awakening to sin and thus to the hope that one may be forgiven is part of a process in which all have responsibility.

Sometimes unintentional sins remain "unknown," and someone must bear the responsibility for disclosing it (note the *hip'il* active

form of the verb, "make known," in 4:23, 28). The text does not specify who makes the disclosure or how it is made, but it clearly recognizes the need for someone to be attentive to transgressions of God's
commandments. It is instructive to imagine that in a community of
faith the burden of addressing sin would be a shared responsibility.
Each one would in effect be a "brother's and sister's keeper." The
priests do not share the assumption on which Cain appears to have
relied when he tried to deflect his responsibility for Abel's welfare to
God. To the question "Am I my brother's keeper?" (Gen. 4:9), the
priests would answer without equivocation "Yes." Brothers and sisters
must care for one another, for if one stumbles, the whole community
staggers as a result. The priests' theology builds on an old truth that
the New Testament embraces and bequeaths to the Christian community. Paul's admonition to the church at Galatia is perhaps the best
example of the model: "My friends, if anyone is detected in a transgression, you who have received the Spirit should restore such a one
in a spirit of gentleness. . . . Bear one another's burdens, and in this you
will fulfill the law of Christ" (Gal. 6:1–2).

Sometimes unintentional sins may remain unknown both to the
offender and to the community, despite their vigilance in caring for one
another. God knows, however, that sin is as much a matter of personal
conscience as of public disclosure. Thus God instructs Moses to keep
the community tuned to the truth of guilt that pangs the conscience
even when there may be no visible or outward signs of sin's effect. When
one becomes unclean, for example, through some unwitting contact
with impurity, it may be guilt that sends the first message that something is wrong (5:3). When one consciously attempts to escape responsibility for sin, a guilty conscience may be the first and most reliable
obstacle to the yearned-for denial that is ultimately unobtainable
(6:4–5; MT: 5:23–24).

The priestly sensitivity to a guilty conscience and its importance in
the move toward confession of sin and the promise of forgiveness is perhaps at odds with modern sensibilities. We have worked very hard in
the postbiblical world, and with a good deal of clinical success, to inoc-
ulate the conscience against the worry and anxiety of guilt. With anti-
depressant drugs, therapy, and a wide range of other strategies for
dealing with negative stress, we have gone a long way toward minimiz-
ing the conscience's hold on us. Without denying the positive gains of
such medical "advances," we may find it instructive to think that consciences formed in the image of God still have a voice in the way we discern and respond to what is happening in our world. The conscience,

55

as Emily Dickinson discerned, has a phosphorescent quality. Like a refracted light from God, it lingers, inspects, instructs, and summons until calmed by a partnered response:

> Who is it seeks my Pillow Nights—
> With plain inspecting face—
> "Did you" or "Did you not," to ask—
> 'Tis "Conscience"—Childhood's Nurse—
>
> With Martial Hand she strokes the Hair
> Upon my wincing Head—
> "All" Rogues "shall have their part in" what—
> The Phosphorous of God—
> (#1598, *Complete Poems of Emily Dickinson*,
> ed. T. Johnson, p. 661)

The hope for forgiveness rests on more than knowledge and guilt. Deliberate breaches of faith require confession before one can be reconciled with God and persons (5:5). The examples cited in 5:1–4 (cf. 6:1–7 [MT: 5:20–26]) indicate that sin must be exposed, articulated, and therefore owned if its destructive effects are to be rectified. It is not enough to understand that one has erred, not enough to feel contrition for a wrong, for knowledge and guilt may result in nothing more concrete than inner resolve. Just as a person's thoughts may be actualized in behavior that is destructive, so a person's resolve to address that destruction must be actualized in behavior that concretizes intention. "To confess in ink," as Robert Frost puts it ("Quandary," *Poetry of Robert Frost*, ed. E. C. Lathem, p. 467), and not only in spirit, requires courage and resolve. It makes public declaration of the intent not only to *think* about repentance but also to *enact* it accountably.

Confession was once highly valued as a virtue. Scripture prizes confession of sin as the truest form of repentance. In the Old Testament one encounters the idea not only in the priestly rituals of Leviticus but also, for example, in the penitential psalms (Psalms 6, 32, 38, 51, 102, 130, 143) and in the prayers of the postexilic period (Ezra 9; Nehemiah 9; Daniel 9; see further Balentine, pp. 103–17). In the New Testament, Jesus uses parables to teach his followers that confession of sin is the requirement for divine forgiveness (e.g., Luke 15:17–21; 18:10–14), and his instruction became a cornerstone for first-century Christians (e.g., James 5:16; 1 John 1:8–10). By the eighth century the idea had become so firmly entrenched in the church's litany that the entire sacrament of penance (contrition, confession, reparation) could be designated with the single word *confession*. Moreover, once confession became an identifiable public virtue, it was appropriated as a dominant form of serious writing that both the religious and the secular could and would read with appreciation. One need only mention Augustine's *Confessions* (fifth century), or James Hogg's *The Private Memoirs and Confessions of a Justified Sinner* (1824), or even James Joyce's *A Portrait of the Artist as a Young Man* (1916) to realize how deeply influential confession became as a means of gaining perspective on life.

The place of confession in today's world has changed significantly. Apart from its role in the legal system and its increasingly infrequent appearance in church liturgies, confession is now perhaps more often associated with the pulp fiction of so-called true confessions that fill the magazine racks in grocery stores. It is instructive, in a double-edged way, that when Milgrom seeks to find a positive analogue in the contemporary world that exemplifies the priestly understanding of confession's importance, he looks not to the synagogue or the church but rather to "The Twelve Steps of Alcoholics Anonymous" (*Leviticus 1–16*, pp. 374–75). Upon joining this informal fellowship, individuals acknowledge *remorse* for their powerlessness over alcohol (steps 1–4), publicly *confess* to God and to those they have hurt the wrongs they have done (steps 5–7), make *restitution* for the damage they have inflicted (steps 8–9), and *pledge* to live more healthily each day of their lives (steps 10–12). Leviticus anticipates what alcoholics have learned: Confession is the cotter pin that joins contrition to reparation and reparation to a public commitment to change. Without confession, sin seeks the camouflage of secrecy, the status remains quo, and brokenness continues to diminish the "very good" world God has created. Perhaps it is a lesson worthy of reconsideration. Perhaps in a world where glossy tabloids pose as the high priests of culture, the instructions for purification and reparation offerings may even be considered as a gift.

The Gift of Ritual. In the priestly world, sin is a real and tangible burden; the hope for forgiveness is abiding and yearns for an equally real and tangible sign that it is obtainable. The modern world is different, of course, and the ancient book of Leviticus (and arguably the Bible itself) seems to many to be ill-suited for playing any significant role in how we plot our course through the maze of new challenges that Israel's priests could not have imagined. Defenders of the faith often do more harm than good, for they seem more concerned with orthodoxy, rigidly construed, than with facing honestly new questions that demand fresh thinking. And yet, whether we aim for orthodoxy or reasoned adjustments that help us to manage, most of us will resonate with the discernment of the noted anthropologist Clifford Geertz, who suggests that ours is a world where "reality threatens to go away unless we believe very hard in it" (Geertz, "Anti Anti-Relativism," p. 264).

Rituals are enactments of belief. Sometimes belief is fervent, and the ritual merely embodies and gestures forth cognitive convictions. For example, we believe in love, and when someone we love is in need, we enact compassion with the rituals of gifts, visits, and other forms of embodied concern. Sometimes belief is dormant, dead, perhaps even unknown and unsought, and the ritual act creates or re-creates a transforming discernment. We may be simply going through the motion of some customary act, for example, attending a wedding or a funeral, only to discover that in the midst of participating in ritualized behavior we are somehow caught up in an experience of unanticipated joy or grief. The priestly rituals of purification and reparation tap both these dimensions of belief. The realities they *reflect* and *generate* are the burden of sin and the hope of forgiveness.

The purification ritual consists of placing blood on parts of the sanctuary believed to be contaminated by sin. The act is "merely" symbolic, and yet it actualizes the belief that the sanctuary is no ordinary place and sin is more than simply a benign abstraction. The sanctuary is holy because it is the visible center of God's presence in the world. When it is defiled, God's presence is compromised, and the world's stability is threatened. When it is ritually cleansed, the sanctuary is believed once again to be a radiating center for holiness that tunes the world to the abiding difference between what Geertz calls the "real" and the "really real" (Geertz, "Religion as a Cultural System," p. 112). The perception of what is "real" comes from a commonsense orientation to the experiences of everyday life. The perception of what is "really real" comes from a lingering awareness that there are other realities, beyond those we may be able to see or verify, which have the capacity to enlarge and correct what would otherwise be accepted as merely given.

The ritual of purification accepts the burden of sin as real. It also enacts the belief that God's forgiveness has a transcendent reality, which supercedes sin with grace that refuses to allow what is given to have the last word. On the one hand, we must believe in the ritual to participate in it meaningfully. On the other, we must participate, meaningfully or not, in the ritual in order to see and feel and touch a belief that may have faded or died. If it is true that the "abdication of Belief / makes the Behavior small" (#1551, *Complete Poems of Emily Dickinson*, ed. T. Johnson, p. 646), it is equally true, from the priestly perspective, that even small, rote deeds—like the sevenfold sprinkling of blood—may restore exiled belief.

The ritual of reparation works in the same way, although it opens a window for reflection on another issue. In ancient Israel as in the modern world, ritual is vulnerable to the criticism that it is only ceremonial piety substituting for concrete acts of justice. Amos's rebuke of the sterility of sacrifice uncoupled from justice and righteousness (Amos 5:21–24), for example, is as much a modern sermon as an eighth-century oracle. This is especially the case in Protestant faith communities, where ritual may be viewed as more an encumbrance to authentic faith than a sacramental enactment of it. Surely, all rituals—secular or religious—may slide into empty acts that have no claim on virtue. For this reason, it is all the more important to pay close attention to the priestly instructions concerning the reparation offering.

Whenever persons break faith with God by violating another human being, they must first make restitution to the person they wronged, then bring their offering to the priest (6:5–6; MT: 5:24–25). The entire process—the enactment of justice and the presentation of the reparation offering—is part of the ritual. Justice is first enacted then ritualized in ceremonial observance. Without the concrete act of restitution, the ritual is formality without substance, which is the point of the prophet's critique. There is, however, another side to this equation. Without the ritual, which regularly calls for restitution of the abused, even when offenders may be disinclined to offer it, justice may be reduced to a legal loophole that may be cleverly finessed without impunity. The priests address the conundrum by insisting that justice is the prerequisite of the ritual. The ritual in turn sacramentalizes justice, thereby both teaching and enacting its imperative as a sacred commitment, not only a legal requirement.

Another observation by Geertz extends the point a step further. He argues that ritual has the capacity to effect in people a "chronic inclination" toward the reality that it symbolizes (Geertz, "Religion as a Cultural System," p. 96). The instructions for the reparation offering invite the faith community to reflect on whether and how such a chronic inclination toward justice for the abused will be manifest in the modern world if rituals of recompense are eliminated from the worship we offer God. Here we may cite once again the observation by Emily Dickinson, this time without any addendum: "The abdication of Belief / makes the Behavior small." On this point, both Leviticus and the New Testament are in accord, for as Jesus taught in the Sermon on the Mount,

> When you are offering your gift on the altar, if you remember that your brother or sister has something against you, leave your gift there before the altar and go; first be reconciled to your brother or sister, and then come and offer your gift. (Matt. 5:23–24)

59

Leviticus 6:8–7:38 (MT: 6:1–7:38)
Further Instructions concerning Sacrifices

The instructions concerning sacrifices are set forth in two sections. The first, Lev. 1:1–6:7, primarily addresses the laity, with corollary instructions for the priests in selective places. The objective is to teach the laity its role in bringing gifts to God. The second, Lev. 6:8–7:38 (MT: 6:1–7:38), primarily addresses the priests, with accompanying instructions for the laity where appropriate (7:11–38). The objective is to teach the priests their role in administering the rituals of sacrifice that comprise cultic worship.

The second set of instructions consists of nine paragraphs: the burnt offering (6:8–13; MT: 6:1–6); the cereal offering (6:14–18; MT: 6:7–11); the cereal offering of the high priest (6:19–23; MT: 6:12–16); the purification offering (6:24–30; MT: 6:17–23); the reparation offering (7:1–10); the well-being offering (7:11–21); the prohibition on eating fat or blood (7:22–27); the priest's portion of the well-being offering (7:28–36); and a concluding summary (7:37–38). Each of these paragraphs begins with a formulaic introduction—either "The Lord spoke to Moses" (6:19 [MT: 6:12]; 7:22, 28) or "This is the ritual (*tôrat*) of the . . . offering" (6:14 [MT: 6:7]); 7:1, 11, 37). In two places both formulas are used together in the same introduction (6:8–9 [MT: 6:1–2]; 6:24–25 [MT: 6:17–18]).

There is considerable overlap between the two sets of instructions, as one might expect, which leaves the reader to wonder, at first glance, why so much repetition is necessary. Two observations lay the groundwork for attending carefully to what is provided here. First, the instructions to the priests are an addendum to chapters 1–5, most likely from later redactors who thought it important to address topics not sufficiently covered in older versions of the sacrificial regulations. This redaction explains in part why 6:8–7:38 goes over much of the same material that has already been covered in the preceding chapters. There is, however, a second factor that merits consideration. Milgrom suggests that the redaction of this material exemplifies the exegetical principle the rabbis later articulated in the following axiom: "Whenever a scriptural passage is repeated, it is only repeated because of the new point contained therein" (*b. Sota* 3a; cited in *Leviticus 1–16*, p. 439). The repetition in 6:8–7:38 may be described therefore as purposefully redundant. Like the second of two parallel lines in poetry, this second list of instructions repeats portions of what has already been stated in order to add new details that enlarge and advance the understanding. The comments below address the principal "new points" in the instructions to the priests that add to our understanding of what God said when "he commanded the people of Israel to bring their offerings" (7:38; cf. 1:1–2a).

1. *The order of the sacrifices.* The instructions in 6:8–7:38 discuss the sacrificial gifts in a different order from chapters 1–5.

Leviticus 1–5	**Leviticus 6:8–7:38**
Burnt offerings	Burnt offerings
Cereal offerings	Cereal offerings
Well-being offerings	Purification offerings
Purification offerings	Reparation offerings
Reparation offerings	Well-being offerings

Leviticus 1–5 presents the sacrifices from the donor's perspective, focusing first on voluntary sacrifices (burnt, cereal, and well-being offerings), then on those that are required (purification and reparation). The sequencing instructs and invites donors to come into God's presence first with joy and when necessary with remorse and confession concerning the sins that have obstructed that joy. Leviticus 6:8–7:38 presents the sacrifices from the perspective of the priests, who must concern themselves not only with the administration of the ritual system but also with its role in reflecting and sustaining the community's vital connection with the holy.

Administration is a practical matter. It involves distinguishing between the regular daily offerings that are part of the public cult (burnt offerings, cereal offerings), those that are compulsory only when someone sins (purification offerings, reparation offerings), and those that are typically personal offerings motivated by thanksgiving, fulfillment of vows, or free will (well-being offerings; cf. 7:11–18).

The priests are also charged with responsibilities that extend beyond efficient management of the ritual system. They must safeguard and sustain the rituals' connection with the holy. Toward that end, the addendum in 6:8–7:38 orders the sacrifices on a descending scale of holiness. The first four offerings in the list—burnt, cereal, purification, and reparation—are identified as "most holy" (6:17, 25, 29; 7:1, 6; for the burnt offering, see 2:3). The well-being offering is distinguished from these by its identification as "holy" (cf. Num. 18:12–19). The "most holy" sacrifices are those whose consumable portions are reserved exclusively for the priests, who must eat them in a "holy place" (6:16, 26). Portions of the "holy" sacrifices may be consumed outside the sanctuary by anyone in the priest's family, and in the case of the well-being offering also by the donors themselves.

61

The architecture of the ritual offerings, which moves from most holy to less holy, recalls and reinforces the priestly understanding of the ordered zones of holiness in the tabernacle (cf. Exodus 25–31, 35–40; Haran, pp. 158–88, 205–29). From the common world outside the tabernacle, one enters ever more deeply into sacred space by passing first into the outer courtyard, then into the Holy Place, and finally into the Holy of Holies. Every aspect of this passage is carefully ordered to ensure that persons, objects, and ritual behavior correspond with and sustain the levels of holiness in the sanctuary. Nonpriests are permitted in the courtyard but no further. Ordinary priests may enter the Holy Place but not the Holy of Holies, which is open only to the high priest. The ritual objects placed within these zones, for example, the altar of burnt offering in the outer court, the incense altar in the Holy Place, and the ark in the Holy of Holies, are constructed from materials that refract the holiness of their respective locations. Moreover, the parallel between the conclusion formula in Exod. 40:33—"So Moses finished the work [of the tabernacle]"—and the statement in Gen. 2:2—"God finished the work [of creation]"—suggests that the priests understood the construction of the sanctuary to be a ritual completion of the work God began in creation (Blenkinsopp, "Structure of P," p. 278).

If the architecture of the sanctuary is the *completion* of God's design for the world, then the architecture of holy rituals may be viewed as a further refraction of that design, which *extends* and *sustains* the sacred through analogous human behavior. The priests are therefore instructed to take care that their ministry inside the realm of the sacred is contiguous with—not counter to—the holiness that God hopes and expects will define them and the world they serve. The ordering of the sacrifices in Lev. 6:8–7:38 serves to keep the priests mindful of their responsibility to match the laity's initiative with a comparable commitment to holiness that honors and actualizes their desire to be connected to God.

2. *"A decalogue of ritual life."* The addendum in Lev. 6:8–7:38 introduces the instructions to the priests with a new term—*tôrâ* (NRSV: "ritual for"; e.g., 6:9)—that invites close attention. The book of Leviticus contains ten *tôrôt* (plural of *tôrâ*). Five of these are concerned with sacrifice: the burnt offering (6:9 [MT: 6:2]), the cereal offering (6:14 [MT: 6:7]), the purification offering (6:24 [MT: 6:18]), the reparation offering (7:1), and the well-being offering (7:11). Five are concerned with impurity: animals (11:46), childbirth (12:7), skin disease (13:59; 14:54–57), purification of skin disease (14:2, 32), and genital discharge (15:32). It is instructive to think of these ten *tôrôt* as a "decalogue of ritual life" (Milgrom, *Leviticus 1–16*, pp. 382–83), half of which inculcates

an ethic of holy behavior in the sanctuary, the other half, "an ethic of bodily existence in the world" (for this suggestive phrase, see Blenkinsopp, *The Pentateuch*, p. 221).

The idea that priestly concern with sacrifice and impurity has the weight of *tôrâ* opens a suggestive window for reflection. The ten *tôrôt* identified above deal with specifically priestly responsibilities. Chapters 1–5, for example, which address sacrifice from the perspective of the laity, do not use the term *tôrâ*. This suggests, as Milgrom notes, that texts which Leviticus designates as *tôrâ* derive from temple archives, which the priests consulted in order to remain current and proficient in their duties (*Leviticus 1–16*, p. 383; cf. pp. 52–57). Leviticus 10:10–11 (cf. 11:47; 14:57) succinctly defines the priestly duties as follows:

> You are to distinguish between the holy and the common, and between the unclean and the clean; and you are to teach (*lĕhôrôt*) the people of Israel all the statutes that the LORD has spoken to them through Moses.

Building on the premise that priestly *tôrâ* consists of teaching people the distinctions between the holy and the common, the clean and the unclean, we may probe a bit further by tracking another question. What is the source of the priestly instruction? Where and how did the priests come into possession of the ten *tôrôt*, which Leviticus retrieves from the priestly archives? It is prudent to concede at the outset that our knowledge of the history and transmission of priestly texts does not yield an unassailable answer to such questions. It is instructive nonetheless to follow the trajectory of the Priestly tradition now preserved in Scripture's final form. If we turn our focus to the composite account of the Sinai pericope (Exodus 19–Numbers 10), there is general agreement that the Priestly strand provides the following basic information: Israel arrives at the mountain in the wilderness of Sinai (Exod. 19:1–2); Moses ascends the mountain and enters the cloud that signals the presence of the "glory of the Lord" (Exod. 24:15–18); God gives Moses instructions for building the sanctuary, which becomes the new locus for the "glory of the Lord" (Exodus 25–31, 35–40) and for establishing the cult that it serves (Leviticus 1–27).

When this sequence of events is isolated from the larger narrative, it is apparent that the Priestly source makes no mention of a covenant at Sinai; it includes no reference to the Decalogue (Ten Commandments; Exod. 20:1–17) or to the statutes and ordinances that comprise the book of the covenant (Exod. 20:22–23:33). These omissions from the Priestly narrative may be, indeed often have been, narrowly interpreted to mean that the priests were preoccupied with "merely" ritualistic behavior. The

63

presumed corollary of this reading is that the priests had little or no concern for the moral exhortations typically associated with covenantal obedience. However, when the Priestly strand is read as an integral part of the composite Sinai narrative, which is precisely what the canonical form of Scripture invites, this negative appraisal must be set aside. The Torah's aggregate vision affirms that at Sinai, God gave Moses instructions that summoned and enabled Israel to become both a covenant community and a worshiping community, a community defined by both justice and holiness (see further Balentine, pp. 59–77). In short, when the Sinai pericope is read holistically, the Priestly contribution is not a reduction but an enlargement of the meaning of *tôrâ*, for it envisions a community of faith where obedience to the "Decalogue" of Ten Commandments and to the "decalogue of ritual life" will have an equal and abiding claim on those who set out for the promised land.

3. *The Tamid.* The Hebrew word *tāmîd*, "continually, always," occurs for the first time in Leviticus at 6:13 (NRSV: "perpetual"; MT: 6:6) and 6:20 (NRSV: "regular"; MT: 6:13). The first occurrence concerns the fire of the burnt offering, which must be kept burning "all night until morning" (6:9; MT: 6:2). The second concerns the cereal offering of the high priest, which is to be presented as a "regular offering," half of it in the morning, the other half in the evening. In both cases, *tāmîd* functions adverbially to describe an action that is done regularly, continually, perpetually.

In the priestly system, *tāmîd* ultimately comes to be used as a noun that denotes an entire regimen of daily rituals, called the *Tamid.* It is not altogether clear what constituted the daily rituals, and it is likely that the practice would have varied in different times, but three cultic acts may be cited as examples (Levine, p. 38): (1) the daily burnt offering of two lambs, one in the morning and one in the evening, accompanied by cereal offerings and libations (Exod. 29:38–42; cf. Num. 28:3–8; Ezek. 46:13–15); (2) the regular lighting of the seven-branched menorah in the Holy Place (Lev. 24:1–4; cf. Exod. 27:20–21; 30:7–8); and (3) the regular incense offering presented each morning when the priest attends the menorah (Exod. 30:7–9; 40:24–27).

It is likely that the priests were required to attend to the details of the *Tamid* rituals for pragmatic reasons. To cite one obvious example, we may reflect on the likely difficulties that would emerge in providing a steady supply of wood for the fire that consumed the burnt offerings. Who had the responsibility for finding the wood and bringing it to the sanctuary? Which trees were best for producing the right amount of smoke, and when was the best time to cut them without jeopardizing the ecological order or too severely diminishing the natural cycles of growth? These and no doubt other practical matters, which are addressed at some length in postbiblical Jewish sources (see Milgrom, *Leviticus 1–16*, pp. 387–88), would surely have been part of the incentive for not letting a fire that was already started ever go completely out.

We may also be sure, however, that practical considerations alone do not explain why attention to the *Tamid* rituals is important. All religious rituals are more than practical or even symbolic acts, as important as these may be. At their core, rituals are a form of liturgical *exegesis* that engages both *mind and body* in the *drama* of theology (Balentine, pp. 148–52, 238–40). Three observations invite reflection on the theology encoded and enacted in the *Tamid* rituals:

- Three times the instructions to the priests stipulate that the altar fire for the burnt offerings must never be allowed to go out (6:9, 12, 13 [MT: 6:2, 5, 6]). These instructions are in effect an exegesis of Lev. 9:24, which reports that the altar fire was lit for the first time at the inauguration of the public cult, when "fire came out from the Lord and consumed the burnt offering and the fat on the altar." It is this fire—divine, miraculous, revelatory—that the priests must safeguard. It is the sign of God's abiding presence, God's pleasure in being available for intimate encounter, God's approval of the worship that enacts and sustains the divine-human relationship. The fire must be "perpetual" (6:13 [MT: 6:6]; *tāmîd*), because each time its embers are stoked, the ritual reenacts and reclaims the truth of God's desire to be in unbroken communication with people. As long as the ritual can concretize this truth and keep it visible, the community of faith may set its compass by the sanctuary's witness. By the same token, whenever the ritual is ignored or denied, whenever the sanctuary's witness is eclipsed or eliminated, more than a symbol is lost. The calamity envisioned by Daniel is case in point. Absent the constant activation of the symbols of God's abiding presence, truth may be cast to the ground, leaving wickedness free rein to mold the world in own design (Dan. 8:11–13; cf. 11:31; 12:11).
- The *Tamid* rituals enact and sustain the creational continuity between day and night. By God's design, day and night are foundational for the creative acts

65

through which God establishes, sustains, and blesses everything the world requires to be "very good" (cf. Gorman, *Ideology of Ritual*, pp. 215–27). The Priestly creation account (Gen. 1:1–2:4a) tracks God's formation of the world with a rhythmic refrain that bears witness to the vital connectedness between beginnings and endings that lead to still further beginnings: "And God said, 'Let there be . . .' And it was so. . . . And there was evening and there was morning. . . . And there was evening and there was morning. . . . And there was evening and there was morning. . . ." The acts of presenting morning and evening burnt offerings and of maintaining the altar fire "all night until morning" are grounded in this creational rhythm. The day begins and ends with ritual gifts that convey wholehearted commitment to be in harmony with God's ongoing hopes and expectations for the world. When the last gift is offered, the means for beginning afresh the next day are already in place. All that remains is for the gift to be actualized anew, whereupon the possibilities that another day brings are received, embraced, and embodied.

• The *Tamid* rituals sacralize the virtue of piety as a perpetual, habitual, constant mode of living. Regular—not occasional—acts of worship anchor life in God. Observance of the rites of faith that is disciplined—not haphazard or sporadic—keeps one tuned to truths that may otherwise slip away or be overwhelmed. The priests are charged with responsibility for *Tamid* rituals that invite and enable a ceaseless orientation to God.

4. *Priests as custodians of holiness.* The instructions to the priests address an array of details that require their careful attention. They are instructed, for example, on the protocols of what priestly garments to wear (6:10–11; MT: 6:3–4), where (6:26 [MT: 6:19]; 7:6) and when (7:15–18) to eat the consumable portions of the offerings reserved for them, and precisely what their portions are (7:31–36). Each of these details is a reminder to the priests of the special nature of their calling and of the care they must take to remain worthy stewards of the ministry God has entrusted to them.

Among the details we encounter here for the first time, one may be singled out for special consideration. The expression "anything that/whatever touches X shall become holy" occurs in 6:18 (MT: 6:11) and in 6:27 (MT: 6:20). Both occurrences deal with the sacrifices designated "most holy," the first with the cereal offering, the second with the purification offering. The meaning of this phrase is disputed, and commentators typically argue for one of two possibilities. M. Haran (pp. 175–88) and Milgrom (*Leviticus 1–16*, pp. 443–56) make the case for understanding the phrase to mean that sacred offerings refract a contagious holiness, which exposes whatever (perhaps also *who*ever) comes into contact with them to its power, for good or for ill. B. Levine, by contrast, resists the idea that holiness was considered to have contagious qualities. His preferred rendering of the phrase, "Anyone who is to touch these must be in a holy state," emphasizes that holiness is not a *result* of exposure to the sacred; it is instead the *prerequisite* for contact with the sacred (Levine, pp. 38–39).

The arguments in support of either of these positions are intricate and susceptible to different valuations. Without denying the complexity of the arguments, we may get our bearings on what is at stake by limiting our focus to certain general issues. First, it is clear that the singular referent for holiness is God. God alone is innately and fully holy. No other person, place, or thing has the capacity for holiness that equals God's. Second, it is equally clear that God is not only able to bestow holiness on and in the world; God is also desirous of doing so. For example, the first time the root word for "holy" occurs in the Bible is with reference to the seventh day of creation, which God blesses and "hallows," that is, "makes holy" (Gen. 2:3). From this primordial act, God's gift of holiness extends to places (principally the sanctuary), objects (especially those associated with the sanctuary), and persons (none more so than the priests but also the laity). There is no clearer summons to the whole community to image God's holiness than that which occurs repeatedly in the book of Leviticus, which devotes no fewer than ten chapters (17–26) to the amplification of what is surely its most important admonition: "You shall be holy, for I the Lord your God am holy" (Lev. 19:2). Third, God's decision to relinquish exclusive dominion of holiness entails both gain and risk. The positive objective is to extend divine holiness, through human agents, ritual symbols, and material objects, to the farthest reaches of the cosmos. The ever-attendant risk is that all nondivine replications of holiness are vulnerable to corruption, distortion, and abuse: Laity and priests sin; the sanctuary can be defiled; sacred rituals can be manipulated, falsified, and ignored.

67

With these general issues in mind, we may return to the instructions in 6:18 and 6:27. The priests must know that when they administer the "most holy" sacrifices, they have entered a realm where God's expectations for the claims of holiness on the world have been entrusted to their hands. Whether we interpret the critical phrase to mean that the priests themselves must be in a holy state when administering the sacrifices or that the priests must oversee the effects of transferable holiness, the fault line for understanding what is at stake is the same. The priests are charged with the awesome responsibility of being the custodians of holiness. What they do and say, the way they live and act, makes a critical difference in the world's potential for holiness. With a ministry that is at once unmistakable and mysterious, the priests may tip the scales of God's decision to share holiness toward either the incalculably positive or the tragically measurable negative.

Perhaps it is the clear definition of just such a fraught responsibility that invites and requires a new chapter in Leviticus. Whatever the history of the transmission of the text, the sequence of the present book, which turns next to instructions for the priests' ordination and for the establishment of the cult they are to serve, hardly seems out of place. Were we to imagine, if only for the sake of entering the world of Leviticus, that we were the priests addressed by these instructions, we might well need a word giving us permission to pause before daring any response at all. That word comes in Leviticus 8–10, which we may prepare for hearing by reflecting on the sage advice of Thomas Wentworth Higginson. In a sympathetic letter to his friend Emily Dickinson, who was throughout her career exceedingly fearful of the public exposure that publication of her poems would bring, he offered this suggestion:

> Such being the Majesty of the Art you presume to practice, you can at least take time before dishonoring it. (Lundin, p.117)

PART TWO

Ordination, Holy Worship, and Unholy Behavior

LEVITICUS 8–10

After seven chapters of detailed instructions concerning the holy sacrifices, Leviticus 8–10 dramatically reports the first public and official enactment of these instructions. On first encounter the style of this report, with its heavy emphasis on ritual prescriptions, seems little different from what has preceded. Thus, chapter 8 describes the ordination ceremony of the priests, with careful attention to the requirements concerning their washing, clothing, anointing, and sacrificial offerings. Chapter 9 follows with an equally detailed description of the first sacrifices offered by the newly ordained priests, their blessing of the people, God's dramatic appearance, and the people's awed response, all of which activates the tabernacle as the central locus for the worship that henceforth is to define Israel. The concern for ritual details, and, more important, for precise adherence to these details, is reinforced by the constant reminder that Moses is to enact every aspect of the process just "as the Lord commanded him," a phrase that repeats no fewer than sixteen times in Leviticus 8–10. By the time we reach the end of chapter 9, the clear first impression is that ritual instruction, with all its rigid but abstract formulation, remains the exclusive preoccupation of this book.

It may come as somewhat of a surprise, therefore, to find that chapter 10 suddenly departs from the style that has thus far been normative. NAB's rendering of 10:1 signals the change: "During this time Aaron's sons Nadab and Abihu took their censers and . . . offered up before the Lord profane fire, such as he had not authorized." Thus begins the one and only extended narrative in the book of Leviticus (for a briefer example, see the commentary on 24:10–23). As the commentary below will make clear, this narrative intrusion into ritual represents more than a mere stylistic anomaly. The report of what Aaron's sons did—and how God responded—is a strategic and important reminder: Holy rituals must always be enacted in *concrete* times and by *specific* individuals who have the capacity both to *honor* the sacred and to *profane* it. Taken as a whole, Leviticus 8–10 insists that readers pause for a careful and thoughtful reflection on the importance of integrating rituals into the vexed story of real life and of living as if life itself is a sacred ritual endowed with holy—but violable—possibilities. Given this "story line," it is perhaps not surprising after all that inside this literary pause is precisely where Leviticus places its most fundamental prerequisite for priests and their congregants: "You are to distinguish between the holy and the common, and between the unclean and the clean" (10:10).

Leviticus 8:1–36
The Ordination of Aaron and His Sons

The ordination ceremony for the priests essentially enacts the instructions God gave to Moses as recorded in Exodus 29 (for discussion of the relationship between Leviticus 8 and Exodus 29, see Milgrom, *Leviticus 1–16*, pp. 545–49). Despite differences in order and detail, it is clear that the present arrangement of the text understands Exodus 29 as the *prescription* for an *envisioned ordination*, which logically awaits the erection of the tabernacle in which the priests will serve (Exodus 35–40) and the instructions for the sacrificial rituals that the priests will oversee (Leviticus 1–7). Once the sacred place and the sacred rites become reality, the ordination of the priests, custodians of the sacred, is the necessary next step in actualizing the worship God invites. Leviticus 8 is the *implementation* of *God's vision* for a priesthood, a vision that has hovered over and shaped the priestly story line of the Torah since Exodus 29. From a literary and theological perspective, therefore, we have come to a moment of high drama in the way Israel tells its story. It is the moment when God's hopes and expectations for a "priestly kingdom and a holy nation" (Exod. 19:6) are finally and fully entrusted to those who will be charged with turning a divine vision into an earthly reality.

The transfer of authority from God to the priests comprises seven steps, each one propitiously marked by Moses' faithful enactment of what "the Lord has commanded" (vv. 4, 9, 13, 17, 21, 29, 36): assembling the materials and the persons (vv. 1–5); washing the priests and clothing Aaron (vv. 6–9); anointing the sanctuary and Aaron and clothing his sons (vv. 10–13); the presentation of the purification offering (vv. 14–17); the presentation of the burnt offering (vv. 18–21); the presentation of the ordination offering (vv. 22–30); and final instructions concerning the consumption of the offerings and the duration of the ordination ritual (vv. 31–36). The seven-step process that "creates" a consecrated priesthood recalls, enacts, and ritually extends God's seven-day process of creating a world that is blessed with the possibility of being "very good." That possibility, from the priestly perspective, is part of an ongoing process. Its journey toward completion is marked by interlinked intervals of sacred "sevens": seven divine speeches that create the world (Gen. 1:1–2:4a); seven acts of obedience through which Moses completes the sanctuary (Exod. 40:19–32); seven divine speeches setting forth instructions for the holy sacrifices (Leviticus 1–7); and now seven consecrated acts that enable ordinary persons to become priests, holy stewards of sacred hopes and visions (Leviticus 8). Inside this heptadic world of ritual enactment, the ordination of Aaron and his sons is a major move founded on the hope that the world of God's creation can in fact be all that God created it to be.

Assembling the Materials and the Persons (8:1–5)

The instructions begin by recapitulating what God previously disclosed to Moses in Exod. 29:1–4. The disclosure had presumably been a private affair, with Moses alone on the mountain and God speaking of what he must do when the time for ordaining the priests arrived. The time has now come for the move from private revelation to public enactment. Moses summons the ordinands, Aaron and his sons, then assembles the materials that will be used in the ceremony. The materials are listed here in the order in which they will be used: the vestments (cf. vv. 7–9, 13), the anointing oil (cf. vv. 10–12, 30), the bull for the sin offering (cf. vv. 14–17), the rams for the burnt offerings (cf. vv. 18–25), and the unleavened bread (cf. v. 26). The ceremony cannot begin until one more decisive preparatory act is completed. The whole congregation must be assembled at the entrance to the tent of meeting (v. 3). As the text will later stipulate, the ceremony that is now ready to begin will last for seven days (vv. 33–35), during which time the priests (and presumably the congregation) will remain at this strategic "entrance" place. What is about to take place, according to Leviticus, is a new beginning, an entrance into a new way of being in relation to God that is as crucial for the priests and the congregation awaiting their ministry as was the first seven-day "beginning" that created the cosmos itself.

71

It is instructive to think of this new beginning as a rite of a passage (cf. Gorman, *Ideology of Ritual*, pp. 115–39; Milgrom, *Leviticus 1–16*, pp. 566–69). When the ceremony begins, Aaron and his sons are part of the laity. When the seven-day ceremony concludes, their role in relation to God, people, and the world will have changed. Henceforth they will be priests, charged to live on the eighth day (9:1), and every subsequent day, with a disciplined stewardship of the holy that images and sustains God's primordial hopes and expectations for the world. The rabbis make the point with a suggestive interpretation of Gen. 2:3, the priestly text that provides the Bible's first occurrence of the word *holy.* After God "blessed the seventh day and made it holy," Ibn Ezra said, God rested in order "[for man] to [continue to] do [thenceforth]" (Sarna, p. 15).

Rites of passage initiate a new status for a person, thus a new way of being in the world. Three distinct stages typically mark the passage: the *separation* of persons from their "normal" roles in a given social context; the marginal or *liminal* stage, in which persons are "betwixt and between" assigned roles and new ones that have yet to be actualized; and the *reincorporation* of persons into society with new self-understandings and new roles. The liminal stage is the critical point of the passage, for here persons are fitted and shaped for the transition from what has been to what is not yet. It is what social anthropologists call the "generative center" in the drama of socialization, a sort of womblike experience that enables the newborn to enter the world specially prepared and uniquely gifted for life. When Aaron and his sons gather with the congregation at the entrance to the tent of meeting, they enter a ritual zone of liminality. Positioned between the common area outside the tent and the holy area that begins just inside its borders, they await the credentialing that will change their lives forever. When they emerge from this ritual as consecrated priests, their ministry will be forever defined by their honed experience as "threshold people," people entrusted with the responsibility of securing the intersection between the holy realm of God and the common realm of the world. On the other side of this threshold, the priests' charge will be both happy and awesome. We might well imagine that before the ceremony begins, Aaron and his sons would feel themselves torn between the desire to proceed and the urge to make a hasty retreat:

> . . . I
> have lingered too long on
>
> this threshold, but where can I go?
> To look back is to lose the soul
> I was leading upwards towards

the light. To look forward? Ah,

what balance is needed at
the edges of such an abyss.
I am alone on the surface
of a turning planet. What

to do but, like Michelangelo's
Adam, put my hand
out into an unknown space,
hoping for the reciprocating touch?
(Thomas, "Threshold," *Poems
of R. S. Thomas*, pp. 149–150)

The Ordination Ceremony (8:6–30)

The ceremony proper begins with the ritual of *washing* (v. 6) and *clothing* (vv. 7–9). The washing ritually cleanses Aaron and his sons, preparing them, in a way similar to what has been described for the animal sacrifices (1:9, 13; cf. 8:21), for contact with the holy. The clothing ritually vests them with garments that visually identify their holy status. Eight vestments in all comprise the attire. Four are worn by the high priest alone (ephod, breastpiece, robe, and the turban with the "golden ornament"; cf. Exod. 29:5–6), and four are common to all priests (tunic, sash, headdress, and breeches; cf. Exod. 29:8–9; 28:40–43). As the high priest is the first to be clothed, his garments are listed first. They are introduced in the order in which they are put on, beginning with the undergarments, then other items, the construction, quality, and symbolic sacredness of which increase with each additional garment.

Based on the details provided in Exodus 28 and 39, the garments may be visualized as follows:

- Linen *breeches* are not mentioned in Leviticus 8. Elsewhere, however, they appear to be one of the priestly undergarments (cf. Exod. 28:42; Lev. 6:3; 16:4). Their omission from Leviticus 8 may imply either that Aaron and his sons were already wearing breeches before the ordination ceremony began (Levine, p. 50) or that the breeches were, strictly speaking, not considered one of the sacred priestly vestments (Milgrom, *Leviticus 1–16*, pp. 385, 1017).
- The *tunic*, a short-sleeved, knee-length garment made wholly of "fine linen" (Exod. 28:39; 39:27), is worn next to the body.

73

- The *sash*, which holds the tunic in place, is woven from fine linen with blue, crimson, and purple woolen threads (Exod. 28:39). The embroidery technique is described with a term that appears to suggest a multicolored weaving process requiring the same skill used in producing the hangings and curtains for the entrance of the tent and the outer court (Exod. 26:36; 27:16). This correlation between the workmanship of the priest's clothing and the workmanship of the materials in the outer court indicates the symbiotic relationship between person and place that holiness requires.

- The *robe*, a poncho-like garment worn over the tunic, is made entirely of a blue-purple wool (Exod. 28:31–35; 39:22–26). It is woven with a technique that seems to be that required for weaving fabrics that are of one piece, rather than multicolored. To the hem of the robe are attached an alternating series of golden bells and woolen replications of pomegranates. The symbolism of the bells is difficult to discern, but we may note that in ancient cultures they were widely understood to be a means both of averting the demonic and of safeguarding the divine (Milgrom, *Leviticus 1–16*, p. 504). The pomegranate is a fruit associated with fertility and abundance (cf. Num. 13:23). We may speculate, therefore, that the priest's robe "enclothes" him with symbolism of both the possibility and the danger that comes from close proximity with the holy.

- The *ephod*, an apron-like garment suspended from the shoulders and tied to the waist by a "decorated band," is made of a blue and crimson wool-linen combination, with golden threads woven into the fabric. Two lapis stones (šōham, NJPS: "lazuli"), each engraved with six of the tribal names for the Israelites, are attached to the shoulder straps of the ephod. According to the Exodus instructions, the priest wears these as "stones of remembrance for the people of Israel" (Exod. 28:6–14), which suggests that each time he enters the holy place, he brings the hopes and fears of the whole congregation into the presence of God.

- The *breastpiece*, worn over the ephod, is made of wool and linen with gold, blue, purple, and crimson threads woven into the fabric. The weaving technique involves a more elaborate process than the style used for weaving garments (e.g., the sash) and materials that are associated with outer court area. Among the tabernacle items that reflect this technique, the most distinctive is the veil that hangs between the inner sanctum and the Holy of Holies (Exod. 26:31–33; 36:35–36). Shaped like a pouch with pockets, the breastpiece was about nine inches square and covered most of the upper chest area. Twelve stones were set in four rows, three stones on each row. Each stone was engraved with the name of one of the tribes of Israel (Exod. 28:15–21). When Aaron entered the holy place, he was to wear these names "on his heart before the Lord continually" (Exod. 28:30). The pockets of the breastpiece contained the Urim and Thummim. The meaning of the two terms and their function is elusive. It is likely that they were two small, flat stones that were cast like dice. Depending on how they turned up, they would provide a yes or no answer to a question put to God by the priest (cf. 1 Sam. 14:41–43).

- The *turban* of the high priest (Lev. 8:9) was different from the *headdress* of the ordinary priests (8:13). The headdress of the ordinary priests was made of fine linen and shaped like a skullcap (Exod. 39:28). The turban of the high priest was wound around the head and perhaps placed on top of the skullcap. Its most distinctive feature is the "golden ornament," or "holy crown," which was fastened to the front by a blue cord. On this piece were inscribed the words "Holy to the Lord." According to the Exodus instructions, when the high priest wore the turban, he took "on himself any guilt incurred in the holy offering that the Israelites consecrate as their sacred donations . . . in order that they may find favor before the Lord" (Exod. 28:38).

After Moses clothes the high priest, he turns next to the ceremony of *anointing* and to the *clothing ritual* that must now be extended to the ordinary priests (Lev. 8:10–13). The anointing oil was a unique mixture of four precious spices: myrrh, cinnamon, cane, and cassia (Exod.

75

30:23–24). Some of this oil was "sprinkled" on the tabernacle and its contents; some was sprinkled—seven times—on the altar and the sancta associated with it; some was "poured" on Aaron's head. The distinctive verbs of application—"sprinkle" and "pour"—underscore the speciality of Aaron's anointing. Whereas the sacred objects (and the ordinary priests; cf. 8:30) are sprinkled, Aaron is anointed more liberally, a fact the psalmist visualizes with graphic hyperbole when he compares the oil that covers Aaron's body with the dew that falls from Mount Hermon (Ps. 133:2–3).

The purpose of anointing was to sanctify the objects and the persons that were to be vessels for the ritual conveyance of the holy. In ancient Israel other persons, most notably kings, were also anointed, thus specially commissioned and empowered for service (cf. 1 Sam. 10:1; 16:13). The anointing of the priests served a different purpose. Among Israel's titular leaders, the priests were uniquely charged with the responsibility for ministering at the intersection between the holy things of God and the common, profane world in which God wishes the holy to be increasingly present and formative. Such a ministry required that they be specially prepared, for unlike kings, who exercise authority in the secular world, where success may be secured and failure corrected by legal statutes, the priests must safeguard God's most distinctive gift to the world—the capacity to be the earthly domain for the holy. On their shoulders, therefore, rests the burden of implementing God's risky investment in the world. When the priests are faithful in their stewardship of the holy, God is present and available to the world. When they fail, the holy is defiled, God's presence is compromised, and the consequences for the cosmos are more severe and more tragic than any statute can correct.

After the anointing, Moses begins the presentation of a series of *sacrificial offerings* (vv. 14–30). First is the "bull of sin offering" (vv. 14–17; cf. Exod. 29:10–14), which is offered along the lines stipulated in 4:3–12. Its function is to purify the altar, presumably of any unintentional sins that may have contaminated it and rendered it unfit for holy offerings. The second is the "ram of burnt offering" (vv. 18–21), which, as previously described in Leviticus 1 (cf. Exod. 29:15–18), symbolizes the priests' total commitment to the holy purposes for which they are being ordained.

The third offering, the "ram of ordination," is the most distinctive of the presentations (vv. 22–30; cf. Exod. 29:19–28). The ritual procedure is similar to that given for the well-being offerings in Leviticus 3 (cf. 7:11–18). Portions of the animal—the fat, liver lobe, kidneys, and right thigh—are turned into smoke on the altar; the breast belongs to the officiating priest, whose role here is necessarily performed by Moses (vv. 25–29). Beyond these similarities, however, the manner in which the blood of the ordination ram is handled (vv. 23–28) indicates that this offering is distinctively shaped for a special ritual significance.

Moses daubs some of the blood on the right earlobes, right thumbs, and right big toes of Aaron and his sons. The rest of the blood he dashes against the sides of the altar. This peculiar manipulation of the blood is often interpreted allegorically as a religious symbol of the priests' preparation for the service of God. Thus Kaiser suggests that "Aaron's ear must be ever attentive to the word of God; his hand ever ready to do the work of God; and his feet ever alert to run in the service of the One who has called him" (Kaiser, p. 1062). Although this suggestion is instructive, it does not adequately explain the function of this daubing rite in the priestly system as a whole.

The only other ritual where blood is placed on the right ears, thumbs, and toes is in Lev. 14:10–20, the ceremony describing the reentry of a recovered leper into the camp. The express purpose of this rite is to "cleanse" or "make atonement for" the leper who is being purified of the disease (vv. 18, 19, 20). This purification enables the leper to return to normal life from a situation that may be likened to death (cf. Num. 12:10–12). In this context, the daubing ritual is the key to the leper's safe passage from the boundaries of death to the possibilities of life.

Gorman has suggested that the daubing of the priests similarly provides for their safe passage between the boundaries of the common and the holy (*Ideology of Ritual*, pp. 131–35; see further Balentine, pp. 153–55). Priestly ordination begins (v. 3) and ends (v. 33) at the entrance to the tent of meeting. Indeed, Moses instructs the ordinands to remain in just this location, at the border between the common world that lies outside the tent and the holy world that begins just inside, for a seven-day period. For the duration of this time, they are to be consecrated according to God's instructions, lest they "die" (vv. 33b–35). When the ordination concludes, however, the priests will be charged to move from this ritual zone framed by the holy and the common. On the one hand, they must go out into the world, where ordinary people will entrust to them common offerings of joy and contrition in the hope that they might be "turned into" sacred and acceptable gifts to God (see the reflections on "Gift as Analogy" in Leviticus 1). On the other hand, the priests must risk entering ever more deeply into the realm of the holy. They must move from the outer court to the inner shrine, and in the case of the high priest, from the inner shrine into the Holy of Holies, the one place on earth where God's presence is most intimately and fearfully concretized. At every step of their journey they are charged

77

with safeguarding the people from the hazards of the holy while ensuring that a right and constructive connection with a holy God will always be attainable (cf. Num. 16:46–48).

The priests are given an awesome responsibility, and they will not always faithfully execute their commission. We have only to read beyond this solemn ordination ceremony to the sad account in chapter 10 of what transpired on the priests' first day on the job to know how fragile and vulnerable the passage between the holy and the common can be. Moses may "fill" their hands with the ordination offering (cf. vv. 22, 33, where the term for the ordination is literally "filling" or "hand-filling"), but priests may decide to use those same hands to offer "unholy fire" that God has not commanded (10:1). The consequences of their failure will be severe, not only for them but also for those they serve. Perhaps this explains why their preparation requires a seven-day period at the intersection of life and death, during which the blood of the ordination ram readies them for the journey that begins with the eighth day.

Final Instructions (8:31–36)

The last paragraph offers additional words of instruction (vv. 31–35) and a concluding statement affirming that the newly ordained priests "did all the things that the Lord commanded" (v. 36). The instructions deal with two matters. First, Moses instructs Aaron and his sons where and how to eat the ordination offering (vv. 31–32; cf. Exod. 29:31–34). The meat is to be boiled and eaten, with the bread, at the entrance to the tent of meeting. What is not consumed is to be burned. These instructions are similar to those that apply to two types of offerings. On the one hand, the consumption of the meat follows the practice observed for most consumable sacrifices (cf. the cereal, purification, and reparation offerings). On the other, the consumption of the meat—a portion reserved for the donors (Aaron and his sons) and a portion reserved for the priest (in this case, Moses; cf. v. 29)—is distinctly similar to the well-being offering.

The ordination offering thus appears to be of a "mixed" type. Its place in the hierarchy of offerings is somewhere between the "most holy" sacrifices, whose consumable portions are reserved exclusively for the priests, and the "holy" sacrifices that are shared by donors and priests. This "ranking" is further suggested by the order of sacrifices in 7:38, which lists the ordination offering *after* the reparation offering and *before* the well-being offering (see further the reflections on "The Order of the Sacrifices" in 6:8–7:38). The "ambiguous" state of the ordination offering appropriately reflects the ambiguous, liminal state of

Aaron and his sons at this penultimate moment in the ceremony (Milgrom, *Leviticus 1–16*, pp. 534–35). They are in transition; their identity is shifting from laypersons to ordained persons; the domain of their service is moving them from the common to the holy.

The second concern of these instructions is to stipulate that the length of the ceremony is seven days (vv. 33–35). Aaron and his sons must remain at the entrance to the tent of meeting for seven days, during which time they are to "keep the Lord's charge" (v. 35: literally, "guard the things of the Lord that must be guarded"). The requirement of a seven-day service is clearly part of the heptadic emphasis that the priestly tradition uses to locate its instructions within the larger context of creation theology (cf. Gorman, *Divine Presence and Community*, pp. 8–10). In the present context, the ordination ceremony is a ritual act of creation that corresponds with and extends God's purposive creation of the world. At the end of seven days, a world that did not exist before God spoke is fully formed and ready to realize its blessed objective of being "very good" (Gen. 1:1–2:4a). At the end of seven days, a priesthood that did not exist until God summoned it into being will be fully consecrated and fully enabled to actualize God's hopes for "a priestly kingdom and a holy nation" (Exod. 19:6).

In this general context of priestly creation theology, we may push beyond the information the text provides to speculate about what the ordinands were to *do* during the seven days of their preparation. Perhaps the actual ceremony described in chapter 8 took place on the first day, in which case Aaron and his sons would have remained another six days in a state of solemn anticipation (cf. Noth, p. 73). It seems more likely that all the rituals described in this chapter—washing, clothing, anointing, and sacrificial offerings—were enacted on each day (cf. Milgrom, *Leviticus 1–16*, p. 536; Levine, p. 54). Although we cannot be certain about these matters, it is plausible to believe that this repetitive seven-day cycle of rites sustains the echo of another repetitive and ever generative liturgy, which henceforth will never be far from priestly consciousness: "And God said, 'Let there be . . .' And it was so. . . . And God said, 'Let there be . . .' And it was so. . . ."

The final verse (v. 36) brings the instructions for the ordination ceremony to a conclusion with the seventh occurrence of the phrase "that the Lord commanded." From the beginning of the chapter, the imperative for the ordinands to hear and respond to what God has commanded through Moses has been of paramount importance. To this point, Moses has faithfully delivered God's instructions to Aaron and his sons. They have consistently been described as the *objects* of his verbs. Now for the first time they become *subjects* of their own verbs. Now for

79

the first time we are told that they *"did* all the things that the Lord commanded."* From this point forward, as the next two chapters make clear, the emphasis shifts from the imperative *to hear* to the imperative *to be and remain obedient.*

Leviticus 9:1–24
The Eighth Day: Holy Worship

The acquired privileges that the priests enjoy carry with them enormous responsibilities to the community on whose behalf they have been consecrated to serve. Thus, after the ceremony of installation, Moses summons the newly ordained priests to begin their public ministry at the tabernacle. The inaugural service of regular public worship begins on the eighth day (v. 1), the first day after the seventh, or Sabbath, day. As with the eighth day of creation, which Genesis assumes with the story that begins to unfold in chapter 3, so now the story of the priesthood and its public ministry begins to take concrete shape. The account begins with further instructions from Moses about what is to transpire (vv. 1–7), once again detailing precisely the offerings that are required. There follows in turn a report of the offerings the priests present for themselves (vv. 8–14) and the offerings they bring on behalf of the people (vv. 15–21). The purpose of all the offerings is stated clearly at the outset: "For today the Lord will appear to you" (v. 4). Three further references to the appearance of the "glory of the Lord" (vv. 6, 23, 24) track the steady movement of this first public worship toward its intended goal. The climax comes with a priestly blessing, a dramatic theophany, and the people's awed response to the God made available to them on this first day in the ministry of priesthood (vv. 22–24).

As we have come to expect from Leviticus, there is considerable repetition in this chapter. All of the offerings listed in vv. 1–7 and again in vv. 8–14 and 15–21 have been described in detail in previous chapters. Some variations immediately stand out, most notably the order of the sacrifices, which begin with purification and burnt offerings (for both priests and people), followed by grain, cereal, and well-being offerings (see the discussion of "The Order of the Sacrifices" in 6:8–7:38) and the description of how Aaron's sons assist him in the ritual procedures (vv. 9, 12–13, 18–20). On a first reading, however, both the tenor and the substance of most of this chapter seem primarily focused on the imperative of strict obedience to details that have by now been thoroughly covered. The strategic reminder that Moses issues and the priests obey "what the Lord has commanded" (vv. 6, 7, 10, 21), a phrase already repeated seven times in the preceding chapter, makes the point that careful adherence to these instructions continues to be definitive for this and all future public enactments of what God has decreed.

Nonetheless, even on a first reading one cannot help but be suspicious of so much emphasis on obedience. Why is it necessary, even in a text about rituals, which by definition deals with rote behavior, to be so repetitive, so tediously insistent on saying what has already been said so often before? The answer comes, in part, in chapter 10, which reports that before this eighth day is over, the priests will have forgotten already what Moses has taken great such pains to teach them. The problem is not the priests' alone. As Jesus makes clear to the disciples who have listened to his teachings in the sure conviction that they will be obedient: "Very truly, I tell you, one of you will betray me" (John 13:21). Had the priests heard Moses speak a similar word, they, like those who would be disciples of Jesus, would likely have responded with incredulity: "Lord, who is it?" (John 13:25). That incredulity—so *convicted* and so *vulnerable* to exposure—explains why the imperative for obedience can never be taken for granted.

Although the repetition in Leviticus 9 may lull us to sleep, the climax of the chapter (vv. 22–24) should stir us to attention, for at last we arrive at the dramatic moment toward which all the preceding chapters have aimed: the conversion of ritual into reality. Aaron lifts his hands toward heaven, faces the people, and blesses them. The words of his blessing are not provided, but many commentators suggest that the priestly blessing in Num. 6:24–26 might have been spoken:

> The LORD bless you and keep you;
> the LORD make his face to shine upon you,
>   and be gracious to you;
> the LORD lift up his countenance upon you,
>   and give you peace.

Moses and Aaron then enter the tent of meeting for the first time, perhaps to offer further prayers that God will honor the ministry that now begins. When they come out, they bless the people a second time. At this very moment, the "glory of the Lord" appears to all the people. The first time the people saw the "glory of the Lord" was at Sinai, where on the seventh day, it appeared like a "devouring fire" on top of the mountain (Exod. 24:15–18). When Moses erected the tabernacle, this same glory, enveloped by a cloud, filled it up (Exod. 40:34–35). With an

81

eye toward the future, the book of Exodus concludes with a promise: Whenever the cloud—and the "glory of the Lord" it portends—is visible, Israel may know that God has taken up residence in its world; whenever the cloud is taken up, Israel must set out on its journey, guided by the promise of God's presence (Exod. 40:36–38). It is this promise that Moses and Aaron enact with the blessing. It is the appearance of the "glory of the Lord," now manifest in the "fire that came out from the Lord" and consumed the sacrifices they had presented, that dramatically confirms not only *God's promise of presence* but also *God's gracious acceptance of the priestly ministry*.

The phrase "all the people" occurs twice in the last two verses, in both instances confirming that God's presence is visible and available to the whole congregation. The promise of God's presence to Moses, Aaron, and the priests is not enough to establish the relationship God intends. The dramatic enactment of God's presence in the tabernacle and its rituals is not sufficient by itself to bear witness to the full truth of God's creative purposes for the world. For the relationship God intends, "all the people" must be able to *hear* the promise of God's presence, *see* the refracted reality of God's presence in the symbols and sancta of their world, and *respond* with worship that declares both spontaneous joy and focused commitment. In this triangulated vision of the divine-human relationship, it is clear that everything moves between the two poles of revelation and response. In between these two poles, at the intersection between what God desires to impart and what people will desire to receive and return, the priests play a critical role. Entrusted with stewardship of the holy, the priests must enable, sustain, and extend the relationship with the world that God intends. That they can and do fulfill their divine commission with faithful and effective obedience is confirmed by the response recorded for "all the people" in v. 24. That they can and do make mistakes in their stewardship of the holy is the witness of the next chapter.

Leviticus 10:1–20
The Eighth Day: Unholy Behavior

After nine chapters of detailed ritual instructions, chapter 10 is the first and only extended narrative "relief" that the book of Leviticus provides. Like most good narratives, this one relates a "story" in three parts: (1) an *introduction* with a presenting problem involving the priests' mis-

82

conduct (vv. 1–7); (2) a word from God that *centers* the drama on divine instructions for priestly behavior (vv. 8–11); and (3) a *conclusion* with another presenting problem concerning priestly behavior and its resolution (vv. 12–20). The narrative's structure makes clear that the framing theme is priestly behavior (vv. 1–7, 12–20), more specifically, priestly error and misunderstanding. At the center of this drama, marked off by the heading "And the Lord spoke to Aaron," is an authoritative word from God about what priests must and must not do (vv. 8–11).

Moreover, the literary context for this drama—priestly misconduct on the eighth day, the first day after everything has been put in place for priestly obedience (Leviticus 8–9)—connects it with two other foundational narratives in the Torah that are of paramount importance for understanding the way Israel tells its story (cf. Gorman, *Divine Presence and Community*, pp. 63–64). The opening chapters of Genesis provide the paradigmatic narrative of God's good creation in seven days (Genesis 1–2), humankind's "eighth day" corruption of God's good creation (Gen. 3:1–6:4), and God's re-creating work that brings resolution and new possibilities (Gen. 6:5–9:28). A second chapter in the same story is recorded in Exodus 19–40. After God has established a covenant relationship with Israel (Exodus 19–24), and after God has begun disclosing the blueprint for the covenant holiness that must be actualized in the tabernacle (Exodus 25–31), the covenant people immediately violate the covenant (Exodus 32). God punishes the people, restores the covenant (Exodus 33–34), and resumes the instructions that make possible the realization of God's abiding objectives (Exodus 35–40). In Genesis 1–9, Exodus 19–40, and now in Leviticus 8–10, the story line is essentially the same: God's *creation*, Israel's *uncreation*, God's *re-creation*. Within this larger narrative pattern, Leviticus 10 is simply another chapter in the same story that began when God risked the paradox of creating a people with the capacity to image the divine but without the capacity to be enough like God to be completely successful (cf. Friedman, p. 99).

Despite the familiar ring of this story, it is intractably complex and difficult to read. In the end, it invites more questions than it answers. What is the mistake signified by the "unholy fire" (v. 1) that Nadab and Abihu bring? Why does this mistake result not only in their death (v. 2) but also in prohibitions against mourning (vv. 6–7) and strong drink (vv. 8–9)? Why is it necessary for Moses to repeat, yet again, instructions on how to eat the priestly portions of the sacrifices (vv. 12–15)? Why was Moses angry about the priests' handling of the purification offering, and why was he satisfied with Aaron's explanation (vv. 16–20)? These and other questions about this story have evoked much speculation, some quite ingenious, but they mostly persist as dangling, loose ends. From

83

a theological standpoint, perhaps the rhetorical "clutter" of this narrative is appropriate, for whenever rituals of faith and worship move from abstract theory to real-life actualization, we should expect the story to get a little messy.

Priestly Misconduct (10:1–7)

On the eighth day, the same day they celebrate their ordination, Nadab and Abihu, Aaron's two eldest sons, take coals from their own censers and offer an "unholy fire" to God. Without any pause for explanation, the text reports that a countervailing "fire came out from the presence of the Lord and consumed them." Apart from the statement that they had done something the Lord "had not commanded," we are mostly left in the dark about the exact nature of their error. It appears that they offered fire from an unauthorized source—their own private censers rather than the sanctuary's outer altar (cf. 16:12; Num. 16:56 [MT: 17:11])—but the report is so brief that it has prompted a wide range of reading-between-the-lines theories. Perhaps they offered the fire at the *wrong time*; perhaps in the *wrong place*; perhaps they were *improperly dressed*. The rabbis, clearly vexed by the lacunae in the text, propose some twelve explanations, including the possibility, inferred from v. 8, that the priests were guilty of officiating while drunk (Milgrom, *Leviticus 1–16*, pp. 633–34). Moses offers what he regards as the explanation by citing something that God has said on a previous occasion—"Through those who are near me I will show myself holy" (v. 3)—the corollary to which would seem to be "Those who are near to me must be holy . . . or else!" (cf. Exod. 19:22). The difficulty is that there is no biblical source for this precise citation, so one wonders how Nadab and Abihu could have known about it beforehand. Alternatively, we may understand God's words as having been spoken simultaneously with the event of transgression, thus as a response that enacts a quid pro quo judgment on the priests' sinful behavior (Milgrom, *Leviticus 1–16*, p. 600). By either interpretation, the essential principle likely remains the same: Priests who have the privilege of being intimately near to God bear awesome responsibilities. By what they do, priests will either secure God's blessings or evoke God's punishment. The New Testament's estimation of the privilege and peril of ministry on God's behalf sustains a similar warning: "From everyone to whom much has been given, much will be required; and from the one to whom much has been entrusted, even more will be demanded" (Luke 12:48).

Moses summons Mishael and Elzaphan, cousins of Nadab and Abihu, to grab the tunics of their dead kinsmen and drag them outside the camp (vv. 4–5). The removal of the bodies is presumably necessary, because otherwise the corpses would defile the sanctuary, which is the situation addressed by the purgation rituals prescribed in Leviticus 16 (see 16:1–2). Moses next instructs Eleazar and Ithamar, Aaron's two surviving sons, not to mourn their dead brothers by disheveling their hair or rending their garments (vv. 6–7). The reason for the prohibition against mourning is not stated; the only explanation the text provides is that once the "Lord's anointing oil" has been placed on the priests, they must not interrupt their sacred duties with anything that would alter their exclusive preoccupation with holy rituals (cf. 21:10–12). The *people* may, and indeed should, mourn the tragedy they have witnessed. The priests, however, must remain focused on the rituals that enable life, even as sin and death threaten to subvert the ministry to which they have been called.

Instructions for the Priests (10:8–11)

In the middle of the two framing texts concerning priestly misconduct (vv. 1–7, 12–20), vv. 8–11 provide the only direct address from God to Aaron by himself that occurs in the Book of Leviticus (the only other instances in Scripture occur in Num. 18:1, 8). The uniqueness of the address signals a moment of high drama in this narrative, for despite the failure of Nadab and Abihu, God's decision to create a priesthood through Aaron remains resolute. Toward this end, God gives Aaron two instructions: the first, a command concerning behavior that is forbidden; the second, a command concerning priestly duties that must never be neglected.

First, priests must refrain from all intoxicating drink while ministering in the sanctuary (v. 9). Specifically prohibited are "wine" and "strong drink," two substances whose impairing effects are frequently condemned in Hebrew Scripture (cf. 1 Sam. 1:15; Isa. 5:11–12; 24:9; 28:7; 56:12; Mic. 2:11). The occurrence in Isa. 28:7, which warns of the hazards these substances hold for the priests and prophets, is particularly instructive: "The priest and the prophet reel with strong drink, they are confused with wine, they stagger with strong drink; they err in vision, they stumble in giving judgment." The penalty for violation of this prohibition is death, which links this command to the sanction against mourning in Lev. 10:6–7. The rabbis, searching for an explanation for the deaths of Nadab and Abihu, infer that they had been guilty of officiating while intoxicated (Milgrom, *Leviticus 1–16*, p. 634). Although such an interpretation is unsupported by the text, it seems clear that the priests are strictly cautioned against using stimulants to induce, enhance, or influence their encounter with God.

85

The second instruction concerns priestly responsibilities that must never be neglected (vv. 10–11). Two infinitives, each conveying the force of an imperative, introduce the essence of God's expectations for the priests. First, God instructs the priests "to distinguish between the holy and the common, and between the unclean and the clean." To be "holy" is to be in the realm of God, whose intrinsic holiness provides the reference point for all "common" or "profane" persons and objects that may, under certain conditions, refract the special status that God alone fully possesses. Persons or objects that are "unclean" or "impure" are prohibited from contact with the holy; only that which is "clean" or "pure" can come near the holy. As we shall see in chapters 11–15, the boundaries between the holy and the common, the clean and the unclean, are static. That which is holy may be defiled, in which case it must be purified and restored to its proper status by appropriate rituals; the common may be sanctified or consecrated and thus rendered fit for proximity with the holy. Of paramount importance is the imperative to sustain and, when necessary, repair the boundary between the holy and the unclean. That which is unclean defiles the holy and diminishes its essence. The custodians of these boundaries, the ones specially charged with the responsibility for securing the proper intersections between the realms of the holy and the common, are the priests. Their commission, here delivered in direct address from God to Aaron, is to "distinguish" the boundaries that define and enable a vital connection with the hopes and expectations of a holy God. Behind this commission lies a fundamental priestly understanding: When they "distinguish" the boundaries between God and the world in which God desires to be present and active, they participate in and extend the primordial acts by which God "distinguished" or "separated" the basic elements of the created order (cf. Gen. 1:4, 6, 7, 18). In sum, the priests' stewardship of the ritual boundaries identified in Lev. 10:10 images God's creation and nurture of a world designed to be "very good."

The second imperative addressed to the priests is "to teach the people of Israel all the statutes that the Lord has spoken to them through Moses" (v. 11). From the outset the book of Leviticus, which clearly concerns priestly duties, claims to be a word from God intended for the *whole community*. Thus, God's first words to Moses from the tent of meeting are "Speak to the people of Israel" (1:2). This phrase (or one comparable to it) occurs twenty times in Leviticus. Indeed, every major pericope in the book—instructions concerning sacrifice (1–7), ordination (8–10), purity (11–15), the Day of Purification (16), and the Holiness Code (17–26)—begins or ends by emphasizing that what has been vouchsafed to the priests from God through Moses is intended to inform the whole community in the ways of being holy before God (7:38; 10:11; 11:1; 15:2; cf. 15:31; 16:34; 17:2; 26:46). It is no surprise, therefore, that the last words of chapter 27 return to the first words of chapter 1 with a climactic reminder: "These are the commandments that the Lord gave to Moses for the *people of Israel* on Mount Sinai" (27:34).

Among ancient Israel's neighbors, the rituals of the sanctuary were commonly understood to be the exclusive prerogative of the priests. The ordinary layperson was, as a rule, barred from entering the sanctuary, and in some instances even from viewing the texts of the rituals (for discussion, see Milgrom, *Leviticus 1–16*, pp. 143–44). As a result, there was a huge and unbridgeable chasm between those entrusted with the secrets of the holy and those for whom such knowledge was denied. From the priests' perspective, privileged access to the divine was an immutable gift that guaranteed status and power. From the laity's perspective, the priestly privileges were rooted in their access to information that was as much esoteric as awesome. The book of Leviticus signals Israel's departure from this understanding of the priestly. Israel's priests are instructed to remember that their commission from God is a sacred trust; only by obeying the command "to teach the people *all the statutes* that the Lord has spoken to them through Moses" can they validate God's investment in their priesthood.

George Herbert offers a Christian perspective on "The Priesthood," which is principally rooted in the Hebraic truth that God has entrusted the sacred to human mediation:

> But th' holy men of God such vessels are,
> As serve him up, who all the world commands:
> When God vouchsafeth to become our fare,
> Their hands convey him, who conveys their hands.
> O what pure things, most pure things those things must be,
> Who brings my God to me!
>   *Complete English Poems*, ed. J. Tobin, p. 151

Priestly Misconduct and a Resolution (10:12–20)

The moment Nadab and Abihu offered "unholy fire" (10:2), the rituals for the eighth day of the ordination ceremony were brought to a full stop. The severe punishment of Nadab and Abihu, coupled with God's specific directives to Aaron "to distinguish" and "to teach," effectively recenters the drama. Thus, Moses resumes his role as mediator of the ceremony by reviewing with Eleazar and Ithamar, Aaron's two remaining sons, the instructions for the priestly consumption of the sacrifices (vv. 12–15). Once more he reminds them to eat the grain offering in a "holy place" (cf. 2:3; 6:14–18 [MT: 6:7–11]; 7:10), the breast and the thigh of the well-being offering in a "clean place" (cf. 7:28–36), for God has designated these as their assigned portions.

Just when the ceremony seems to be back on track, however, a new problem emerges (vv. 16–20). Moses is concerned specifically with the disposal of the goat for the sin offering of the people. According to the prescriptions already given (6:24–30 [MT: 6:17–23], the priests must consume the remains of the goat in a holy place. The consumption is obligatory, because it effects the purgation of the community by removing their guilt. Yet when Moses inquires about the matter, he discovers that the remains have already been burned, not consumed. When Moses angrily demands an explanation, Aaron alludes to the tragic events of the day—"such things as these have befallen me" (v. 19)—and returns a question to Moses: Given what has happened, would the eating of the sacrifice have been agreeable to God? Would it have been proper to consume the sin offering in the sanctuary on the very day that the transgressions of Nadab and Abihu had defiled the sanctuary and arrested the ordination rituals? The text concludes with a brief statement: "When Moses heard that, he agreed" (v. 20).

It is not clear why Moses becomes so enraged about the failure to consume the sin offering, or why Aaron's response appears to satisfy his anger. That the ritual for the sin offering has to do with the removal of sin seems clear, but why is it mandatory that the offering be ingested in order for this ritual to be complete? In an extensive discussion of the question, Milgrom has proposed the most compelling explanation to date (*Leviticus 1–16*, pp. 635–40). The remains of the animal sacrificed for the sin offering may be understood to have symbolically absorbed the impurities and iniquities of the people. Because the priests are the personification of the holy, they are endowed with the capacity to nullify sin by ritually consuming it. Milgrom makes the point as follows: "When the priest consumes the *ḥaṭṭāʾt* [sin offering] he is making a profound theological statement: holiness has swallowed impurity; life can defeat death" (*Leviticus 1–16*, p. 638).

If consuming the sacrifice is obligatory for ritually enacting sin's defeat, why then did Eleazar and Ithamar fail to comply with such a crucial part of their priestly mandate? Aaron's defense of their conduct suggests that they were uncertain about what to do in light of the tragic events of the day. The deaths of Nadab and Abihu would certainly have impressed upon them the need to show proper respect and reverence for the awesome power of the holy God they served. They may have logically concluded that it was better to err on the side of caution than to adhere rigidly to the procedures for a ritual that seemed so fatally

88

flawed. Aaron's question—"If I had eaten . . . would it have been agreeable to the Lord?"—indicates that he had given the matter careful consideration. Surely God would not disapprove of a genuine effort to be a faithful priest, even if the realities of life required an alteration of the prescribed ritual. When the text reports that Moses "agreed" with what he had heard, it invites readers to consider that on this matter Aaron was right.

Thus ends the "story" of Israel's first ordination ceremony. The priests are duly consecrated. They are specifically commissioned "to distinguish" and "to teach." And before they even begin to fulfill their responsibilities, they have already failed, been judged, and been forced to ponder deeply what it means to stand in between the demands of the holy and the frailties of the common. Given this candid report of the difficulties that accompany the divine imperative to become " a priestly kingdom and a holy nation" (Exod. 19:6), it comes as no surprise that the next words from Moses to the newly ordained priests comprise a lengthy discussion of just what will be required if they are "to teach" the people of Israel "to distinguish between the unclean and the clean."

PART THREE

Instructions on Purity and Impurity

LEVITICUS 11–15

Leviticus 11–15 deals with a variety of situations that produce uncleanness, situations that defile one's body or environment and thus limit a person's ability to come near to God's holy presence. The concerns address four primary situations: clean and unclean animals (chapter 11); the uncleanness of childbirth (chapter 12); the uncleanness of skin diseases (chapters 13–14); and the uncleanness of genital discharges (chapter 15).

The instructions in these five chapters collectively shift the focus from the sanctuary (chapters 1–10) to the sphere of everyday life, especially the customs and practices observed in the home and at the table. Toward this end, the instructions offer a bridge between the sacred and the common. On the one hand, they respond to God's mandate to Aaron in Lev. 10:10: "You are to distinguish between the holy and the common, and between the unclean and the clean." On the other, they anticipate and prepare for the great Day of Atonement that will be described in Leviticus 16. The rituals on that day are for purifying the sanctuary "because of the uncleannesses of the people of Israel" (16:16). Thus the stipulations concerning the "clean" and the "unclean" are framed by instructions and rituals that are set within the context of community worship. Their purpose is to render the community "clean," that is, fit for life in the presence of God. Sandwiched between the instructions for the consecration of the cult and its priests (Leviticus 8–10) and the purification of the sanctuary (Leviticus 16), these purity laws teach that how one lives *outside* the sanctuary is no less important than the rituals one offers *inside* the sanctuary. God's expectations for holiness are all-encompassing.

Despite this claim for the importance of Leviticus 11–15, it is likely that on first encounter many will find its concerns with uncleanness not only extreme but perhaps also bizarre. The ritual prescriptions for cleansing a person recovered from leprosy, for example, stipulate that the priest slaughter one bird over fresh water in an earthen vessel, then take a second bird, along with cedarwood, crimson yarn, and hyssop, and dip it in the blood of the slaughtered bird. He then sprinkles this blood seven times on the one who is to be pronounced clean, after which this person must wash his clothes, shave his head, and bathe himself in water (14:2–9). Our response to such a strange practice may be similar to that described by Nathan Englander in the short story titled "The Gilgul of Park Avenue" (*For the Relief of Unbearable Urges*, pp. 107–37).

Englander, a former yeshiva student from New York who now lives in Israel, knows well how strange orthodox Judaism can seem to the outsider. The story opens with Charles Lugar, a middle-aged financial analyst, sitting in the backseat of a New York cab. All of a sudden and with no forewarning it happened: "Ping! Like that it came. Like a knife against glass" (p. 109). This man who had been a nonbeliever all his life suddenly realized he was Jewish. He leaned forward and knocked on the plexiglass divider that separated him and the cab driver. The driver looked into the backseat through the rearview mirror. "Jewish," Charles said. "Jewish, here in the back." The driver opened the window so he could hear more clearly. "Oddly, it seems that I'm Jewish. Jewish in your cab." "No problem here," the cab driver said casually. "Meter ticks the same for all creeds."

If the cab driver had no problem with his sudden confession, Charles knew his wife, Sue, would. He dreaded telling her when he got home, and so he waited for just the right moment. In the meantime he tried to act Jewish in private. He observed the dietary laws forbidding milk and meat, gave up the suits that were blended of the forbidden mixture of linen and wool, and refused to punch in the elevator numbers on the Sabbath day. Out of respect for the prohibition against work, he simply rode up and down until someone pushed the button for his floor. Finally, after waking up Sue one Friday night by stumbling in the bathroom because he would not turn on the light, Charles knew the time had come to confess his conversion.

So, one evening Charles prepared a candlelit dinner and tried to set a pleasant scene for his confession. Finally he broached the subject. "I'm Jewish," he said. Sue sat still. "Is there a punch line?" she asked. "Or I am supposed to supply that?" (p. 117). Charles tried to explain that this was not a joke. He was right. She did not respond well at all.

> What you're really trying to tell me is: Honey, I'm having a nervous breakdown. . . . I've been waiting for your midlife crisis. But I expected something I could handle, a small test. An imposition.

Something to rise above and prove my love for you. . . . Why couldn't you have turned into a . . . liberal Democrat? Slept with your secretary . . . Any of those and I would've made do. (pp. 118, 122)

Charles tried to reassure her. "Honey, this should make you happy for me. I've found God" (p. 121). Sue was not comforted by this explanation at all.

Exactly the problem. You didn't find our God. I'd have been good about it if you found our God—or even a less demanding one. A deity less queer. . . . Today the cheese is gone. You threw out all the cheese, Charles. How could God hate cheese?

The story ends with Charles and Sue still trying to learn how to live with each other now that he is Jewish. Englander's last paragraph leaves us with a final image that may serve as an introduction to the "strange" concerns for purity in Leviticus 11–15:

He [Charles] tried to appear open before her, to allow Sue to observe him with the profound clarity he had only so recently come to know. He struggled to stand without judgment, to be only for Sue, to be wholly seen, wanting her to love him changed. (p. 137)

The instructions for purity, indeed all the instructions in the book of Leviticus, require a deeper and more profound clarity than Sue could muster. A first step toward attaining that clarity is to attend carefully to the concerns of these chapters, for in them Leviticus insists, as Kaiser has noted, that "without cleanness, there can be no holiness" (Kaiser, p. 1074). If we permit ourselves to live imaginatively inside this claim, we may discover that there is more truth in the familiar adage of John Wesley than we have yet realized: "Cleanliness is indeed next to godliness."

Leviticus 11:1–47
Clean and Unclean Animals

The instructions concerning clean and unclean animals are set forth in two blocks. Verses 2–23 deal with land animals (vv. 2–8), fish (vv. 9–12), birds (vv. 13–19), and winged insects (vv. 20–23). Verses 41–45 complete this survey with instructions concerning swarming land creatures. This same sequence of animals occurs also in Deut. 14:4–21, which appears to be dependent on Leviticus 11 (for discussion of the complex relationship between Leviticus 11 and Deuteronomy, see

Milgrom, *Leviticus 1–16*, pp. 698–704). Verses 24–40, generally regarded as a later insertion into the chapter, interrupt the listing of impure animals with instructions concerning the ritual procedures for purification in the case of defilement by contact with unclean carcasses. A summary statement in vv. 46–47 concludes the chapter with a reminder of the purpose of the instructions: "to make a distinction between the unclean and the clean."

The rationale for the dietary laws, as for the instructions that follow in chapters 12–15, is elusive. Despite an enormous amount of scholarly work on the question, no single explanation has as yet proved completely persuasive (for a concise summary of the theories, see Kaiser, pp. 1074–76). Nevertheless, two foundational discernments have gradually emerged, both heavily influenced by the work of two scholars, Jacob Milgrom (e.g., *Leviticus 1–16*, pp. 704–42) and Mary Douglas (e.g., *Leviticus as Literature*, pp. 135–94). First, we may posit that a *religious/theological* reason undergirds the concerns for purity in dietary and other matters. The first clue comes in Lev. 11:44, a direct address from God that explains why Israel must not defile itself by eating forbidden animals: "Sanctify yourselves therefore, and be holy, for I am holy." Israel must strive for holiness, because its primary commission, rooted in God's expectation for all humanity, is to live "in his image" (Gen. 1:27). In explicating God's "image," Genesis 1, the Priestly version of the creation story, places considerable emphasis on God's careful ordering of everything in the world "according to its/their kind." This concern repeats no fewer than ten times in Genesis 1 (vv. 11, 12 [twice], 21 [twice], 24 [twice], 25 [three times]). The text with the next most frequent number of occurrences of this phrase is Leviticus 11, which specifies that the dietary laws are similarly defined by the concern to categorize clean and unclean animals "according to its/their kind" (the key term, *min,* "kind, species," occurs nine times: vv. 14, 15, 16, 19, 22 [four times], 29). From a priestly perspective, distinguishing between clean and unclean animals is an act of faith that mirrors God's work in establishing and sustaining the "very good" design of creation.

Second, we may understand that the theological rationale includes a *moral/ethical* imperative. God's primordial act of creation is grounded in the principles of justice and righteousness (Murray, pp. 94–125). Imitating God's holiness, therefore, requires living according to God's ethics. Toward this end, the dietary laws inculcate a reverence for life that mirrors God's compassion for all creatures, especially those whose constitution may render them vulnerable to violence or abuse. Douglas has suggested, for example, that the forbidden animals in Leviticus 11 exemplify sufferers from injustice. In the blindness of worms, the vulnerability of fish without scales, the ceaseless labor of ants, we may discern an analogy to human counterparts: the beggar, the orphan, the defenseless widow. The summons to refrain from eating certain animals is not a license to avoid or shun them. It is a word of caution not to prey on them. As Douglas puts it, "Holiness is incompatible with predatory behavior" ("Forbidden Animals in Leviticus," p. 22; cf. *Leviticus as Literature*, pp. 134–51). When the mandate for holiness is ritualized in concerns with diet, then theological sensitivity may be gestured forth in ethical behavior that is both concrete and pragmatic.

The Categorization of Clean and Unclean Animals (11:2–23, 41–45)

The delineation of clean and unclean animals generally corresponds to the classification of animals in Genesis 1, which focuses on the three domains of land, water, and air. *Land animals* (vv. 2–8) that are clean, therefore edible, are those that walk on split hoofs and chew the cud. Leviticus 11 does not specify which animals meet these criteria, but Deut. 14:4–5, a later text, identifies the ox, the sheep, and the goat, plus seven other wild animals. Animals that do not meet both these criteria—the camel, the rock badger, the hare, and the pig—are forbidden. The pronouncement concerning each disqualified animal is that "it is unclean for you" (*ṭāmēʾ hûʾ lākem*; vv. 4, 5, 6, 7), a phrase that applies only to cases of impurity that are irreversible (Milgrom, *Leviticus 1–16*, p. 648). Verse 8 amplifies the prohibition by warning against eating these animals or touching their dead carcasses. No purification ritual is provided for one who ingests forbidden animals; presumably consumption renders one irrevocably impure. Verses 24–28 will describe the purification ritual for those who inadvertently touch the carcass of an unclean animal.

Water creatures (vv. 9–12) that are edible are those that have fins and scales. All marine life that does not meet these criteria is declared "detestable (*šeqeṣ*) to you" (vv. 10, 11, 12). Milgrom has argued that the term *šeqeṣ* is reserved for animals whose consumption is forbidden but that do not defile if only touched (*Leviticus 1–16*, p. 656). Douglas has noted that *šeqeṣ* does not convey the negative emotion we normally associate with something that is detestable, or as we might say, contemptible or loathsome. Instead, she suggests that something that is *šeqeṣ* must be avoided or shunned not because it is evil but because God has placed it off limits (*Leviticus as Literature*, pp. 166–69).

The *creatures of the air* (vv. 13–23) that are declared "detestable" include certain birds and winged insects. The list of forbidden birds numbers twenty species in all (vv. 13–19). Because the identification of many of these birds is uncertain, the characteristics that make them unfit are difficult to determine. In general, they are all birds of prey (e.g., falcons, vultures, owls, and ravens) and thus are excluded because they feed on dead carcasses and consume flesh with blood in it. The primary issue appears to be the concern to keep faith with God's postflood commandment not to eat "flesh with its life, that is, its blood" (Gen. 9:4; cf. Lev. 3:17; 7:26; 17:10–16). From all those who violate this commandment, which God imposes on *both animals and humans*, God will "surely require a reckoning" (Gen. 9:5). Winged insects (vv. 20–23) that "walk upon all fours" are "detestable," perhaps because their means of movement, walking rather than flying, makes them an anomaly in the domain of air creatures. Winged insects with "jointed legs" that allow them to hop in the air as well as walk on the land are declared edible. Four specific insects are identified: the locust, the bald locust, the cricket, and the grasshopper.

The final category deals with *"all creatures that swarm upon the earth"* (vv. 41–45). Those that are declared "detestable" are identified by three characteristics: crawling on the belly, moving on all fours, and having many legs. These characteristics appear to supplement at least some of those that have been previously identified, hence it is unclear specifically which animals are meant to be included in this prohibition. One clue may be found in vv. 29–30, which list eight rodents and reptiles that are "unclean for you among the creatures that swarm upon the earth." The concluding statement in vv. 43–45 provides a theological rationale for obeying the instructions: "Be holy, for I am holy." Just as God's holiness is manifest through concrete acts on earth—"I am the Lord who brought you up from the land of Egypt" (v. 45)—so Israel must image its God through concrete behavior that honors and sustains the purity and order of God's creational design (cf. Gorman, *Divine Presence and Community*, pp. 75–76).

The theological rationale for obedience—"be holy, for I am holy"—reflects the style and thematic emphasis of the Holiness Code (cf. 19:2; 20:7; see further the commentary on Leviticus 17–27) and thus may be a supplement to the dietary laws provided by a later Priestly redactor (Milgrom, *Leviticus 1–16*, pp. 691–98; Knohl, p. 69). It is likely, however, that the redactor is developing an ethical mandate deeply rooted in the Priestly understanding of God's reverence for all life in creation. As noted above, both Genesis 1 and Leviticus 11 stress God's ordering of everything in creation "according to its/their kind." Leviticus builds on this discernment by stipulating that only the animals that reflect the normal characteristics of their kind are edible. Those that do not possess these characteristics are not only different; they are disadvantaged, because they lack the means for survival that are common to their species. Thus land animals that walk on feet are edible, but those that must move about on paws (cf. v. 27) must not be pursued as game. Marine animals with fins and scales are edible, because they have the capacity to move about in water in a way that gives them full access to the resources of their natural environment. Water animals that do not have fins and scales must survive by other means; their vulnerability means they should not be considered as food for human beings. In general, birds of the air are edible, provided they do not use their ability to fly to prey upon the carrion and blood of animals that can no longer defend themselves against attack.

But why should Leviticus be so concerned with such a careful delineation of the animal world "according to its kind"? The explanation lies in the Priestly understanding of humankind's violation of the creational boundaries God has established. By God's design, all creation is endowed with the capacity to flourish, to be "very good" (Gen. 1:31), specific creaturely limitations and obstacles notwithstanding. However, when human beings transgress creation's boundaries with a greedy desire to consume what God has placed off limits, an escalating violence against life threatens the world's capacity to be all that God desires (Genesis 3–6). God's response to human sinfulness is to purge the world by flood, then re-create it, complete with blessing and commission (Gen. 9:1, 7). In the postflood world, God recognizes that divine intentions must be worked out in the midst of the "fear and dread" that falls on "every animal of the earth, and on every bird of the air . . . and on all the fish of the sea" because of human dominion (Gen. 9:2). God therefore places a new restriction on humankind that serves to protect the animal world from exploitation and abuse: "Every moving thing that lives shall be food for you. . . . Only, you shall not eat flesh with its life, that is, its blood" (Gen. 9:3–4). Any violation of this imperative will eventuate in a divine reckoning, which includes not only "human beings" but, where appropriate, "every animal" as well (Gen. 9:5). Both the promise and the responsibility that define life in this new world are anchored to the "everlasting covenant" that God establishes with all humanity and "with every living creature of all flesh that is on the earth" (Gen. 9:16; cf. vv. 9, 12, 15, 17).

The restrictions on diet in Leviticus 11 are testimony to the fact that the Priestly tradition takes this covenant between God and every living creature with utmost seriousness (cf. Milgrom, *Leviticus 1–16*, pp. 704–5; Douglas, *Leviticus as Literature*, pp. 134–37). To be in covenant with God and every living creature is fundamentally incompatible with

97

an unrestrained consumption of the animal world. To be holy as God is holy (Lev. 11:44), human beings must aspire to moral and ethical relationships with the world that reflect and sustain God's compassion for all creatures, especially those that live in "fear and dread" of violence. Only then can the ultimate reward for covenantal fidelity so evocatively envisioned by the prophets *and* the priests—perfect peace and harmony between all creatures on earth (cf. Lev. 26:6; Isa. 11:6–9; Hos. 2:18; Ezek. 34:25–31)—move from promise to reality.

Ritual Procedures for Purification (11:24–40)

These verses comprise a unified block of material that deals with impurities resulting from contact with carcasses. Both the style and substance of this section suggest that it is a later insertion into the chapter, possibly designed to supplement the concern with impurities conveyed by humans (chapters 12–15) with a corresponding emphasis on communicable impurities by animals (Milgrom, *Leviticus 1–16*, p. 693). Verses 24–25 establish two general principles, both informed by the belief that contact with a corpse is dangerous, because it brings one near the forces of death: (1) incidental contact with a corpse renders a person unclean "until the evening," and (2) carrying a carcass, which presumably involves a more intense or more lengthy form of contact, not only makes persons unclean "until the evening" but also requires that they wash their clothes. Verses 26–40 amplify these principles with instructions concerning the carcasses of unclean land animals (vv. 26–28), unclean "swarming" creatures and the impurities they convey in various situations (vv. 29–38), and the carcasses of edible animals (vv. 39–40).

The most detailed instructions concern the uncleanness of "creatures that swarm upon the earth" (vv. 29–38). The list of eight reptiles and rodents (vv. 29–30) suggests a focus on small creatures that commonly "invade" and contaminate the cooking area, where food is stored and prepared (cf. Carroll, pp. 120–24). Both *persons* and *objects* that come into contact with the carcasses of these animals are defiled. If the carcass touches anything made of wood, cloth, skin, or sackcloth, that object becomes unclean "until the evening." It must be immersed in water and set aside until the next day, when it becomes clean and acceptable for use again (v. 32). If the carcass falls into an earthen vessel, that vessel becomes unclean and must be shattered. Standing water in such a vessel contaminates any food or liquid that it touches (vv. 33–34). Similarly, any oven or stove that comes into contact with these carcasses becomes unclean and must be broken (v. 35).

98

There are two exceptions to the polluting power of animal carcasses (vv. 36–38). First, anyone who touches a carcass that has fallen into a spring or cistern will become unclean, but these water sources themselves are not contaminated. Second, if the carcass touches a seed that has been watered, that seed becomes unclean, perhaps because its growth process has been corrupted before it has even begun. But if the seed is dry, that is, if its growth process is still to be determined by natural rainwater, then it remains clean. The principle that guides these two exceptions is difficult to determine. Water is clearly an ambiguous agent. On the one hand, it is a necessity for life and for purification. On the other, water that has become polluted conveys impurities that bring whatever it touches into the realm of death. It appears that the priests wished to preserve the necessary distinction between these two states: Water that is naturally associated with the earth—such as springs, rain, and rainwater collected in cisterns—remains an incorruptible resource for life in God's good creation; water that is "unnaturally" collected in humanly constructed vessels or water that is "artificially" placed on seeds (by human hands?) may be polluted, in which case it conveys the impurities that may have been contracted from external sources.

The Purpose of the Instructions (11:46–47)

The dietary laws conclude with the statement: "This is the law pertaining to . . ." There are twelve such formulaic statements in Leviticus, ten of which are strategically positioned to mark one aspect of the *tôrâ* this book imparts (see the discussion of "A Decalogue of Ritual Life" at 6:8–7:38). The first five *tôrôt* deal with the requirement of holy sacrifice that the priests must administer in the sanctuary (6:9, 14, 24; 7:1, 11). The second five deal with the requirement of holy behavior that priests must teach and people must practice in everyday life. Priests and people alike must obey the *tôrâ* concerning clean and unclean animals (11:46), the uncleanness of childbirth (12:7), the uncleanness of skin disease (13:59), the purification of skin disease (14:57; cf. 14:32, 54), and the uncleanness of genital discharge (15:32). From the priestly perspective, these ten *tôrôt* are equally binding on the people who know themselves called by the God of Sinai to be "a priestly kingdom and a holy nation" (Exod. 19:6). *Without priests* to teach them the holy sacrifices that enable them to draw near to God in the sanctuary, the people cannot be the *priestly* kingdom that God envisions. And *without obedience* to the priests' instructions concerning their conduct outside the sanctuary, they cannot be the *holy* nation that mirrors God's investment in them of the hopes for the world. In sum, if priests and people do not

99

demonstrate a commitment to the ethics of holiness *outside the sanctuary*, in the ordinary affairs of everyday life, they will give the lie to the profession they offer through pious rituals *inside the sanctuary*. From the priestly perspective, the fragile but generative first step toward becoming the people God believes in and hopes for is to make a distinction between the clean and the unclean. To be obedient to this *tôrâ* is to walk faithfully in the footsteps of the One who (re)created the world and gave it a second chance to reverence all creation with a God-like compassion.

Leviticus 12:1–8
The Uncleanness of Childbirth

Within the purity laws, chapters 12–15 shift the focus from a concern with uncleanness that has its source outside the human body—animals and carcasses—to that which has its origins in the human condition itself (cf. Kaiser, p. 1084). The concern with bodily impurities, of both males and females, is signaled by the two chapters that frame this text unit. Chapter 12 deals with the impurities females incur in giving birth. Chapter 15 addresses the impurities that both males and females incur in genital discharges. In between these two chapters, Leviticus 13–14 treats the related issue of skin diseases that may mar any person's body, whether male or female (on the structure of chaps. 12–15, see Douglas, *Leviticus as Literature*, pp. 176–78). The structure of the last four chapters in this unit indicates, therefore, that the principal concern is with the impurities of the human body as a whole. Although some of the concerns are gender-specific—only females discharge menstrual blood, only males discharge semen—these instructions as a whole do not discriminate between the worth of men and women or the susceptibility of their bodies to impurity.

The salient details of the concern with the uncleanness of childbirth are relatively clear. If a woman bears a son, she is "ceremonially unclean" for seven days (cf. 15:19–24). On the eighth day, the son is to be circumcised, which is the sign of his entry into the covenant community (cf. Gen. 17:10–14). The mother undergoes an additional thirty-three days of purification, during which time she may not enter the sanctuary or touch any holy object (vv. 2–4). At the end of her purification process, a period of forty days in all, she must bring to the priest the requisite offerings that he may enact the purification ritual on her behalf. If she has the economic means, she must offer a lamb for a burnt offering and a pigeon or a turtledove for a purification offering. If she cannot afford these offerings, she may substitute two turtledoves or two pigeons (vv. 6–8). If a woman bears a daughter, the time period for her impurity is doubled: the initial period is fourteen days rather than seven; the period of purification is sixty-six days rather than thirty-three (v. 5). The purification ritual at the end of this period, eighty days in all, is the same as that required for the birth of a son (vv. 6–8). Upon the completion of the purification ritual, women who have given birth may resume their regular activities in the life and worship of the community.

Despite this text's seemingly straightforward approach, it invites a number of questions, not only about the priestly understanding of a woman's status in ancient Israel but, perhaps more formidably, about the relevance of this understanding for the contemporary world. The following observations suggest a foundation for further reflection:

1. *The concern with ritual impurities resulting from childbirth is widely shared by different cultures throughout the world.* It is by no means a unique or peculiar fascination limited to ancient Israel; it is a global issue. In support of this claim, Milgrom cites parallels not only in societies that are culturally contiguous with ancient Israel, such as ancient Babylon, Egypt, Persia, and Greece, but also in such diverse primitive societies outside Israel's cultural environment as the Tahitian, the Indian, the Sinaugolo of British New Guinea, and the Ba-Pedi of South Africa (*Leviticus 1–16*, pp. 763–65). Moreover, we may note that similar concerns continued to be addressed in rabbinic Judaism and in the early church; indeed, to this day among Christian faith communities, the Greek Orthodox Church prohibits menstruating women from participating in the sacrament of confession. It is the case, of course, that different cultures address the issues in ways that reflect their peculiar values. Nevertheless, the fact that postpartum purification rituals are so widely attested confirms that Israel was not alone in viewing the miracle of childbirth with both awe and anxiety. As Milgrom puts it, the concern with the impurities from childbirth "cannot be traced to a creed or a ritual but must reside in some universal human condition that has evoked the same response all over the globe. In a word, we have to do with the human psyche" (*Leviticus 1–16*, p. 765).

Given the universality of this concern, Israel's priests would have been unique, perhaps even strange, had they *not* developed purification rituals for childbirth. This point deserves consideration, especially from a cultural-historical perspective, because it turns our modern suppositions on end. We may be tempted to dismiss the priestly thinking

101

as oddly, even tragically out of step with any reasonable religious assessment of what happens when a woman gives birth. The comparative data indicate just the opposite. In a world where virtually every culture regarded purification rituals for parturients and menstruants as vital for the religious welfare of the society, Israel's claims for its God could not have passed muster as a bona fide religion without dealing with the impurities associated with childbirth. Indeed, Douglas plausibly suggests that Israel's priests might well have believed that in the religious pluralism of their world, "holiness was a competitive business" (*Leviticus as Literature*, p. 171). In the high-stakes game of proving their religious doctrines were comprehensive and sufficient for every situation in life, the priests could not afford to be silent on issues that everyone would have expected them to address.

2. *A woman's uncleanness at childbirth does not imply that the female's worth or value is intrinsically less than a male's*. Consideration of this issue is necessary because of the stipulation that a woman's impurity after giving birth to a daughter is twice as long—eighty days compared to forty—as that for a son.

Some have suggested, usually by appealing to Lev. 27:2–7, which states that the redemption price of women is about half that of men, that the disparity reflects ancient Israel's understanding of the relative status of the sexes (cf. Wenham, p. 188; Noth, p. 97). The logic of this interpretation is faulty for at least two reasons. First, Leviticus 27 assigns a higher value to males (and younger persons) because of their ability to carry out the heavy labor associated with the sanctuary, not because of their inherent worth. Second, the rationale behind the priestly purity system would suggest that the potential for defilement is related to an object or a person's power, not weakness. Thus, if a female's impurities require more attention, it might well be argued that she must be accorded more regard, not less, than a male. At the very least, before assuming that Leviticus 12 (or Leviticus 27) implies a woman's inferiority, we should heed the caution urged by Gruber: "Greater defilement is not necessarily an indication of lesser social worth" (Gruber, p. 43 n.13).

Although it must be conceded that the rationale behind the doubling of the purification times for the female is unclear, two further possibilities merit consideration. First, ancient Israel was not the only society to require a longer purification period for the birth of a daughter. Milgrom cites similar requirements from cultures as diverse as southern India and the ancient Hittites (*Leviticus 1–16*, p. 750). Moreover, there is evidence to suggest that this practice was based on a commonly held biological assessment. Both Jewish and Greek sources affirm the ancient understanding that the female embryo requires a longer formation period than the male, a judgment that at least one modern physician has partly defended on scientific grounds (Macht, pp. 253–60). Even if such a view would not be validated by modern medicine, that it was widely believed in Israel's world suggests it could have been a part of the priest's rationale.

The second possibility is that a mother and a newborn daughter require a longer period of purification because they are more vulnerable. A woman's loss of blood at childbirth leaves her in a weakened condition that to the Israelite mind makes her susceptible to sickness and potentially to death. The same threat applies to her daughter, who as a mother-to-be will one day share the experience of losing some of her life in order to bring life into the world. Through the discharge of semen, males also experience a risky diminution of life, yet by virtue of the rite of circumcision, they enjoy the protection of the covenant from the eighth day of their birth. The woman's place in the covenant is more tenuous, for her status depends first on her relationship with her father, then her husband. Her vulnerability is therefore twofold. Her condition at childbirth subjects her not only to physical complications but also to unethical abuse by those who might wish to take advantage of her weakened condition. Given the possibility that the purity laws are fundamentally connected with the desire to image and sustain God's compassion for all life (see the discussion at 11:2–23, 41–45), we may speculate that the priests were concerned to protect women, no less than other vulnerable creatures, from harm and injury (cf. Douglas, *Leviticus as Literature*, p. 182).

3. *A woman's impurity at childbirth is not equated with sinfulness.* When a woman "produces seed" (v. 2; NRSV: "conceives"), she is in fact sharing in the procreative capacities that God has entrusted to creation. When she conceives and bears a son or a daughter, she is no less obedient than the plants and fruit trees that "produce seed" in accord with God's expectations (Gen. 1:11–12). Although it should be obvious, the priestly affirmation of childbirth deserves to be underscored. Indeed, a woman's capacity to bring new life into the world is a critical part of the generative process that God blesses and decrees to be "very good" (cf. Gen. 1:28–31).

Further confirmation that a woman's impurity is not a moral failure comes from observing that when her purification period is completed, she once again becomes "clean" (vv. 7, 8). Her defilement is a ritual one, not a moral one. When the priest effects expiation on her behalf, he in effect recognizes that her uncleanness has already been eliminated. She is not "forgiven" in the sense that is implied in the previous cases where "purification offerings" are required (cf. 4:1–5:13). Indeed, at no point does chapter 12 say or suggest that the either the priest or God has judged the woman to have "sinned" or "brought guilt" on herself or the community. Rather, once she brings the required offerings, she is "cleansed" from a natural impurity that has only temporarily restricted her normal participation in the life and worship of the community. In this connection, it is instructive to note that the New Testament records a similar ritual cleansing for Mary following the birth of Jesus. After Jesus was circumcised, Mary and Joseph brought him to Jerusalem and offered the sacrifices prescribed in Lev. 12:8 "according to what is stated in the law of the Lord" (Luke 2:21–24). The narrative goes on to report that "when they had finished everything required by the law of the Lord," Mary, Joseph, and Jesus returned to Nazareth and resumed their regular activities (Luke 2:39–40).

Leviticus 13–14

The Uncleanness of Skin Disease

These two chapters comprise three speeches—13:1–59; 14:1–32; and 14:33–53—through which God offers instructions concerning a variety of skin diseases and the requisite rites of purification. Each speech is marked off by an introductory formula—"The Lord spoke to Moses (and Aaron), saying" (13:1; 14:1, 33)—and a concluding summary—"This is the ritual for . . ." (13:59; 14:32, 54; cf. Hartley, pp. 180–83). The first speech addresses seven skin diseases that render a person unclean (13:2–44), the prescribed behavior for persons afflicted by these diseases (13:45–46), and a concomitant concern with mold or fungus that makes clothing unclean in a manner similar to bodily skin diseases (13:47–58). The second speech, 14:2–32, describes the purification ritual for a person who has recovered from a skin disease. The third speech, 14:33–53, provides complementary purification rituals for a house that has become unclean because of mildew or mold.

Although these three speeches contain an enormous amount of detail, several repeating emphases combine to produce a generally systematic presentation: (1) The dominant word for "disease" throughout is ṣāraʿat. The NRSV, along with most commentators, associates the term with leprosy (for discussion, see Hartley, pp. 187–89; Milgrom, *Leviticus 1–16*, pp. 816–20). While this may be generally true, it is clear that

Leviticus uses the term to refer to a wide range of irritations, swellings, eruptions, or other surface changes that affect not only humans but also fabrics and houses. (2) The priest functions not as a medical doctor who treats and cures a patient but as a cultic specialist who identifies impurities and administers rituals that enable the community to separate the "unclean" from the "clean" (cf. 10:10). (3) The diagnosis that a person or an object has become unclean depends on the coloration of the lesion and the degree to which it has spread. (4) The purification rituals involve examination, a period of quarantine, reexamination, and final disposition. If the priest determines that the presenting symptoms have passed, then he will restore the person or object to normalcy. If he determines that the symptoms persist, he will confine the person, fabric, or house to isolation until such time as a change merits further review.

One further issue in these chapters requires careful consideration. The words *clean* and *unclean* occur in these two chapters more than sixty times. There can be no doubt, therefore, that the integrity of the body, as well as of material objects closely related to the body, has a serious impact on the wholeness and holiness of the community. To be clean is to be whole; to be whole, without blemish, is to be holy and acceptable for communion with God. By the same token, it is noteworthy that these chapters do not use the word *sin* to define the blemishes they address, nor do they require a confession of sin from the afflicted person. It is true that outside Leviticus the Old Testament associates ṣāraʿat with both God's wrath and God's punishment. The cases of Miriam (Num. 12:1–15), Gehazi (2 Kgs. 5:25–27), and Uzziah (2 Chron. 26:16–21) are perhaps the parade examples. Such examples likely reflect a widespread popular belief that skin diseases *could be* a telling sign that God was punishing a sinful person.

Against this backdrop, the lack of sin language in Leviticus 13–14 may be more than a curious omission. It is plausible to suggest that the priests were aware of the popular connection between affliction and sin and sought to reframe the issue in a ritual context that permitted a different assessment. Skin disease *may* be a sign of divine judgment, *but it is not necessarily so*. Sometimes, perhaps even most of the time, disease is caused by nothing other than a breakdown of the body's defense mechanisms against foreign invasion. In such cases, the priestly purification rituals provide a nonaccusatory way for a society to recognize, protect, and provide for the possible restoration of innocent victims. One indication that ancient Israel was aware of both the regnant assumptions about disease and their potential for destructive application is the book of Job. The assertion that God condemned the friends (cf. Job 42:7–9) for unjustifiably linking Job's "loathsome sores" (Job

2:7) with sin provides an important caution against assuming that disease is always a metaphor for divine judgment. (For further discussion, see the reflections below: "Have You Considered My Servant Job?")

The First Speech: Skin Diseases and Related Matters (13:1–59)

The first speech divides into three parts: skin diseases that render a person unclean (vv. 2–44), the behavior prescribed for persons with skin diseases (vv. 45–46), and "diseases" that make fabrics unclean (vv. 47–58). An introduction (v. 1) and a concluding statement (v. 59) frame these parts as the *tôrâ* on skin disease that applies to all persons (*ʾādām*).

Skin Diseases (13:2–44). God's instructions to Moses and Aaron address seven types of skin conditions that make a person unclean: shiny patches (vv. 2–8); discoloration (vv. 9–17); boils (vv. 18–23); burns (vv. 24–28); sores on the scalp and in the beard (vv. 29–37); rashes or blisters (vv. 38–39); and bald spots on the head that are discolored (vv. 40–44). The medical terms for these conditions are in many cases a matter of conjecture. Such uncertainty, however, has only a minor effect on the interpretive process, for by listing *seven* diseases, the text puts the reader on notice that its primary objective is to provide a representative survey of all the sores and lesions that may be considered.

The condition that is described first (vv. 2–8) provides the essential criteria for diagnosis and the basic paradigm for response, which repeats with some variation in the succeeding cases. When any person has a skin condition, the priest will look for three symptoms: (1) a "swelling" that produces an abnormal protrusion; (2) an "eruption," perhaps something scab- or scalelike that appears on the skin; or (3) a shiny "spot" that indicates an inflammation of some sort (v. 2). M. Fishbane has noted that these three symptoms occur in the following verses in an almost perfect chiastic pattern ("On Colophons," pp. 442–43). Thus, in v. 2 the order of the symptoms noted above is 1, 2, 3; in vv. 3–17 it is 3, 2, 1; in vv. 18–23 it is 1, 2, 3; in vv. 24–28 it is 3, 2, 1; and in vv. 29–44, where number 1 is lacking, the order is 2, 3. Such a systematic presentation invites the speculation that the priests may have relied on a mnemonic device—1, 2, 3, then 3, 2, 1—to help them remember these instructions (Hartley, p. 185).

If any one of these symptoms has turned the hair white and the affected area is deeper than the skin, the priest will declare the person "ceremonially unclean" (v. 3). If the presenting symptoms are inconclusive, that is, if the affected area is not deeper than the skin and the hair has not turned white, the priest will quarantine the person for a period of fourteen days (vv. 4–6). On each seventh day the priest will reexamine the condition, and if the condition has not spread at the end of this period, he will declare the person to be "clean" (v. 6). Such persons must then wash their clothes, after which they may resume normal activities. If, however, the priest finds that the condition has not abated but spread, he will declare the person "unclean," for the evidence now confirms that the condition must be regarded as *ṣāra'at* (v. 8).

The six cases that follow this paradigmatic example show slight variations in keeping with the specifics of the presenting condition. Nevertheless, all of the conditions defined as *ṣāra'at* share one thing in common: Whether because of "swelling," "eruption," or "spotting," the skin's condition makes the body seem as if it is rotting away. Such an appearance suggests disintegration, which, if left unchecked, results in the person's death. And just as Israel must avoid defilement by contact with unclean carcasses (Leviticus 11), so must it guard against the disintegration of the *body of the person* and the *body of the society*.

For understanding both the fear and the compassion that inform each of these instructions concerning *sara'at*, the case of Miriam is particularly instructive. When Aaron saw that Miriam had been stricken with leprosy (*ṣāra'at*), he said to Moses, "Let her not be like something stillborn, whose flesh is half eaten away when it comes from the womb" (Num. 12:12, REB). In response to this plea, Moses cries, "Lord, not this! Heal her, I pray" (Num. 12:13, REB). God's response is telling. Miriam must remain outside the camp for seven days, during which time the people must not advance any further on the journey toward the promised land. Only when Miriam's quarantine is over and she is brought back into the camp may Israel resume its journey (Num. 12:15–16). Miriam's condition is dangerous, for both her and her community, but her exclusion is not the final word. The final word is about restoration, inclusion, and the resumption of the journey toward becoming the people God intends.

When we attend carefully to Israel's stories about those afflicted, for whatever reason, with *ṣāra'at*, it is not at all surprising to find that the New Testament portrays Jesus as one who faithfully embodies the legacy of his Jewish forebears. We may cite but one of the several examples the Gospels provide. Mark 1:40–45 reports that when a person with "leprosy" implored Jesus to make him clean, Jesus was "filled with compassion" (v. 41) and responded by saying, "Be made clean!" To emphasize Jesus' respect for the Torah, Mark adds that Jesus also said, "Go, show yourself to the priest, and offer for your cleansing what Moses commanded" (v. 44). The episode's final scene confirms that whatever exclusion the leper had previously experienced, his healing now restored him to a full (and vocal) role in society: "The man went away and made the whole story public, spreading it far and wide" (v. 45, REB; for further discussion, see Kazmierski, pp. 37–50).

The Behavior Prescribed for Persons with Skin Disease (13:45–46). Persons with certified cases of ṣāraʿat must tear their clothes, dishevel their hair, cover their mouth, and cry out, "Unclean, unclean." This symbolic enactment of affliction confirms that they know themselves to have become repugnant to the community. They must cry out a warning, lest others inadvertently come too close to their impurity, and they must banish themselves from the community by living alone outside the camp for the duration of their affliction (cf. Num. 5:1–4). Isolated from the community, where the observance of holy statutes and ordinances defines the fullness of life God enjoins (cf. Lev. 18:5), they now reside in a place where deprivation, shame, and abandonment mark them as the living dead. The only thing that stands between them and a final dismissal to the grave of the forgotten is the very ritual that has mandated their exclusion. One day, perhaps, the priest will say, "He is clean" (v. 17; cf. vv. 6, 13, 23, 28, 34, 35, 37, 38, 40). Until then, the afflicted must wait and hope. In the words of John Updike, whose lifelong battle with psoriasis offers firsthand knowledge of the mental anguish of those whose skin diseases make them society's lepers, they must eke out an existence under the cloud of "another presence coöccupying [their] body and singling [them] out from the happy herd of healthy, normal mankind" (Updike, p. 42).

"Diseases" That Make Fabrics Unclean (13:47–58). The same word used for skin diseases that afflict the body—ṣāraʿat—is also applied to items of clothing, specifically those made of wool, linen, or leather. In such cases the presenting symptoms are greenish or reddish spots that disfigure the surface of a garment, giving it the appearance of something that has begun to rot or deteriorate (vv. 47–48). The condition is best associated with mold or fungal growths.

The ritual procedure is very similar to that which has been previously described. When a garment appears to be infected, it is shown to the priest, who places it in quarantine for seven days and then reevaluates it. If, at the end of this period, the condition has spread, the garment is declared "unclean," and it must be burned (vv. 51–52). If the condition has not spread, the priest orders that it be washed and confined for an additional seven days. If, upon reexamination, the spot has not changed color, the garment is unclean and must be burned (vv. 53–55). If the spot has faded after having been washed, then the priest will tear out the affected area. If, however, the spot reappears, then it is clear that the infection is still spreading, and the garment must be burned (vv. 56–57). If the spot disappears after the first washing, then the garment must be washed a second time, and if it then continues to appear normal it is pronounced "clean," and its normal use may be resumed (v. 58).

The Second Speech: The Purification Ritual for a Person Recovered from a Skin Disease (14:1–32)

The second speech resumes the concern for persons afflicted with a skin disease (13:2–46). The resumption is significant because it serves notice that the ultimate concern of these instructions is not to banish persons as outcasts but to anticipate the day when they may be restored to a full and normal life within the community. The movement from affliction to healing and from banishment to restoration is ritually enacted through an eight-day process comprising three stages (day one: 14:2–8; day seven: 14:9; day eight: 14:10–32). The length of the process recalls the priestly paradigm for God's creation of the world. In its own way, the ritual ceremony is itself a creative act; upon its completion on the eighth day, there will be a new person who has made the scarring journey from death to life.

Day one (vv. 2–8) begins outside the camp, where life for the afflicted has been defined until now by conditions that approximate the "formless void and darkness" of primordial chaos (13:45–46; cf. Gen. 1:1–2). When persons have been healed of a skin disease, the priest must go to them outside the camp in order to inspect their recovery. Once the priest certifies that the disease has disappeared, he initiates the ritual process. From this point forward, the person is no longer referred to as "skin diseased" (14:2) but rather as "the one who is to be cleansed" (vv. 4, 7, 11, 17, 18, 19, 25, 28, 29, 31). The cleansing ritual requires two birds, cedarwood, crimson yarn, and hyssop (v. 4). The birds must be alive, healthy, and ritually clean. It is not clear why birds, rather some other animal, are required, but given the nature of the ritual details that follow, it is probable that they were chosen at least in part because of their ability to transport the impurity of the disease to a distant place (cf. v. 7). Cedarwood and crimson yarn, both red materials, may have been selected because their color is similar to blood, which the priestly ritual associates with the power of life (Milgrom, *Leviticus 1–16*, p. 833). Hyssop, which is also associated with purification (Num. 19:6; cf. Ps. 51:7 [MT: 51:9]), is a plant that acts somewhat like a sponge. When dipped into a liquid, for example, into the blood of the slaughtered bird (v. 6), its leaves retain enough of the substance to allow it to be sprinkled onto another object.

109

When the ritual materials are gathered, the priest orders that one of the birds be killed and its blood collected in an earthen vessel filled with fresh water—literally, "living water" (v. 5), that is, water from a stream or spring that is flowing. The other bird, still living, along with the cedarwood, crimson yarn, and hyssop, is dipped into the mixture of blood and water that has been collected in the earthen vessel. The priest sprinkles this mixture, presumably by means of the hyssop, seven times on the one who is being cleansed. The living bird, now daubed with both the blood and water, is then freed to fly away (vv. 6–7).

The symbolism of these acts is open to multiple interpretations. It is reasonable to assume, however, that the mixture of blood and water, both of which are clearly associated with life, indicates that the one whose affliction has meant a deathlike existence has now been freed to live without shame or diminishment. The sevenfold sprinkling with blood and water enacts a new birth, a re-creation; it is, in sum, a ritual reenactment of God's seven-day creation of a world blessed and ready to fulfill its Maker's highest expectation (see further the commentary on 4:3–12). The last rite of day one extends the symbolism. The person being cleansed washes the clothes, shaves, and bathes the body (v. 8). Each act is a ritual embodiment of the cleansed and new life that now awaits one who is ready to reenter a world formerly forbidden and closed.

On *day seven* (v. 9), the healed and ritually cleansed person is readmitted to the camp, with the proviso that he (or she) must remain outside the tent for seven days (v. 8b). For a second time, this time more thoroughly, the person shaves all the hair—head, chin, and eyebrows—launders the clothes, and bathes the body. Thoroughly cleaned of even the smallest residue of the affliction, the person is virtually like a new-born child, unspoiled, unblemished, fresh from the protective womb that is now ready to release its perfect work into the outside world (cf. Hartley, p. 196). Like creation itself on day seven, the ritual has reenacted a journey toward life that now has the potential once again to be "very good" (cf. Gen. 1:31–2:3).

The ritual concludes on *day eight* (vv. 10–32) with sacrifices that complete the transition from death to life and ritually enact the joy and the commitment of those who know themselves to have been reinstated with their community and reconciled with their God. The materials for the rite comprise the following: two male lambs without blemish, one yearling ewe lamb, a cereal offering of three-tenths of an ephah of flour, and a measure of oil. The person brings these to the priest, who performs the final rite at the entrance to the tent of meeting (vv. 10–20). If persons cannot afford these materials, they may substitute less expensive sacrifices: one male lamb, one-tenth of an ephah of flour, and two turtledoves or pigeons (vv. 21–32). Whether one is well-to-do or poor, the prescriptions concerning sacrifices in chapters 1–5 are presumed to apply to all these offerings.

Four primary types of sacrifices are offered: the reparation offering (cf. 5:14–6:7 [MT: 5:14–26]), the purification offering (cf. 4:1–5:13), the burnt offering (cf. 1:1–17), and the cereal offering (cf. 2:1–16). Of these, it is the reparation offering (vv. 12–18) that provides the key for understanding the ritual. The priest takes some of the blood from the reparation offering and some of the oil and places it on the person's right earlobe, right thumb, and right big toe. He dips his right finger in another portion of the oil and sprinkles it seven times before the Lord. The remainder of the oil he places on the head of the one being cleansed. By these acts the priest effects "atonement." The key word is *kippēr* (v. 18), which in ritual texts, as has been previously noted (see the commentary on 4:13–21), has the specific meaning of "purge" or "purify."

The reparation offering effectively sets right or reconciles whatever improper contact the diseased person may have had with the holy things of God. Once the reconciliation is complete, the person is free to enter the sanctuary and to resume full participation in the rituals and festivals that are part of every Israelite's life. In this connection, Milgrom has noted that the threefold occurrence of the word *kippēr* in vv. 18, 19, and 20 is strategically complemented by a triple repetition of the word *ṭāhēr*, "clean," in vv. 8, 9, and 20 (*Leviticus 1–16*, pp. 858–59). Together, these rhetorical markers trace the three stages of the recovered person's journey from death to life. At the end of day one, the cleansing signals the initial return to the camp (v. 8). At the end of the seventh day, the cleansing permits the person to move inside the camp to the tent (v. 9), thus to the threshold of a reentry into community life. At the end of the eighth day, the final cleansing, now ratified by three expiatory acts (*kippēr*), completes the rehabilitation process. From this point on, the person is fully integrated into the life of the community and the worship of God.

The most suggestive aspect of this eighth-day restoration ritual is its similarity to the ordination ceremony for the priest (see 8:22–30). Two comments are in order. First, it is apparent that the daubing of the blood on the extremities of the body enacts a rite of passage for both the priest and the healed person. In both instances persons move from outside to inside the tent, from a greater to a lesser distance from God, and from an existence associated with death to one that promises life. In both cases the ritual effects a person's changed status in relation to God and community.

111

The second discernment is admittedly more speculative. Because the priest and the person healed of skin disease are the only examples of persons who receive this particular daubing rite, we may be permitted to wonder if perhaps there is a subtle and peculiar connection between priesthood and suffering. Is it the case that only those who have traveled the life-scarring road from being condemned and ridiculed to being restored and embraced can really know what it means to minister to the afflicted? Is it the case that priests who stand in the gap between a holy God and fragile world are most attuned to their world when they know themselves to be "wounded healers" (Nouwen, pp. 81–96)? To be sure, the restoration ritual in Leviticus 14 appears to be solely focused on matters far more immediate and practical than such abstract theological ruminations. Even so, the picture of a priest daubed from head to toe with holy oil administering the same rite to a leper invites a wonderment about why and how we include (or exclude) the afflicted from the promise of life that we have claimed. Perhaps the credo of priest and leper alike shares a common Lear-like discernment: "If thou wilt weep my fortunes, take my eyes" (Shakespeare, *King Lear*, 4.6).

The Third Speech: Purification Rituals for an Unclean House (14:33–53)

The instructions concerning the purification of unclean dwellings would seem more logically to follow those dealing with leather and fabrics (13:47–58). Their location here may be due to the fact that the ritual is in many respects similar to that which applies to skin-diseased persons. In both cases the affliction is described as *ṣāra'at*, which suggests some type of fungus like mold or mildew. As with many of the rituals described in Leviticus 11–15, the purification of houses is a rather common cultural practice in the ancient Near East (cf. Meier, pp. 184–92). It may be noted, however, that whereas Israel's neighbors associated "diseased" houses with the displeasure of the deity, these priestly instructions stop short of attributing motives to God. Although God "puts" (v. 34) the disease on the house, there is no causal connection to sin or disobedience. Clearly, the house has not sinned! Moreover, no confession of sin or sacrifice for sin is required from the owner of the house (cf. Milgrom, *Leviticus 1–16*, pp. 867–68).

Any growth or disease that appears in a house must be reported to the priest, who, having ordered the removal of all the contents, will make an examination (vv. 35–42). If the priest finds greenish or reddish spots in the walls that appear deeper than the plaster surface, he orders the house to be closed for seven days. On the seventh day a second inspection occurs, and if the priest determines that the condition has spread, he orders the removal and disposal of the affected areas to an "unclean place outside the city" (v. 40), presumably to protect the city from further contamination. The walls are to be scraped and repaired. If the condition reappears, the priest declares the house "unclean" (v. 44) and orders that it be torn down and all the rubbish taken to an unclean place outside the city. Persons who have entered the quarantined house, whether to eat or sleep, must wash their clothes and wait until evening before resuming normal activities.

If, after replastering, the condition does not reappear, the priest shall pronounce the house "healed" and instruct the owner to enact a purification ritual (vv. 48–53). The ritual is essentially the same as that prescribed for persons who have recovered from a skin disease (14:1–7). The house is sprinkled seven times with a mixture of blood, water, cedarwood, and crimson yarn into which a living bird has been dipped. This act ritually "cleanses" ("decontaminates"; v. 52) and effects the purgation (v. 53) that restores the house for normal use.

For Further Reflection:
"Have You Considered My Servant Job?"

We may pause for a moment to reflect on what it might mean, from the victim's perspective, to live inside the gap between Leviticus 13:45–46 and Leviticus 14. On one side of this gap are the priestly instructions concerning the seven skin diseases that render a person ritually unclean and therefore unable to come near to God's holy presence. On the other side of this gap, Leviticus 14 describes the purification ritual for persons who have recovered from a skin disease. Leviticus 13:45–46 offers the only description of what diseased persons should do inside this painful interim between affliction and restoration. They must tear their clothes, dishevel their hair, cover their mouths, and cry out, "Unclean, unclean!" The question this prescription invites is "Will such instruction be adequate for those who must live inside the gap between suffering and healing?" The question may be addressed through the lens of another, which perhaps offers additional perspective on both the power and the burden of ritual: "Have you considered my servant Job?" (Job 1:8).

What brings Job into the orbit of Leviticus is his affliction with "loathsome sores" (2:7). The term for his condition is *šĕḥîn*, which is one of the generic words Leviticus uses to describe the various skin diseases the priest is empowered to diagnose (Lev. 13:18–23). Job's affliction

113

locates him among the persons who merit the priest's counsel on what to do when adversity places them outside the normal boundaries of God's available presence. Job's response to affliction is, of course, both more extensive and more extreme than what Leviticus 13 appears to envision. I suggest, therefore, that Job's radical exploration of life on the ash heap, where every cry for help seems to ricochet off the walls of an empty cosmos, permits a new understanding of what it means to wait in the hope and expectation of one day hearing the priest say, "He is clean."

Between Job 2 and 38 is a gaping chasm of divine silence. On one side is God's painfully permissive address to the *śātān*: "Very well, he is in your power" (2:6). On the other side is God's blustery but enigmatic response from the whirlwind (chaps. 38–41). Between relinquishment and revelation, Job is on his own, surrounded by what may be described as nothing more than God's "ontological stammer" (Sontag, p. 199). Job has, of course, the "comfort" of his friends, who try to explain God's silence with two recurring arguments: (1) They read Job's affliction as a metaphor for sin and divine judgment, and they urge him to repent so that God may be present for him once more (8:3–6; 11:13–19; 22:23–28); and (2) they read silence as a metaphor for God's inscrutable wisdom, which is necessarily too deep and too high for mere mortals like Job to comprehend (8:8–9; 11:7–9; 15:7–8; cf. 33:12–14). Job should not misread silence as absence, they insist. If he will only submit obediently to what God gives and withholds, then he can be "at peace" with God and with himself (22:21).

Job is not persuaded. Against the notion that affliction is a metaphor for sin, Job insists that the reality, the very physicality, of his pain shatters every attempt to give suffering a name that belongs to something else. "*Look at me*, and be appalled," he says to the friends, "and lay your hand upon your mouth" (21:5; cf. 6:28). If they would but look into his eyes, red-raw with weeping, if they would but touch his body and feel the hurt that has been stitched like sackcloth into his very skin (16:15–16), then they would know that moralisms can never bandage physical pain. Against the notion that silence is a metaphor for God's benevolently mysterious transcendence, Job insists that it is instead a sinister ruse (10:13–17) for God's malignant abandonment of good to evil and justice to injustice (10:1–17; 16:6–17; 19:6–12; 27:7–12; and especially 24:1–17). Like Salieri, the musician in Peter Shaffer's play *Amadeus*, whose career was derailed by Mozart's brilliant but disrespectful talent, Job takes his stand against any God who cannot be bothered to intervene on behalf of the righteous. In Salieri's words, "They say the spirit bloweth where it listeth: I tell you NO! It must list to virtue or not blow at all" (Shaffer, *Amadeus*, p. 74).

114

Job resists the metaphorical trappings the friends offer for his suffering and for God's silence. He also resists the limitations of the ritual stipulated in Lev. 13:45–46. He knows himself to have become someone the community regards as "unclean" and too repugnant for inclusion in their company (cf. 17:2, 6;19:13–20; 30:1–15), but he persists in believing, against all evidence to the contrary, that neither his suffering nor God's silence can be permanent if God is God. Sitting on the ash heap of suffering and silence, Job explores a different metaphor, one that exceeds the priestly ritual and subverts the friends' moralisms. For a brief explication of this metaphor, I turn to the evocative meditation on the quest for wisdom in Job 28.

Job 28 is a soliloquy on the question "Where shall wisdom be found?" (vv. 12, 20). The speaker is reflecting, turning things over and over in the mind, speaking them out loud to hear how they sound, then mulling them over again to find new levels of meaning that may not have been discerned on the mind's first pass through. The first section of this soliloquy, vv. 1–14, provides a good example of how this works. The governing metaphor is the miner's search for precious metals and gems. Miners have the capacity to "put an end to darkness" (v. 3). They can cut and carve through almost any obstacle until they see "every precious thing" and "bring to light" whatever is hidden (vv. 10–11). Yet for all their skill and resolve, they search in vain for the most prized possession of all—wisdom and understanding (v. 13). In an earlier speech, Zophar chided Job by asking rhetorically, "Can you find out the limit of the Almighty?" (11:7). The presumed answer is no. Indeed, Job has been pushed to concede that the full truth about God's work "at the boundary between light and darkness" (26:10) defies comprehension. At a first level, therefore, the miner's limitations serve to remind Job that even his best efforts to obtain wisdom sufficient for his situation will never be fully satisfying.

At a second level, however, the mining metaphor seems to evoke from Job the consideration of a different response to Zophar's question. A number of verbal and thematic connections between *what miners do* and *what God does* suggest that for all their limitations, humans in fact possess a certain Godlike capacity. When humans "put an end to darkness" (v. 3) and bring "hidden things . . . to light" (v. 11), they imitate the creative activity of God, whose word "Let there be light" provides the foundation for the world in which all creatures are to find their place (Gen. 1:2–3; cf. Job 12:22). When humans risk probing the limits of their world (v. 3b), they reach for the very boundaries that God sets in place to prevent the collapse of light and darkness (cf. 26:10). The correspondence between God's power and human power extends to the

115

specific measures described in vv. 9–11. The miner's power to "overturn mountains" (v. 9) compares with the power that manifests God's peculiar wisdom in governing the world (9:4–5). The ability to "see every precious thing" (v. 10a), even "hidden things" (v. 11b), approximates God's ability to "see everything under the heavens" (28:24), including wisdom, the most elusive treasure of all (28:27). The capacity to "cut out channels in the rocks" (v. 10) to get to the source of water evokes the image of God "splitting" rocks to create water for the people in the wilderness (Ps. 78:15; cf. Hab. 3:9).

In short, this soliloquy indicates that Job has thought deeply and on several levels about what humans can and cannot accomplish in the world. He can see that the world is full of things precious and desirable. Some of the world's greatest treasures—silver and gold—are buried so deep that their acquisition requires extraordinary human courage and skill. Other treasures—wisdom and understanding—are so elusive that even the best efforts to find them do not succeed. At this juncture, Job remains uncertain about what these possibilities and limitations mean for him. Should he focus on the limitations that humans must live with, as the friends have urged him to do—and as the priestly ritual seems to endorse—and resign himself to search only for those things that he has a reasonable chance of obtaining? Should he focus on the possibilities that tempt humans to reach for treasures that inevitably exceed their grasp? Job's experience has provided ample reason to believe that his friends are right. He understands that at a basic level human beings are slaves to destinies they do not choose. They live and they die, and in between they must simply endure whatever joy or sorrow God apportions to them (cf. 7:1–6; 14:5, 10–12).

Still, even as he is tempted to yield to limitations that cannot be refuted, Job has wondered if in some mysterious way he may be endowed with significance and power that can make a difference in the way the world works (cf. 7:12, 17). Having listened to all the reasons the friends give for why he should abandon such foolish thoughts, Job now contemplates a model for human striving that invites him to hold on to his imagination. It is the miner who fixes Job's reflections on what he can and cannot do. If it is possible for the miner to search inaccessible places and obtain some of the world's most unavailable treasures, then perhaps Job's search for the elusive God is not so foolish after all. If the miner can reach to the very limits of what is possible and in the process bring what is hidden to light, then perhaps Job can reach for the boundaries between silence and response, absence and presence. In the process, perhaps he too can see into the hidden things that defy com-

116

prehension. And if the miner must concede that some treasures, like wisdom, elude even the most determined efforts, perhaps the resolve to "overturn" and "split open" and "see" offers Job a model that in fact brings him as close to God as it is humanly possible to be.

Like a person who rubs two sticks of wood together to make a spark, I have rubbed two texts together in the hope of generating an idea. The text from Leviticus offers a ritual for identifying, addressing, reviewing, and potentially restoring those whose afflictions make them society's outcasts. Outside the gate, these persons cry out, "Unclean, unclean!" and wait for a word from God's priests that will remove the barriers between them and the life they once enjoyed. The ritual's promise is that the religious establishment will not let first discernments concerning affliction be the last; all persons who are cut off from God's presence deserve a second chance to have their case reviewed and their situation reversed. At the same time, the ritual is limited, even short-sighted; it contemplates no response from the afflicted other than patient submission. The texts from Job offer another picture of those whose affliction consigns them, for "no reason" (Job 2:3), to live outside the gate on ash heaps of affliction. If Job is any model, we should not be surprised to hear these persons cry out not "Unclean, unclean!" but "Injustice, injustice!" If Job is any guide, these persons will question and probe faith's foundations until they explode the boundaries of every ritual that denies them access to the world where they believe God's presence must be real and available.

Inside the gap between affliction and restoration, perhaps people of faith need the witness of both Leviticus and Job. Without rituals to mediate the explicable and inexplicable gaps that separate the holy from the common, all God-talk risks becoming nothing other than "pointlessness posing as a purpose" (for this suggestive phrase, see Woods, p. 254). By the same token, until and unless the rituals of faith are broken open and transformed by the shrieks of the Jobs of the world, they risk becoming vapid pronouncements that promise nothing more than sacramental nonsense.

For the bruising journey inside the promise and the burden of faith's rituals, there is perhaps one further word to ponder. It comes from the same God who posed the question "Have you considered my servant Job?" to those entrusted with the challenge of his affliction. "You have not spoken of me what is right, as my servant Job has. Now therefore take seven bulls and seven rams, and go to my servant Job, and offer up for yourselves a burnt offering; and my servant Job shall pray for you" (Job 42:7–8).

117

Leviticus 15:1–33

The Uncleanness of Genital Discharges

Chapter 15 completes the instructions concerning human bodily impurities that began with Leviticus 12. Taken together, the two chapters frame the priestly concern for impurities that both males and females must address. The chiastic structure of the chapter underscores the understanding that men and women, in their distinctive ways, share a common concern for bodily purity (cf. Hartley, pp. 205–7).

A Introductory statement (vv. 1–2a)
  B Abnormal discharges in males (vv. 2b–15)
    C Normal discharges in males (vv. 16–17)
      D Discharges in sexual intercourse that render men and
        women unclean (v. 18)
    C' Normal discharges in females (vv. 19–24)
  B' Abnormal discharges in females (vv. 25–30)
A' Concluding statement (vv. 31–33)

As the outline above indicates, v. 18 is the cotter pin that links together the two halves of the instructions. In their respective sexualities, men and women in intercourse share the responsibility for circumspection, lest their normal activities outside the tabernacle compromise the holy rituals they perform inside the tabernacle.

The following observations on the priestly concern with sexuality provide a reference point for interpretation:

> • Priestly thinking locates discharges from the reproductive organs within the larger context of ritual purity. The guiding principle is that the integrity of the body is vitally connected to the wholeness and holiness of the community. To be clean is to be whole; to be whole, without any breach of the body's physical boundaries, is to be holy and acceptable for communion with God. Both the normal discharge of seminal fluid and menstrual blood and abnormal genital emissions represent a penetration of the boundaries that the priests associate with anatomical wholeness, health, and security.
> • Breaches of the body's limits that are associated with the penis and the vagina are of particular concern in

the priestly system because they have to do with the creation of life. Moreover, because the procreative act involves a loss of semen for the man and a loss of blood for the woman, it brings both man and woman dangerously close to the sphere of death. In effect, both partners in the sexual union lose some of their own life, symbolized by the loss of vital fluids, in creating a new life. The collapse of the boundaries between life and death, even in the quite natural act of intercourse, is always a principal concern for the priests, who steward the responsibility for safeguarding God's creational boundaries between order and chaos.

• That Israel's priests viewed the sexual sphere as a matter of ritual concern indicates neither a unique nor a repressive attitude toward the importance, worth, and enjoyment of sex. On the one hand, we may note that religions both ancient and modern regard sexual activity with both awe and fear. Love, passion, procreation, pregnancy, and birth are believed to be endowed with the special, divine creative energies that sustain the cosmos. As such, they must be experienced and exercised with both care and caution. Mary Douglas makes the point as follows:

> It may be remarked that religions which ritualize sex are usually more in favour of it than against. To suppose that the numerous sexual regulations of Leviticus exhibit a narrowly puritanical attitude to sex would be like expecting a culture with numerous food rules to condemn good food. It is where sex is recognized as a potent elemental force, at once the source of desire, fulfillment, and danger, that religion seeks to appropriate sex and bind it with rules. (*Leviticus as Literature*, pp. 178–79)

On the other hand, it is clear that priestly instructions concerning sexual purity have continued to evoke reflection and discussion, not only in the Mishnah and Talmud but also among a wide range of peoples who share similar concerns about such matters. Particularly striking is the evidence that suggests the objective is not to demean or deny the natural passions of men and women but instead to

119

engender an environment of mutual respect in which neither has sovereign rights over the other. In this respect, Gerstenberger cites the example of Vera Lúcia Chahon, an orthodox Brazilian woman, who describes the obligations the purity regulations in Leviticus impose on the husband during his wife's menstruation:

> The Jewish faith prevents a husband from living out his sexual desires in an uncontrolled manner. Thus he is to understand that the woman is not the object of his desire. He is to understand that she is a person, that she has a personality and rights just as he himself does. Thus by keeping the waiting periods *a man learns to acknowledge his partner as a being deserving of his complete respect.* (Gerstenberger, p. 207; emphasis added)

Male Discharges (15:1–17)

Instructions concerning male discharges are divided into two categories: abnormal emissions (vv. 2b–15) and normal emissions (vv. 16–17). The first category treats secretions that are not semen-related. A variety of medical conditions have been suggested as plausible explanations of what is meant by the ambiguous term *zab*, "flow" (v. 2; NRSV: "discharge"), including diverticulitus, hemorrhoids, and gonorrhea. At a minimum, we may understand the condition to involve abnormal or inordinate discharges of some mucus-like substance from the genital area that renders a male ceremonially unclean (v. 3).

Such discharges render both the affected person and anyone or anything that comes into contact with him temporarily unclean (vv. 4–12). Thus anyone who touches a person with a discharge or comes into contact with the bed on which he sleeps, the seat on which he sits, or the spittle from his mouth becomes unclean "until the evening." Persons who contract impurity by such means must wash their clothes, bathe in water, and wait until evening, at which time they become clean once more and may resume their normal activities. Similar instructions apply to cooking pots—earthen and wood vessels—that become unclean by contact with the affected person.

The purification ritual for the affected person himself involves additional requirements (vv. 13–15). When the discharge has ceased, the recovered person must wait seven days, the customary period for the ritual crossing of the boundaries from unclean to clean, then wash his clothes and bathe himself in "fresh (i.e., 'living') water." On the eighth day, which is symbolic of the first day of life in a world now restored to its normal and blessed state, he must bring a sacrifice of either two turtledoves or two pigeons. The priest presents one as a purification offering, in order to cleanse the sanctuary of the person's communicable impurities; the second he presents as a burnt offering, which enacts the person's thanksgiving for recovery. With these offerings, the priest "effects purgation" (*kippēr*) for the person, who may now resume normal participation in the life and worship of the community.

Instructions concerning the emission of semen, a normal function of the penis, receive briefer treatment. Any discharge of semen, whether accidental (vv. 16–17) or in the act of intercourse (v. 18), renders a man ritually unclean. The "accidental" discharge appears to refer to what Deut. 23:11 calls a "nocturnal emission," that is, an emission not associated with intercourse. If a man experiences such a discharge, he must bathe his body, launder any clothes that have come into contact with the semen, and wait until evening to become clean. After this process, he may resume normal activities.

Sexual Intercourse (15:18)

From a structural standpoint, this single verse stands as the rhetorical center of the chapter, for it completes the instructions about male discharges in vv. 2–17 and anticipates the instructions concerning female discharges in vv. 19–30. Both biologically and ritually, the discharge of semen in intercourse joins man and woman together in a "unitary whole" in which both bear responsibility for circumspection in matters of sexual activity (cf. Whitekettle, p. 33). In terms of God's creational commission to "be fruitful and multiply" (Gen. 1:28), the man and the woman "become one flesh" (Gen. 2:24). The uncleanness that results from normal sexual activity is therefore relatively minor, as the purification process suggests. Both the man and the woman must bathe themselves in water; each remains unclean only until the evening.

In view of the creational commission noted above, in which God blesses the sexual union of man and woman, we may be surprised by the suggestion that intercourse generates impurity. Two principal explanations are instructive for assessing the priestly concern. First, we may note that it was common in ancient cultures to require ablutions following intercourse before resuming normal cultic activities. Similar rituals are attested among the Egyptians, Arabs, Persians, Hittites, and Greeks (for examples, see Milgrom, *Leviticus 1–16*, pp. 957–68). Within this cultural continuum, the priestly concern for sexual purity preserves the

121

boundary between the common and the holy. Intercourse is not to be practiced at the sanctuary, nor is it to be conflated with cultic observances that bring persons into a sacred and ritually exclusive union with God, the ultimate progenitor of life. Second, the priestly system associates semen and vaginal blood with the forces of life; the loss of these fluids represents a person's vulnerability to death. In intercourse, these vital bodily fluids are not so much lost as mixed, and as such they produce an ambiguous but potentially dangerous collapse of the boundaries between life and death. The priests are the stewards of these boundaries. Whenever the powers of life and death are in close proximity, the potential for impurity escalates and the threat of chaos becomes palpable and urgent. The priests are especially attentive therefore to the need for men and women to exercise caution in their sexual relations, lest they ignore the boundaries between the blessing that sustains life and an irresponsible sexuality that has the potential to subvert that blessing.

Female Discharges (15:19–30)

The instructions concerning female discharges are essentially a mirror image of those for the male. They deal with two kinds of discharges: normal menstrual flow (vv. 19–24) and abnormal or irregular discharges that extend beyond menstruation (vv. 25–30). For the duration of her normal menstrual period, here reckoned to be seven days, the woman is ritually impure. During this period, her impurities may be conveyed to whoever touches her (v. 19), to the bed on which she lies (vv. 20–21, 23), and to anything on which she sits (vv. 20–23). The purification ritual requires that persons who touch a menstruating woman or the things that have come into contact with her launder their clothes, bathe themselves in water, and wait until evening before resuming normal activities (vv. 21–23). Further, if a man lies with her during her menstruation and some of her impurity "falls on him," he remains unclean for seven days, the same period of time that applies to the woman herself, and he can convey uncleanness to any bed on which he lies during this time (v. 24).

The priests' anxiety about menstrual discharge and its potential for communicating impurity is understandably difficult, perhaps even offensive, for modern notions about the sexuality of both women and men. With justification, feminist and other scholars have been critical of a priestly system that advantages men by imposing severe social and religious controls on women. The fact that Israel's priesthood was exclusively limited to men only reinforces the view that these instructions served to legitimate a social hierarchy—a patriarchy—that many today would judge to be both unethical and unworthy of God's blessing (cf. Plaskow, pp. 171–210; Nelson, pp. 94–98). For all its limitations, however, the priestly concern about menstruation may not be as one-sided as it appears.

In addition to several observations previously noted (see the commentary on 12:1–8 and the introductory suggestions at the beginning of 15:1–33), two small but important aspects of the instructions in 15:19–24 deserve careful consideration. First, unlike the man, who must wash his hands lest he convey genital impurities to anything he touches (vv. 11–12), the menstruating woman is not prohibited from touching anyone, nor is she required to wash her hands. As a result, we may understand that during her menses she is not in fact isolated from human contact or banished from society, as some commentators infer (e.g., Kaiser, p. 1105). The second observation extends this point and sets it into greater relief. Among Israel's contemporaries, and likely within Israel itself, the menstruant was widely regarded as a metaphor not only for impurity but also for that which society shuns as repulsive. It is all the more striking, therefore, that against these common assumptions the priests seem concerned to ensure that the menstruating woman *not* be isolated or shunned. Instead, she remains at home, presumably fully engaged in the normal affairs of the family and household (for both these observations, see further Milgrom, *Leviticus 1–16*, pp. 936–37, 948–53). In view of the criticism that the priests were concerned to preserve a status quo that disadvantaged women, it is instructive to consider whether their legislation might in fact have provided an alternative model that protected women, at least in some small way, from the repression common in other cultures.

Verses 25–30 deal with abnormal discharges, that is, chronic or irregular bleeding that is not associated with normal menstruation. For the duration of her discharge the woman is unclean and may communicate uncleanness to other persons, to her bed, and to anything on which she sits. Anyone who touches these objects that have contracted impurity becomes unclean. They must wash their clothes, bathe themselves in water, and wait until evening to become clean once again. When the woman herself becomes clean, she observes the same purification ritual as the male (cf. vv. 13–15). She must wait seven days after the discharge has stopped. On the eighth day she brings to the priest two turtledoves or two pigeons. One bird he sacrifices as a purification offering, the other as a burnt offering. By these means the priest "effects purgation" on the woman's behalf.

123

Concluding Statement (15:31–33)

The conclusion to chapter 15 contains two statements. The first (v. 31) serves to summarize the concerns of chapters 11–15. The priests are once more reminded of their commission to teach the people to distinguish between the clean and the unclean (cf. 10:10). The language here is supplemented by two specific concerns: (1) Israel must "separate" (*hizzîr*) itself from uncleanness. The imperative recalls the obligation of the Nazarite (*nāzîr*) not only to *refrain from* practices that dishonor God but also to *engage in* dedicated service to God's holy presence in their midst (cf. Numbers 6). (2) Of particular concern is the potential for the defilement of "my tabernacle that is in their midst." As chapter 16 will make clear, the purity of the tabernacle, the one place on earth that is filled with the "glory of God" (Exod. 40:35), is of paramount importance for the relationship with people that God desires. Toward this end, the solemn rituals of the Day of Purification mark both the burden and the promise of faithful attention to these instructions for purity.

The second concluding statement follows in vv. 32–33. On first encounter this statement appears out of place, for it actually serves as a specific summary of Leviticus 15. On further reflection, however, it may be a strategic reminder that such mundane matters as bodily discharges, reciprocal respect for the sexuality of both men and women, and a nurturing of the life forces that both embody are indeed critical parts of the *tôrâ* (v. 32; NRSV: "ritual") that binds God and people together.

PART FOUR

The Day of Purification

LEVITICUS 16:1–34

The annual Day of Purification marks a major rite of passage, both structurally and theologically, in the book of Leviticus. From a structural perspective, this chapter stands at the center or *liminal* point of the book (see further the discussion at 8:1–5). Everything that has preceded in chapters 1–15 describes the "gifts" (*qorbān*; 1:2) that people and priests must bring to God as evidence of their commitment to live obediently inside the boundaries between "the holy and the common, and between the unclean and the clean" (10:10). Through sacrifices offered inside in the sanctuary and through the enactment of purity commitments outside the sanctuary, both people and priests signal their desire *to separate* themselves from the claims of the status quo. On the other side of Leviticus 16, chapters 17–27 reprise the "gifts" (*qorbān*; 17:4) that all the people must bring to God, this time with instructions for *reintegration* into the world that are weighted with the mandate to embody Godlike justice, Godlike holiness, in the everyday affairs of life. The all-embracing standard of conduct that God requires is stated succinctly in 19:2, the keynote passage in the book: "You shall be holy, for I the Lord your God am holy." Between chapters 1–15 and 17–27, Leviticus 16 is a structural reminder that all effective rites of passage involve both ritualized expression and bodily enactment. Ronald Grimes makes the case as follows:

> The magic of ritual takes effect only if there is *work* behind a rite. If the only work is that which appears *in* the rite, the result will likely be self-deception, a saying that only makes it *seem* so. Saying can make it really so, but only if the saying *is* a doing or if the saying is *underwritten by* a doing. (Grimes, p. 323)

From a theological perspective, the journey from *gifts of ritual* to *gifts of justice* is fraught with difficulty and failure. As the narrative in chapters 8–10 candidly concedes, even those consecrated for holiness

125

succumb to the temptation to substitute their own "unholy fire" for what God truly requires. In the middle of the twin mandates for ritual probity and ethical holiness, Leviticus 16 bridges the gap between God's expectations and human failure with the promise of forgiveness. Once a year the high priest is empowered to cleanse both the sanctuary and the people from the sin that diminishes their witness and compromises God's presence. Inside the ritual for this Day of Purification, Israel yields to the requisite liminality that refits and reshapes it with second chances to continue the journey as the stewards of God's image in the world.

The outline of the chapter is difficult to discern. In part this reflects the complexities of the ceremony itself; in part it reflects the editorial process through which the final text has passed. In general, an introduction (vv. 1–2) and a conclusion (v. 34b) frame three major sections: preparations for the ritual (vv. 3–10), the ritual proper (vv. 11–28), and instructions for regularizing the ritual as an annual ceremony (vv. 29–34a).

Precautions (16:1–2) and Preparations (16:3–10)

Before the preparation for entering the sanctuary can begin, the introduction sounds a word of warning (vv. 1–2). Aaron must approach the holy presence of God with care, for as the tragic experience of his sons Nadab and Abihu makes clear (chap. 10), what one offers God is a matter of life and death. When they offered "unholy fire" they sinned, and both their deed and their death defiled the sanctuary. If Aaron is to enter the inner sanctum and stand before the "mercy seat" over which the cloud of God's presence appears, he must exercise due caution. As with Moses at Sinai (Exod. 24:15–18), so now with Aaron in the sanctuary, the fire of God's holy presence is all-consuming. The "mercy," literally, the "purgation," that God offers is at once uncompromisable and unlimited. The Day of Purification therefore begins with a charged solemnity that places Aaron between the memory encoded in the words "they died" and the promise that he "will not die" if he is faithful to these instructions.

The preparations for the ceremony are set forth in two parts (vv. 3–5, 6–10). First, Aaron must assemble the required materials and prepare himself for the ceremony (vv. 3–5). He brings for himself and his household (cf. vv. 6, 11) two animals, a bull for a purification offering (cf. 4:1–5:13) and a ram for a burnt offering (cf. 1:10–13; 8:18–21). From the congregation he takes two male goats for a purification offering and a ram for a burnt offering. He prepares for the ceremony by

126

bathing his body in water, thus ritually purifying himself, then clothing himself with linen garments—tunic, breeches, sash, and turban. These are not the ornate garments normally worn by the high priest. The repeated emphasis on "linen" suggests that they are more ordinary, which perhaps represents the priest's being enclothed with humility (see the discussion at 8:6–30). But these garments are also more than ordinary, for elsewhere linen vestments are associated with the attire of angels who are permitted to appear before the throne of God (Ezek. 9:2–3; cf. Dan. 10:5–6). There is therefore a "mixed" symbolism in these garments, which is appropriate for one entering a liminal zone. The priest "wears" the signs of both the sacred and the common.

These preparations appear primarily intended to inform the laity, for they omit several details that would seem to be necessary if they were meant as a complete guide for the priest. Milgrom calls attention to the lack of any instructions concerning Aaron's spiritual preparation (*Leviticus 1–16*, pp. 1015–16). On this point, it is instructive to note that rabbinic tradition stipulates a seven-day preparation period for the priest before the enactment of the purification rituals. Included among the exercises during this period are required readings from the biblical books of Job, Daniel, Ezra, and Nehemiah (*m. Yoma* 1:6). The inclusion of Job in this lectionary of texts is highly suggestive. Although the rabbis do not explain the reason for this selection, we may speculate that the legendary story of the man from Uz, who suffered the ineffective ministry of friends who could not or would not deal honestly with his search for God, would have been particularly apt for a priest preparing to represent *all* his congregation before God (see further the reflections at Leviticus 13–14: "Have You Considered My Servant Job?").

The second part of this section (vv. 6–10) provides the "liturgical order" for the ceremony (Hartley, p. 227). Aaron must first offer the bull for his own purification offering. Next he will take the two goats for the people's purification offerings. He casts lots to determine which one is designated "for the Lord" and which one is "for Azazel" (see vv. 20–22). The goat "for the Lord" will be sacrificed as a purification offering for the sanctuary. The goat "for Azazel," by which the purification of the people is to be enacted, will be stationed alive before the Lord, then dispatched to the wilderness.

The Ritual Proper (16:11–28)

127

The ritual proper proceeds in three general stages: (1) the purification of the sanctuary (vv. 11–19); (2) the purification of the people

(vv. 20–22); and (3) the sacrifice of the burnt offerings and the cleansing of the participants (vv. 23–28).

1. *The purification ceremony for the sanctuary* begins with the sacrifice of the bull that the priest presents for himself and his fellow priests (v. 11). The aspersion of this bull's blood, along with the blood from the goat "for the Lord" that the people bring for themselves (v. 15), is the key to the ritual. Before the aspersion can begin, however, Aaron must engage in one further preparatory act. He fills a censer with coals from the fire burning on the outer altar, adds two handfuls of finely ground aromatic incense, and brings this mixture into the Holy of Holies. The result is a cloud of thick smoke that covers the mercy seat and presumably fills the whole of the inner sanctum (vv. 12–13). The purpose of this act is ambiguous. In part, the smoke offers a screen that prevents the priest from looking directly on the place symbolizing God's most intimate presence. The phrase "lest he die" (v. 13; NJPS) further suggests that the smoke protects Aaron from the potential danger of such close proximity to the holy.

At the heart of the ritual outlined in 16:11–19 is the concern to "purge" the sanctuary completely—inner sanctum (vv. 14–16a), outer sanctum (v. 16b), and outer altar (vv. 18–19). The process begins in the inner sanctum. Aaron first takes some of the blood of the slain bull he offers for himself and sprinkles it with his finger before the mercy seat seven times. He repeats the procedure with some of the blood from the slain bull offered by the people. The objective is to cleanse the inner sanctum of the "uncleanness," the "transgressions," and "sins" of the people that have polluted the sanctuary. The second of these three "sin" words—"transgressions" (*pĕšā'îm*)—refers specifically to moral violations, thus indicating that what are being addressed are not only Israel's ritual impurities but also its ethical transgressions. Next, Aaron moves out to the outer sanctum, then to the outer altar, where he repeats essentially the same aspersion ritual. In the case of the outer courtyard, he daubs (*natan*; v. 18) some of the blood from both bulls on the horns of the altar, then sprinkles (*hizzah*; v. 19) some seven times upon the altar. These two applications indicate that the altar is first cleansed from all the "uncleannesses of the people of Israel," then reconsecrated as a holy and acceptable place for the offering of sacrifices that effect Israel's expiation.

The tripartite cleansing of the sanctuary reflects the priestly understanding of sin's capacity to defile not only persons but also institutions. In the ritual world conceptualized by the priests, sin, whether manifest as moral transgression or ritual impurity, has a malignant power. It spreads its cancer through the world, as Milgrom puts it, like "an aerial miasma that possessed magnetic attraction for the realm of the sacred" (*Leviticus 1–16*, p. 257). Moreover, Milgrom has shown that sin's defilement of the sanctuary may be placed on a continuum: the more serious the sin, the more extensively the sanctuary is compromised (*Leviticus 1–16*, pp. 257–58; see further the reflections above on "The Burden of Sin, the Hope for Forgiveness, and the Gift of Ritual" at Lev. 5:14–6:7). Inadvertent sins of an individual defile the outer altar and the outer courtyard (Lev. 4:22–35). Inadvertent sins by the high priest or the entire community are more powerful, for they penetrate into the outer sanctum (Lev. 4:3–21). Most serious of all are intentional unrepented sins, which extend their reach into the inner sanctum and to the very throne of God. During the course of the year, inadvertent sins and their defilement may be purged as they occur through the ordinary sacrifices outlined in Leviticus 4–5. However, because intentional sinners are prohibited from bringing offerings to the sanctuary (cf. Num. 15:27–31), their transgressions must await the special rites of the high priest on the annual Day of Purification.

In sum, the sanctuary is a barometer that measures not only the *spiritual health of the community of the faith* but also, more important, the *stability of the world God has created* (Balentine, pp. 164–67). Both measurements are vitally important. First, the community of faith must be attentive to the sanctuary's role in its life, because it knows that a holy God will not reside in an unholy dwelling. The holiness of the sanctuary is therefore inextricably tied to the conduct of God's people. When they are faithful to God's expectations, the sanctuary radiates their commitment, sustains their witness, and secures their identity as a holy people. The reverse is also true. When they forsake their commitments, the sanctuary reflects their failing, and if it is not cleansed, God may depart and leave the community of faith to flounder in self-constructed futility. Such a scenario is described by Ezekiel, a prophet of priestly descent, in Ezekiel 8–10. Having been shown the abominations piled up in the temple (8:10–16), Ezekiel looks on as God abandons the holy place and the city of Jerusalem to certain destruction (10:2, 4, 18). Ezekiel's cry of alarm and God's pathos-filled response bear witness to the high cost of Israel's wrong choices:

> "Ah, Lord GOD! Will you destroy all who remain of Israel as you pour out your wrath upon Jerusalem?" He said to me, "The guilt of the house of Israel and Judah is exceedingly great; the land is full of bloodshed and the city full of perversity; for they say, 'The LORD has forsaken the land, and the LORD does not see.' As for me, my eye will not spare, nor will I have pity, but I will bring down their deeds upon their heads." (Ezek. 9:8–10)

129

Second, Israel must guard against the defilement of the sanctuary, because it embodies the hope for the realization of God's creational plan for the entire cosmos. In Priestly thinking, the sanctuary is a microcosm of the world (see the commentary on Lev. 1:1–2). The heptadic patterning that structures the account of the sanctuary's design (Exodus 25–31) and of Moses' instructions for its erection (Exodus 35–40) and the numerous verbal links between the completion of the sanctuary (Exodus 39–40) and the completion of creation (Genesis 1–2) reinforce the Priestly conceptualization of the sanctuary as an orderly world that carefully marks and sustains the boundaries between the sacred and the common. When these boundaries are in place, the world enjoys order and harmony. When they are ignored or breached, the world teeters on the brink of chaos and collapse. From this perspective, the defilement of the sanctuary and the potential of God's consequent departure threaten far more than the local community's welfare. They threaten the fraying of the fabric that swaddles the entire universe in God's protective plan. The rituals on the Day of Purification, therefore, engage the community of faith in an active restoration of the sanctuary, *not for its own sake alone but for the sake of the world.* When the sanctuary is holy, God is present, and the world is secure, because heaven and earth are joined in common pursuit of God's creational intentions.

2. *The purification of the people* requires the offering of the goat "for Azazel" (vv. 20–22). The meaning of the term ʿăzāʾzēl, which occurs only four times in the Old Testament, all in this chapter (vv. 8, 10 [two times], 26), has been the subject of much debate. Three explanations deserve consideration (for a succinct summary, see Wright, "Azazel," pp. 536–37).

- First, the Septuagint and the Vulgate appear to understand the Hebrew term ʿăzāʾzēl as a combination of two words, ʿēz, "goat," and ʿāzal, "to go away." This rendering has been highly influential in English translations, which frequently adopt the term *scapegoat* (e.g., KJV, NAB), coined by William Tyndale in the sixteenth century, to describe the function of the animal that is sent away bearing the blame of others.
- Second, the rabbis interpret ʿăzāʾzēl as a geographical term that designates the place—"a rocky precipice" (Rashi; cf. *Targum Pseudo-Jonathan*)—to which the goat is sent away. There is some support for this interpretation in Leviticus 16, which states

that the goat for Azazel is sent away into the "wilderness" (v. 10) and to a "barren region" (v. 22).

- Third, there is strong evidence in support of understanding ʿăzāʾzēl as the personal name of a divine being. D. P. Wright has called attention to Hittite banishment rites in which leaders of the army seek relief from a plague by decorating rams with colored wools, then driving them into the open country as offerings of appeasement to whatever god has caused the plague (Wright, *Disposal of Impurity*, pp. 50–55). By analogy, we may understand the goat offered to "Azazel" as the counterpart of the goat offered to the "Lord"; at some point traditional rituals may have understood both recipients of the offering to have been supernatural beings. Despite a number of congruencies between such Near Eastern rites and Leviticus 16, Wright notes that in Israelite thinking Azazel is portrayed as neither personal nor demonic. Milgrom makes the same point when he observes that although other cultures may have regarded Azazel as a demonic figure, Israel's priestly legislators have effectively "eviscerated" this name of any demonic powers (*Leviticus 1–16*, p. 1021).

It is apparent nonetheless that some postbiblical Jewish texts reflect the connection between Azazel and demonic figures (Grabbe, "Scapegoat Tradition," pp. 152–67). To cite but two of the exemplars, both *1 Enoch* 6–16 and *Apocalypse of Abraham* 13–14 develop a trajectory of interpretation that links Azazel with demonic leaders who foment rebellion against God and are punished by being banished (cf. Isa. 14:12–15). Moreover, the New Testament also likely reflects this tradition, albeit rather obliquely, by associating the one who opposes God with the figure of Satan, who, like Azazel, will be bound and cast into the abyss in the final judgment that ushers in the eschatological kingdom of Christ (cf. Rev. 20:1–6, 10). However much the New Testament may draw upon this Jewish tradition of interpretation, it also shapes it in accordance with distinctive Christian affirmations. In the principal New Testament discussion of the Day of Atonement, Hebrews 6–9, the role

131

of the "scapegoat" is transformed by the work of Christ, whose own blood, shed on a cross outside the city, bears for all eternity the sin of the people.

Of the three understandings reviewed above, the comparison with Near Eastern banishment rituals offers the most plausible explanation for the treatment of the "goat for Azazel." That Israel adapted such rituals is evidenced by the rites performed for a person recovered from a skin disease in Lev. 14:2–8. In that situation two birds were offered: One was slain, and its blood cleansed the person of impurity; the second was set free, carrying the impurities "into the open field" (14:7). The treatment of the living goat designated for Azazel is similar. The priest places both hands on the head of the animal, thus symbolically enacting the transfer of iniquity from the people to the goat. The transference ritual is accompanied by a confession (v. 21), which, as has been previously stipulated (5:5), is required only for deliberate and presumptuous breaches of faith (see further the reflections on "The Burden of Sin, the Hope for Forgiveness, and the Gift of Ritual" at 5:14–6:7). The words of the confession are not recorded in Leviticus, but the Mishnah provides the following account:

> [The High Priest] came to the scapegoat and laid his two hands upon it and made confession. And thus he used to say: "O God, your people, the house of Israel, have committed iniquity, transgressed, and sinned before you. O God, forgive I pray, the iniquities and transgressions and sins which your people, the house of Israel, have committed and transgressed and sinned before you; as it is written in the law of your servant Moses, 'For on this day shall atonement be made for you to cleanse you: from all your sins you shall be clean before the Lord.'" And when the priests and the people who stood in the Temple Court heard the Expressed Name come forth from the mouth of the High Priest, they used to kneel and bow themselves and fall down on their faces and say, "Blessed be the name of the glory of his kingdom for ever and ever!" (m. Yoma 6:2)

After the confession, the goat is set free, bearing "on itself" the sins of the people to a "barren region" (v. 22), literally, to a "cutoff land" where their destructive powers can no longer be effective.

Although the full meaning of the banishment ritual may elude us, its combination with the ritual of purification for the sanctuary (vv. 11–19) is clear enough. On the Day of Purification, the people of Israel confess that their transgressions have defiled the sanctuary and diminished their witness in the world. Their objective is twofold. First, they desire to cleanse the sanctuary, thereby restoring its capacity to sustain creation's sacred intersection between the presence of a holy God and the common life of the people. Second, they desire to purify themselves by removing the sins that fray their commitment and subvert their covenantal partnership with God. Toward this end, the goat for Azazel is banished to the wilderness, which in the ritual world that is gestured forth on the Day of Purification symbolizes the domain of disorder and chaos. In the primordial liturgy of creation, God separated the dark from the light, thus creating a sacred zone where humans might enact their divine commission to be stewards of God's hopes and expectations for the world. Now, in this ritual re-creation of the world God desires, Israel reenacts the separation between darkness and light that releases them once more from the malefic power of sin. In the liturgy for the Day of Purification, as in the liturgy of creation, chaos is not removed or eliminated. Its power to control people can, however, be contained and restricted within the grand design of creation's order. Viewed from this perspective, the ritual banishment of the goat to the wilderness reestablishes the creational boundary between order and chaos that makes a holy life in the presence of a holy God possible.

3. The ritual concludes with the *sacrifices of the burnt offerings and the cleansing of the participants* (vv. 23–28). Upon the completion of his role in cleansing the sanctuary and the people, Aaron removes the linen garments he had worn, ritually bathes himself once more (cf. v. 4), and reclothes himself with the more ornate garments that symbolize his high-priestly status. Other participants in the ritual—the person who supervises the release of the goat for Azazel (v. 26) and the person who disposes of the remains of the burnt offerings (v. 28)—will undergo similar ablutions. Finally, Aaron presents the burnt offerings, a bull and a goat, which ritually complete the purification of both the priests and the people (v. 24). The fat of the offerings is "turned into smoke" (v. 25; cf. 1:3–9); the hides, the flesh, and the dung of the slain animals are brought outside the camp and incinerated. The procedure serves as a further reminder of the ritual transformation that has been accomplished. Those once unfit for communion with a holy God now present gifts that bear witness to a new reality: What they offer has now been ritually "turned into" an offering that is acceptable and pleasing to God.

Instructions for Regularizing the Ritual (16:29–34a)

These verses are widely regarded as a later addition to the text, the primary purpose of which is to regularize what originally was a ritual performed by the high priest "at any time" (v. 2) an emergency occurred

133

into a solemn ceremony to be observed only "once in the year" (v. 34; for further discussion, see Milgrom, *Leviticus 1–16*, pp. 1064–65). In its final form, the text now addresses the people directly for the first time. They are to observe the Day of Purification on the tenth day of the seventh month. The seventh month marks a critical place on Israel's liturgical calendar (cf. Leviticus 23), for it represents the intersection between the ending of one year and the beginning of the next. In this seventh month, this "sabbath month," Israel is to make the Day of Purification a "sabbath of complete rest" (v. 31). Of all the holy days in Israel's liturgical calendar, only the Sabbath day and the Day of Purification require a complete cessation of work (Lev. 23:3; Exod. 35:2). In place of the normal labor that is required to make one's way in the world, the people are to practice a self-denial that reconnects them both to their dependency on God and to their commission to be God's servants in the world.

The nature of the self-denial is not specified. It is generally associated with fasting, which is often practiced as part of rituals that express repentance and a desire for God's mercy (e.g., Ezra 8:21–23). But it most assuredly would have required more than contrition, as necessary as this is. One clue may be discerned from the way Reform Judaism observes the liturgy for this day. On the morning of Yom Kippur, congregants hear a reading from Isa. 57:14–58:14, which keeps them mindful that the *ritual of forgiveness* must not be uncoupled from the *ethical mandate* to be stewards of God's justice. Two excerpts from this reading illustrate the twin commission that must be pondered, then enacted, each time the Day of Purification is observed:

> For thus says the high and lofty one
>   who inhabits eternity, whose name is Holy:
> I dwell in the high and holy place,
>   and also with those who are contrite and humble in spirit,
> to revive the spirit of the humble,
>   and to revive the heart of the contrite.
>
> (Isa. 57:15)

> Is not this the fast that I choose:
>   to loose the bonds of injustice,
>   to undo the thongs of the yoke,
> to let the oppressed go free,
>   and to break every yoke?
> Is it not to share your bread with the hungry,
>   and bring the homeless poor into your house;
> when you see the naked, to cover them
>   and not to hide yourself from your own kin?

> Then your light shall break forth like the dawn,
>   and your healing shall spring up quickly;
> your vindicator shall go before you,
>   the glory of the LORD shall be your rear guard,
> Then you shall call, and the LORD will answer;
>   you shall cry for help, and he
>   will say, Here I am.
>   (Isa. 58:6–9)

The appendix to Leviticus 16 effectively returns us to the observations offered at the beginning of the chapter. When the instructions for the Day of Purification conclude, all Israel stands at a critical juncture between the promise of forgiveness and the mandate for justice. Both the promise and the mandate define the "gifts" that Israel presents to the Holy One in its midst. The gift of the ritual symbolizes the commitment to be clean and holy receptacles for God's presence in the world. The gift of justice concretizes ritualized commitment in specific behavior that repairs the havoc that sin wreaks on a world. On the Day of Purification, all creation yearns for a chance to hear God say once again, "Everything I have made is indeed very good" (cf. Gen. 1:31).

The echo of creation's liturgy could not be clearer. As God rested on the seventh day in order to celebrate and enjoy a world perfectly fitted for the best life could offer, so Israel must image God by setting aside this day for a time of celebration and renewal in order that it may resume the life God has ordained. On this day, when Aaron enacts the paradigm for priestly ministry that each of his successors will follow (v. 32), when he cleanses the sanctuary, the priests, and "all the people of the assembly" (v. 33), both Israel and the world it serves stand at the juncture between past and future. When we turn to chapter 17 and the "Holiness Code" it introduces, both the structure and the substance of the book of Leviticus will insist that the ritual for forgiveness is but the necessary first step in heeding God's summons to all creation to live obediently at the tensive intersection between the sacred and the common. Toward this end, the summative report that "Moses did as the Lord had commanded him" makes a down payment on the promise commemorated by the "everlasting statute" that is the Day of Purification (v. 34).

An "Everlasting Statute" . . .
for Jews and Christians?

To a very real and quite palpable degree, the Jewish community of faith has indeed observed the ritual described in Leviticus 16 as an "everlasting statute." Yom Kippur, the traditional name for the tenth

135

day of the seventh month, remains to this day the best known and most observed of the Jewish high holy days. On this day, which typically falls on the Gregorian calendar somewhere between the beginning of September and the end of October, Jews all over the world, from diverse communities and different religious traditions, gather to observe the ancient ritual by fasting, abstinence, and prayers for the forgiveness of sin.

The situation is, of course, different for the Christian community, and this fact invites reflection on how and to what degree, if at all, the ritual of Leviticus 16 remains an "everlasting statute" for Christians. At issue is the New Testament's clear and certain affirmation that Jesus, not Aaron, is the perfect high priest whose death effects atonement "once for all" (Heb. 9:12). That Christians are encouraged to interpret Leviticus 16 as "prologue" to the central story of Jesus' death and resurrection is signaled by the fact that commentaries conventionally connect the Day of Atonement with the witness of Hebrews 9–10, the New Testament's most sustained and direct engagement with the idea. Although space does not permit a full treatment of this important text, it is instructive to consider the discernments of two commentators who exemplify a Christian approach (for further discussion of the issues, see Nelson, pp. 141–68).

In his discussion of "The Day of Atonement in the NT," G. Wenham observes, as do many commentators, that Hebrews sets forth a number of important differences between the ministry of Aaron and the ministry of Jesus (Wenham, pp. 237–38). His list is succinct and informative:

- Whereas Aaron was a sinner who needed to offer a sacrifice for himself, Christ is sinless and thus needs to offer no sacrifice for himself (Heb. 7:26–27).
- Whereas Aaron was required to present the sacrifices regularly, "once a year," Christ offered a sacrifice of himself "once for all" that secured an eternal redemption (Heb. 9:6–14, 25–26).
- Whereas Aaron's rituals allowed him entry into an earthly sanctuary, Christ's death led him into the heavenly temple of God (Heb. 9:24).
- Whereas Aaron's sacrifice had to be repeated because of the persistence of sin, Christ's once-for-all sacrifice effected a permanent forgiveness of sin: "For by a single offering he has perfected for all time those who are sanctified" (Heb. 10:1–18; see especially v. 14).

F. Craddock's reflections on Hebrews 9–10 also call attention to the differences between the priestly ministries of Aaron and Jesus and set them in still greater relief (Craddock, pp. 116–18). He suggests that preachers of this text pay particular attention to the way the Hebrews writer uses the rhetorical device of repetition and contrast to make a forceful and new point for the Christian community. The contrasts between Aaron and Jesus that he regards as heuristic are listed in a bipolar fashion: "old/new, dead/alive, ineffective/effective, apparent/real, endless repetition/once for all, shadow/substance." To put the edge on this discernment, he cites Heb. 10:11–12 as case in point:

> At 10:11–12, two images are offered. One is of a priest, standing, working in the relentless cycle of the day-after-day repetition of the same words and actions. It is the picture of *futility*. The other image is of a priest who has made a single offering, a one-time-only act, and is now seated, waiting for the full harvest of benefits from that never-to-be-repeated sacrifice. It is the picture of *finality*. Much that is presented from desk and pulpit is, of course, properly framed as "both-and." However, in most recitals of events and relationships there are also discontinuities that beg for crispness and clarity. The writer of Hebrews offers a model for casting such material "on the one hand/but on the other hand." (Craddock, p. 118; emphasis added)

Both Wenham and Craddock couch their reflections on Hebrews 9–10 within a summons to the Christian community not to neglect Leviticus as a necessary theological primer for understanding the sacrifice of Christ. Their sensitivity notwithstanding, however, it is not difficult to imagine that the sharp distinctions they draw—old/new, dead/alive, apparent/real, futility/finality—do little to encourage Christians to embrace Leviticus 16 as an "everlasting statute." Faced with such contrasts, the church has too often sadly slipped from a "both-and" model for relating to its Jewish roots to an "either-or" one. Either Christ is the true high priest, or he is not. Either his atonement connects us once-for-all to God, or it does not. Either we have eternal salvation through his death and resurrection, or we do not. When this position becomes entrenched in Christian thinking, it is but a short step to the assumption that we have little in common *either* with Leviticus *or* with those who embrace it as sacred Scripture. The issue and the caution that such an assumption invites are clearly stated by the Jewish theologian Abraham Heschel:

> The problem to be faced is: how to combine loyalty to one's own tradition with reverence for different traditions? How is mutual esteem between Christian and Jew possible?

A Christian ought to ponder seriously the tremendous implications of a process begun in early Christian history. I mean the conscious or unconscious dejudaization of Christianity, affecting the Church's way of thinking, its inner life as well as its relationship to the past and present reality of Israel—the father and mother of the very being of Christianity. The children did not arise to call the mother blessed; instead, they called the mother blind. Some theologians continue to act as if they did not know the meaning of "honor your father and mother"; others, anxious to prove the superiority of the church, speak as if they suffered from a spiritual Oedipus complex.

A Christian ought to realize that a world without Israel will be a world without Israel's God. (*I Asked for Wonder*, p. 111)

Must we opt either for Hebrews 9–10 or Leviticus 16? Must we "dejudaize" our faith in order to be Christian? If Christ is our high priest, are Aaron and his children no longer our partners in the journey toward realizing the "very good" world that God has created? "This shall be a statute to you forever" (Lev. 16:29). Whether we are Jewish or Christian, this command from God freights the questions we pose and the answers we contemplate. We might do well to consider that when we approach God, we must come as those whose path has been prepared by the abiding ministries of both Aaron and Jesus. As G. Herbert (1593–1633), the English rector and poet, puts it, even those whose "doctrine [is] tuned by Christ" are invited to come as "Aaron's dressed":

> Holiness on the head,
> Light and perfections on the breast,
> Harmonious bells below, raising the dead
>   To lead them unto life and rest.
>   Thus are true Aaron's dressed.

> Profaneness in my head,
> Defects and darkness in my breast,
> A noise of passions ringing me for dead
>   Unto a place where is no rest.
>   Poor priest thus I am dressed.

> Only another head
> I have, another heart and breast,
> Another music, making live not dead,
>   Without whom I could have no rest:
>   In him I am well dressed.

> Christ is my only head,
> My alone only heart and breast,
> My only music, striking me ev'n dead;
>   That to the old man I may rest,
>   And be in him new dressed.

So holy in my head,
Perfect and light in my dear breast,
My doctrine tuned by Christ (who is not dead,
But lives in me while I do rest),
Come people; Aaron's dressed.
(Herbert, "Aaron," *Complete English Poems*,
ed. J. Tobin, p. 164)

PART FIVE

The Holiness Code

LEVITICUS 17–27

For more than a century, the conventional view of Leviticus 17–26 (27) has been tied to the judgment of A. Klostermann, who described these chapters, which he labeled the "holiness code," as a distinct collection of legal materials (Klostermann, pp. 368–418). The name Holiness Code suggested itself because of the repeated emphasis throughout this corpus on the theme of holiness, nowhere more succinctly or memorably stated than in the summons of 19:2: "You shall be holy, for I the Lord your God am holy." Building on this discernment, J. Wellhausen argued that these chapters were literarily independent of the priestly material in Leviticus 1–16. In his judgment, the distinctive concerns in chapters 17–27 with ethical and moral behavior were wholly uncharacteristic of the priests, who were largely understood to have been preoccupied with the more arcane matters of sacrifice and ritual. Ethical and moral laws were more at home in Israel's prophetic tradition, which, he believed, antedated the priestly tradition and provided the likely impetus for the concerns addressed here (Wellhausen, pp. 376–80).

In the wake of these early studies, both the so-called distinctive (i.e., nonpriestly) emphases of these chapters and their redactional history have been the subject of enormous scrutiny and debate (for a survey of the history of research, see Hartley, pp. 251–60). Despite the many revisions and new hypotheses these additional studies have generated, the conventional presumption that chapters 17–27 are a late insertion betraying essentially nonpriestly concerns has remained a staple of the ongoing discussion. This presumption, which only thinly masks typical Protestant biases against Scripture heavy weighted with ritual concerns (cf. Gorman, "Ritual Studies and Biblical Studies," pp. 13–21), has, however, been recently challenged. The most compelling and instructive work comes from I. Knohl and J. Milgrom, both of whom have argued that Leviticus 17–27 derives from a priestly "holiness school" that postdates the priestly circles who produced the bulk of the "Priestly Torah" in Exodus, Leviticus, and Numbers (Knohl, pp. 212–16; Milgrom, *Leviticus 17-22*, pp. 1332–64). They date this Holiness School to the eighth century, specifically, to the reigns of Ahaz and Hezekiah (ca. 743–701 B.C.E.), a period in Israel's history that coincides with the classical prophets and their persistent criticism of priestly ritual for neglecting the weightier matters of social justice (e.g., Isa. 1:10–17; Amos 2:6–16; Mic. 3:9–12). In sum, the Holiness School represents an inner-priestly response to the prophets' call for a "moral refinement" of the cult (Knohl, p. 216). Indeed, it may be argued that the priestly emphasis on holiness, especially as exemplified in the summons to moral and ethical integrity in all aspects of life, not only responds to the prophets' concerns about social justice but also, at least potentially, offers concrete measures to resolve them (see especially the commentary on the jubilee year in Leviticus 25).

The commentary below on the individual chapters in the Holiness Code will offer additional perspective on some of the interpretive ramifications of the approach advanced by Knohl and Milgrom. In advance of that discussion, two broad and summary theological observations may be singled out as foundational for the readers' reflection. First, inasmuch as chapters 17–27 are integral, not ancillary, to the concerns so evident in 1–16, it becomes apparent that the priests neither envisioned nor sanctioned any disjunction between the summons to ritual purity and the summons to ethical conduct. Obedience to both these summons is in fact the irreducible minimum of what it means to be holy as God is holy. In this respect the New Testament's caution against separating one's love of God from one's moral obligation to enact that love in the human community God has created is part of one and the same commandment:

> Those who say, "I love God," and hate their brothers and sisters, are liars; for those who do not love a brother or sister whom they have seen, cannot love God whom they have not seen. The commandment we have from him is this: those who love God must love their brothers and sisters also. (1 John 4:20–21; cf. Matt. 25:38–40, 44–45)

Second, however we may assess the redactional history of chapters 17–27, their location in the final form of the book of Leviticus suggests that the rituals of holy worship are not only inextricably wedded to the ethics of holy living; they are also fundamentally *generative* of the community's motivation to obedience. The placement of these chapters after the instructions concerning the sacrifices offered in the sanctuary (chaps. 1–7), after the consecration of the priests who serve in the sanctuary (chaps. 8–10), and after the instructions concerning purity and impurity in the everyday affairs of life outside the sanctuary (chaps. 11–15) indicates that fidelity to ritual has the capacity to *create* ethical sensitivity.

A subtle but persistent reminder of ritual's creative potential is the rhetorical use of the number seven, which occurs frequently not only in Leviticus 1–16 (e.g., 8:1–36; 14:1–32; 16:11–28) but also throughout chapters 17–27. Milgrom has helpfully listed the examples, of which the following may be mentioned as representative (*Leviticus 23–27*, pp. 1323–25). In chapter 21 the word *holy* occurs seven times with respect to the behavior required of priests (vv. 6–8). Chapter 22, which continues with corollary instructions concerning the required holy behavior of the laity, uses the words *Israel* (vv. 2, 3, 15, 18 [three times], 32) and *acceptable* (vv. 19, 20, 21, 23, 25, 27, 29) seven times each. Chapter 26, which pronounces the blessings and curses that fall upon the land in relation to Israel's obedience, uses the key word *eat* seven times (vv. 5, 10, 16, 29 [two times], 38).

In all these texts the number seven is not only a rhetorical device for calling attention to the idea of perfection and completion; it is also a theological reminder of God's heptadic design for creation itself (Gen. 1:1–2:4a). From the priestly perspective, both the rituals inside the sanctuary (Leviticus 1–16) and the code of holy behavior required for life outside it (Leviticus 17–27) are *no less necessary* and *no less generative* for the "very good" world God has designed than the seven-day process with which it all began. Thus, when readers embark on the journey through the instructions in the Holiness Code, they do so with these words as their guide: "In the beginning when God created the heavens and the earth, . . . God said, 'Let there be . . .'" (Gen.1:1–2); and "The Lord summoned Moses and spoke to him from the tent of meeting, saying: . . . 'When any of you bring an offering . . .'" (Lev. 1:1–2); and "The Lord spoke to Moses: Speak to Aaron . . . and to all the people of Israel and say to them: This is what the Lord has commanded. . . ." (Lev. 17:1–2).

Leviticus 17:1–16
The Slaughter and Consumption of Meat

Leviticus 17 returns to instructions concerning the "gifts" (*qorbān*; v. 4) of sacrifice, which were first introduced in chapter 1 (1:2). Whereas the first instructions were addressed primarily to the priests, these now

143

focus on all Israelites (v. 2), who here and throughout chapters 17–27 are summoned to know that holiness in the presence of God requires more than priestly ritual. It extends to each and every person, and it must be embodied in every area of life. The principal concern of this chapter is the slaughter and consumption of meat, both sacrificial and nonsacrificial. Thus, at issue is the meat offered to God in the sanctuary and the meat that is consumed at the table in the home.

After an introduction (vv. 1–2), the chapter comprises a pentad of instructions (vv. 3–7, 8–9, 10–12, 13–14, 15–16), each prefaced by a varying formula, "If anyone of the house of Israel . . ." (vv. 3, 8, 10, 13; cf. v. 15: "All persons"). Other repeating structural markers include a rationale for obedience (vv. 5–7, 11–12, 14) and a prescribed penalty for disobedience (vv. 4, 9, 10, 14, 16). The first three instructions convey prohibitions—actions the people must refrain from doing—arranged in an increasing order of severity. The last two give positive commands—actions that must be performed—arranged in decreasing order of importance. Of the five, the third or middle instruction (vv. 10–12) prohibiting the ingestion of blood, and its rationale—"For the life of the flesh is in the blood" (v. 11)—is the hub around which the whole of the chapter revolves (Schwartz, pp. 42–43). The overall structure serves thus to remind Israel both to *refrain from* and *engage in* actions that body forth in practical ways the holiness God requires.

The First Three Prohibitions (17:1–9)

The Holiness Code begins by announcing that distinctions that otherwise apply between priests and laypersons are fundamentally erased when it comes to God's expectations for holy living. Thus, for the first time in Leviticus, God instructs Moses to address "Aaron and his sons" and "all the Israelites" simultaneously (v. 2; see also 21:24; 22:18). While the two groups surely have different roles to play in the arena of public worship, neither is exempt from the obligation to live holy lives in the presence of God. The priests must teach Israel to distinguish "between the holy and the common, and between the unclean and the clean" (10:10); Israel must practice what the priests teach. The laity's role in supplying holy sacrifices and in maintaining purity in the spheres of everyday life has been addressed in chapters 1–7 and 11–15 respectively. The Holiness Code now begins to enlarge upon this picture. From this introduction in verse 2, and from a second occurrence in 21:24, where Moses ends instructions to the priests concerning their conduct in mourning rituals with the same address to "Aaron and to his sons and to all the people of Israel," we may infer that the laity also had a supervisory role with respect to the priests. Perhaps they were charged with the responsibility of seeing to it that the priests officiated in ways that did not diminish their common concerns to maintain holiness in the presence of God (Milgrom, *Leviticus 17–22*, pp. 1409–10, 1451). In short, the introductory address in 17:2 suggests that the responsibility for holiness cannot be fully upheld by either priests or laity alone. It is a reciprocal responsibility; if either the priests or the laity fail to attend to what God expects of them, all efforts toward holy living will be diminished.

The first two instructions comprise prohibitions related to meat from sacrificial and nonsacrificial animals. In each case the concern is with potential violations, in an escalating order of seriousness, that laypersons should avoid.

Any Israelite who slaughters an ox, a lamb, or a goat must present it as an offering, a "gift," to YHWH at the entrance to the tent of meeting (vv. 3–7). Failure to do so results in bloodguilt (v. 4: "he has shed blood"), a phrase elsewhere associated with premeditated murder of innocent human beings (e.g., Gen. 9:6; Num. 35:33). The penalty for this violation is that the perpetrator will be "cut off from the people," which likely means that the offender will have no descendants in this world and perhaps no possibility of being gathered with his ancestors in life after death. The rationale behind the prohibition is that the blood of a slaughtered animal equates with the death of one of God's creatures and thus is an infringement on God's sovereignty in matters relating to life and death. There is also the possibility that Israelites will be tempted to adopt the practice of some of their neighbors and offer the blood to "goat-demons" (v. 7), that is, to foreign gods often identified with the underworld (for the association of goat-demons with desolate, foreboding places, see Isa. 13:21; 34:14).

There is debate concerning whether this first instruction requires that all animals be slaughtered at the central sanctuary or only the triad of domesticated quadrupeds—ox, lamb, and goat—that are to be sacrificed to God. The verb *šāḥaṭ*, which is used to refer to both sacrificial and nonsacrificial slaughter, has invited both a broad and a restricted interpretation. The majority of commentators, citing the legislation in Deut. 12:15–16, which permits nonsacrificial slaughter away from the altar, favor a restrictive interpretation: Only sacrificial animals must be slaughtered at the altar (e.g., Hartley, p. 271; Levine, pp. 112–13; Kaiser, p. 1118). Milgrom, however, has made a strong case for the broader view. He argues that Lev. 17:3–7 calls for a complete ban on the slaughter of all animals—sacrificial and nonsacrificial—away from the sanctuary. If Milgrom is correct, then we are invited to understand that the author of the Holiness Code espouses an innovative and radical revision of Priestly thinking, which previously presumed that nonsacrificial animals could be slaughtered away from the sanctuary. The significance of Milgrom's interpretation is the suggestion that the Holiness School advocates a more encompassing view of the manifold ways holiness must lay claim on routine matters of everyday life: Even meat intended for common consumption in the home must be initially treated as an offering to God (*Leviticus 1–16*, pp. 28–34; *Leviticus 17–22*, pp. 1452–54).

The second instruction (vv. 8–9) builds on the first. Both sacrificial animals—now specifically identified as "burnt offerings"—and nonsacrificial animals must be offered at the altar. This applies not only to Israelites but also to all resident aliens, that is, to non-Israelites who have taken up permanent residence in the land of Israel and who therefore must live in accordance with Israel's civil and religious laws. While resident aliens were held to a more lenient standard when it came to religious law (religious conversion, for example, was not required), they were required to observe the prohibitive commandments, for a violation in these areas was believed to generate impurity that defiled the land, thus compromising God's presence for all its inhabitants (see further Milgrom, *Leviticus 17–22*, 1416–20, 1463–64). The first two instructions are both motivated by similar reasoning: Whether animals are slaughtered for food or for sacrifice, they must be offered "to the Lord," a point underscored by the sevenfold repetition of this phrase in vv. 3–9 (vv. 4 [two times], 5 [two times], 6 [two times], 9).

The Central Prohibition: "No Person among You Shall Eat Blood" (17:10–12)

The third of the five instructions is the hub of the chapter. The prohibition on eating blood, that is, ingesting meat that contains blood, is stated twice. The first statement in v. 10 includes the penalty for disobedience: The offender will be "cut off." A restatement of the prohibition occurs in v. 12, without the penalty. In both cases the importance of the injunction is signaled by the inclusivity of the terms designating the addresses: "anyone of the house of Israel," "the aliens who reside among them," "the people of Israel," "any person" (v. 12). While the prohibition against blood consumption is widely attested in the Old Testament (Gen. 9:4; Lev. 3:17; 7:26–27; Deut. 12:16, 23–25; 15:23; 1 Sam. 14:32–34), this prohibition elevates it to a still higher plane. Every human being, not just Israel, is enjoined to obey this directive. As Milgrom notes, not even the Ten Commandments have such a far-reaching claim, for they were given exclusively to Israel. The Holiness Code, however, insists that there can be no "viable human society" unless all humankind lives in accordance with this injunction against the consumption of blood (Milgrom, *Leviticus 17–22*, p. 1470).

Such a framing for this instruction's importance immediately begs the question "Why?" Sandwiched between the double statement of the prohibition, v. 11 offers the Old Testament's most explicit answer: "For the life of the flesh is in the blood, and I have assigned it to you for making expiation for your lives upon the altar; it is the blood, as life, that effects expiation" (NJPS). Unfortunately, this answer is open to different interpretations. On the one hand, it is evident that this answer can be traced back to Gen. 9:3–6. In the aftermath of the flood, God concedes that, beginning with Noah, the human community, which God originally intended to be vegetarian (Gen. 1:29), may consume animal flesh, provided that it "not eat flesh with its life, that is, its blood" (Gen. 9:4). In Genesis, this prohibition against ingesting animal blood is followed by a warning against the shedding of human blood (9:6), which effectively ties the slaughter and consumption of animal blood to the crime of homicide. Blood, whether animal or human, is a metaphor for life; when it is spilt—and in the case of animals, consumed—by a human being, God's creation is diminished by the loss of that life. Within this same trajectory of understanding, Lev. 17:11 now reiterates that "the life of the flesh is in the blood." The clear inference is that the loss of blood equates with the loss of life. From a Priestly perspective, neither a holy God nor a human community seeking to image God's holiness will ever be unconcerned about the loss of life.

On the other hand, Lev. 17:11 goes on to say that blood on the altar is "for making atonement." The critical and much-debated question is, how does blood effect atonement, or expiation? Two views deserve attention. Perhaps a majority of commentators understand blood to function as a "substitute" for the life of the offerer. In this view, the life of the slain animal bears the sin of the offender, whose guilt has caused God's anger. When a life is offered back to God, God forgives the sin and ransoms the sinner from judgment. This position typically includes (1) associating the verb *kippēr*, "make expiation," with the related noun *koper*, "ransom" (see the parallel use of both terms in Exod. 30:12); and (2) referencing the principle of *lex talionis*, "life for life," which the Old Testament embraces, for example, in Exod. 21:24 and Lev. 24:20. No doubt the attractiveness of this argument is enhanced, especially in Christian circles, by the fact that substitutionary atonement can be seen as exemplified in a unique way in the shedding of Christ's blood on the cross, which effects forgiveness and reconciliation between God and

147

sinners (see, for example, the expositions of Hartley, pp. 279–80; Kaiser, pp. 1120–21; Wenham, pp. 246–48).

Another view, principally associated with the work of Milgrom, understands the meaning of Lev. 17:11 as more specifically tied to the primary concern of this chapter: the danger of consuming blood when eating meat (see the commentary above on vv. 3–7). Although he also argues that the ritual use of the blood effects a "ransom" for the guilty party, Milgrom interprets this as a specific reference to the sacrifice of well-being, not as a general theory of atonement that applies to the entire Priestly sacrificial system. Elsewhere in Leviticus, as previously discussed, the Priestly tradition associates the expiatory capacity of blood principally with the purification and reparation offerings; other sacrificial offerings may also have expiatory functions, but the sacrifice of well-being, which concerns the provision of food for the table, seems originally not to have been used for this purpose. Milgrom argues that the author of the Holiness Code now innovatively reinterprets the well-being offering in order to make clear that killing animals for food, that is, for personal consumption, is so dangerously close to the taking of human life for selfish reasons, it is tantamount to homicide. Unless the blood of the slaughtered animal is offered on the altar to God, the one who has taken the life of one of God's creatures is guilty and punishable for the crime of manslaughter. When the blood of the slain animal is placed on the altar, it ransoms the life of one who has taken a life (for further discussion, see Milgrom, *Leviticus 1–16*, pp. 217–25, 1079–84; *Leviticus 17–22*, pp. 1472–79).

On first inspection, Milgrom's interpretation, if correct, may appear less theologically instructive than the substitutionary view discussed above, especially for readers looking for the relevance of ancient priestly rituals to Christian life. It is wise to note, however, that priestly rituals have a theological profundity in their own right, apart from their application to Christianity. This complex and difficult instruction concerning the prohibition of consuming blood is a case in point. At its core it insists that every aspect of life, animal and human, be reverenced as a gift from God, not in an abstract (merely theological) way but in a concrete, tangible respect for blood, for as this text makes clear, "the life of the flesh is in the blood."

Two Positive Commands (17:13–16)

148   The fourth and fifth instructions contain performative commands related to the consumption of food from animals not previously addressed. The fourth (vv. 13–14) stipulates that when wild game and

fowl are hunted and killed for food, the blood from the slaughter must be poured on the ground and covered with earth. The rationale for not consuming the blood (v. 14) restates the principle of v. 11: "For the life of every creature—its blood is its life." There are a number of possible explanations for why the blood should be covered by earth, but most likely the concern is that the blood be disposed of in such a way as to ensure that it will not be used for any purpose whatsoever. The penalty for disobedience is that the offender will be "cut off."

The fifth and final instruction (vv. 15–16) concerns the eating of meat from any animal that has died of natural causes or from an attack by another animal. Such animals are edible, but because the eaters cannot know if the animal's blood has congealed in its body or drained away, they might inadvertently consume blood, thus becoming unclean. In such cases, persons must wash their clothes, bathe in water, and wait until morning, at which time they may resume their normal activities. Should they fail to observe this purification procedure, they must "bear their guilt." The punishment is not explicitly stated, but in the majority of cases where this idiom occurs, the penalty is either being "cut off" (e.g., Lev. 7:18; 19:8; Num. 9:13) or death (e.g., Exod. 28:43; Lev. 22:9; Num. 18:22).

Leviticus 18:1–20:27

"You Shall Be Holy,
for I the Lord Your God Am Holy"

The signature of the book of Leviticus, as often noted, is the summons to holiness, which occurs most succinctly and memorably in 19:2: "You shall be holy, for I the Lord your God am holy." With this summons as its anchor, Leviticus 19 has become an enormously important and influential resource, not only for Jewish communities of faith that regularly recite its mandate in the readings assigned for the high holy days of Yom Kippur but also for Christians who are directed to remember and embrace its imperative by the author of 1 Peter: "As he who called you is holy, be holy yourselves in all your conduct; for it is written, 'You shall be holy, for I am holy'" (1:15–16). With good reason, therefore, faith communities have affirmed that holiness is central to the biblical understanding of who God is ("I am") and who God's people must be ("You shall be"). "What we have learned from Jewish history," the esteemed rabbi Joshua Heschel reminds all who would seek to respond with Israel to the summons to be a "holy people," is that

149

if a man is not more than human then he is less than human. Judaism is an attempt to prove that in order to be a man, you have to be more than a man, that in order to be a people we have to be more than a people. Israel was made to be a holy people. (*I Asked for Wonder*, p. 104)

Despite the popular embrace of Lev. 19:2, the all-important context for its singular imperative to holiness, chapters 18–20, has seldom received the attention it requires. Perhaps this is understandable in one sense, for on first encounter this larger context addresses concerns, especially sexual transgressions, that may seem quite distant from those typically associated with holiness. There are, however, important structural and theological connections between these chapters that invite and require closer inspection.

In terms of literary structure, chapters 18 and 20 provide a frame for issues that lead to and derive from the centerpiece text in chapter 19 (see Figure 2). Chapter 18 begins (vv. 1–5) and ends (vv. 24–30) with exhortations to observe and keep God's statutes and ordinances. In between these exhortations, the chapter treats sexual transgressions (vv. 6–20, 22–23) and child sacrifices to Molech (v. 21) that constitute disobedience to the summons. Chapter 20 uses similar exhortations (vv. 7–8, 22–26) to envelop and expand on virtually the same concerns, presented now in reverse order: sacrifices to Molech (vv. 2–5) and sexual transgressions (vv. 9–21). Chapter 18 presents the prohibitions in apodictic form (categorical imperatives, "You shall not do X"), followed by a general statement of penalty (the violator will be "cut off"; v. 29). Both the prohibitions and the penalty focus on the *negative* consequences of behavior that is to be avoided, especially the exile from Canaan: "Do not defile yourself in any of these ways . . . otherwise the land will vomit you out for defiling it" (18:24, 28). Chapter 20 presents the prohibitions in casuistic form ("If/When X occurs, then Y will result"), typically including more specific and in some cases more severe sanctions (e.g., death, vv. 10–16; childlessness, vv. 20–21). These prohibitions and the penalties that accompany them also warn of *negative consequences for disobedience*, but their primary focus is rather on the *positive result of engaged obedience* that enables people to attain holiness, especially as this is manifest in faithful possession of the promised land: "You shall keep all my statutes and all my ordinances. . . . You shall not follow the practices of the nation that I am driving out before you. . . . But I have said to you: You shall inherit their land, and I will give it to you to possess, a land flowing with milk and honey" (20:22–24).

As structural bookends, chapters 18 and 20 resolutely insist on an acutely theological valuation: The holiness enjoined by Leviticus 19 encompasses much more than religious devotion to God. It has also to

Figure 2

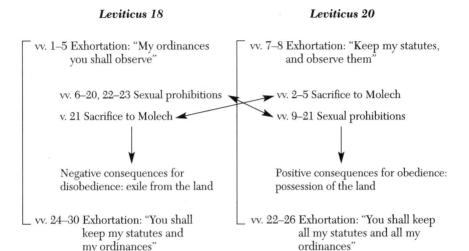

do with the way human beings treat one another. Indeed, given the preoccupation of chapters 18 and 20 with the most intimate form of human conduct—sexual relationships—these texts invite us to understand that the requirement of holy love for others is equal to, if not greater than, the requirement of holy love offered to God. In sum, this frame insists that theology is ethics, and ethics, when directed and evaluated by the abiding summons to be holy, is the highest expression of the most fundamental of all theological assertions: God is holy.

Framing Exhortations
(18:1–5, 24–30; 20:7–8, 22–26)

Two sets of opening and closing exhortations provide the literary and theological context for understanding the summons to holiness. Taken together, these exhortations invite reflection on four primary issues.

1. *The God of Sinai.* The formulaic phrase "I am the Lord your God," which occurs for the first time in 18:2, is the semantic equivalent of God's self-introduction at the beginning of the Decalogue (Exod. 20:2; Deut. 5:6). The repetition of this phrase, in slightly varying form, twenty-six times in chapters 18–20 punctuates all these instructions

151

with the constant reminder that they are an integral part of what the God of Sinai requires if Israel is to realize its covenantal commission to become not only a "priestly kingdom" but also a "holy nation" (Exod. 19:6; see Figure 4, below). Two additional statements underscore the importance of this phrase. First, v. 4, which implicitly recognizes that instructions from other presumed authorities will compete for Israel's allegiance (see below), emphasizes that Israel must obey God and God alone. The NJPS nicely captures the point with its translation: "*My rules alone* shall you observe." Second, v. 5 links obedience to God's instructions to the gift of life itself: "by doing so one shall live." The syntax of the phrase in Hebrew (*wāḥay bāhem*) is unusual and open to multiple interpretations. The most attractive is that proposed by Milgrom, who understands *bāhem*, "in them," to mean "life is built *into them*." These instructions have an "inherent power to grant life," a power that is equaled only by God (Milgrom, *Leviticus 17–22*, pp. 1522–23).

2. "*You shall not do as they do in the land of Egypt . . . and . . . in the land of Canaan*" (18:3; cf. 18:24; 20:22). Obedience requires saying yes to God and no to other powers that vie for Israel's allegiance. The challenge is identified with Egypt and Canaan. The former is the power that enslaved Israel in the past, the latter the power that will tempt Israel in the future. Both are reputed to have built their powerful hegemonies in conjunction with sexual practices that chapters 18 and 20 prohibit, especially incestuous marriages (e.g., father-daughter, brother-sister). Israel's history contains the memory of how influential such practices could be on its own ancestors. The cases of Abraham and Sarah (Gen. 20:2, 12), Judah and Tamar (Gen. 38:12–19), Reuben and Bilhah (Gen. 35:22), Amram and Jocebed (from whose union came Aaron and Moses; Exod. 6:20), and Amnon and Tamar (2 Sam. 13:7–14) are cases in point. Whether and to what extent the Egyptians and Canaanites actually practiced such behavior and whether or not the cases just mentioned are true examples of Israel's conformity with these practices, there is no reason to doubt that the strictures in Leviticus are grounded in realistic concerns. Toward that end, Leviticus 18 warns Israel, no fewer than seven times, not to behave like those who serve other gods (vv. 3 [two times], 24, 26, 27, 29, 30).

3. *Moral impurity defiles the land.* Leviticus 1–16 is deeply concerned with *ritual impurities* that defile the cult, violate the sanctuary, and threaten a holy God's abandonment of an unholy people. The priestly solution to ritual impurity is purification and atonement, ritual enactments that promise God will forgive the transgressions and repair the breach in the divine-human relationship. The closing exhortations in 18:24–30 and 20:22–26 warn that *moral impurities*, principally the

sexual abominations listed in these chapters, pollute the land with consequences that are even more serious than ritual transgressions. If Israel succumbs to the temptation to embrace the practices of its neighbors, it will be guilty of sin that so defiles the land that it will vomit them out (18:25, 28; 20:22). If the transgressions are committed by individuals, they will be "cut off" (18:29) by God from their communities. But if the transgressions are community-wide, if moral impurity becomes so rampant that it is the norm, not the exception, for society, there can be no ritual remedy. Like a sensate human being, the land will become so sickened by what it has ingested from its inhabitants that it will automatically regurgitate them in order to cleanse itself (on the personification of the land, see Joosten, pp. 152–54).

In tracking this issue, Milgrom has perceptively discerned two important theological implications (*Leviticus 17–22*, pp. 1572–80). First, there is a creational motif at the root of the idea about sin's capacity to defile the land. The first human sin against God's primordial design for a "very good" world was a violation that resulted in ecological upheaval: "Cursed is the ground *because of you*" (Gen. 3:17). In the aftermath of this act, Genesis records the escalation of violence that humans inflict on one another. As a result, the earth itself cries out for justice (Gen. 4:10–12), and a grieving God concedes there is no other option short of destroying the very earth on which divine hopes had rested (Gen. 6:5–8,13). From these tragic beginnings, the biblical record proceeds with a sad litany of testimony bearing witness to sin's potential to wound the land (e.g., Num. 33:33–34; Deut. 24:1–4; Isa. 24:5–6; Jer. 3:1–10; Ezek. 33:16–18; Ezra 9:10–11). Given this witness, the exhortations in Leviticus 18 and 20 are freighted with urgent concerns; if they are not heeded, creation itself is jeopardized.

Second, Milgrom has argued that the Priestly tradents of the Holiness Code offer a radical internal critique of the priestly understanding of impurity. The priestly authors responsible for Leviticus 1–16 use the word *ṭāmēʾ*, "impure, unclean," to refer to *ritual* impurities that defile the holy, most palpably the sanctuary, thereby rendering it unsuitable for God's presence. In this view, it is religious or spiritual obedience that provides the measure for Israel's fidelity to God. Leviticus 18 and 20 expand on this understanding by extending both the cause and the effect of impurity. *Unethical* and *immoral* human conduct outside the sanctuary defiles the world with consequences no less catastrophic than religious infidelity. The measure of Israel's obedience to God is not only the *purity of its rituals*; it is also the *morality of its everyday conduct*. In point of fact, unethical behavior is more serious than religious transgression, because it wounds the land in ways that no ritual can repair.

153

Unethical behavior can and will be punished, but it cannot be expiated. It can only be expelled, in the hope that the victim (the land) might recover the capacity to be whole and healthy.

This trenchant critique of moral impurity cautions those who may too quickly assume Israel's priestly tradition is preoccupied with arcane ritual matters that are largely unrelated to urgent issues of social justice. This assumption, often widespread among Christians and especially among Protestants who are more likely to set their spiritual compass by the prophets instead of the priests, is turned on its head by a close reading of Leviticus 18–20. For all the concern about sacrifices, dietary laws, and rites of expiation, the authors of the Holiness Code invite us to understand that Israel's priestly tradition refuses the easy disconnect between ritual and ethics.

4. *"Consecrate yourselves therefore, and be holy"* (20:7). The imperative in 20:7 is a repetition of 11:44. Both texts likely derive from the authors responsible for the Holiness Code. In both texts the summons is directed to priests and laity alike. The significance of the appeal is the affirmation that both priests and laypersons can refract holiness, which God alone inherently possesses, in reciprocal ways. The Priestly source behind Leviticus 8–10 understands Aaron's ordination as a founding ritual through which his descendants acquire holiness as a permanent priestly virtue. Leviticus 20:7 expands on this understanding in two ways. First, the priests' bequeathed holiness is unique, entitling them, and them alone, to officiate at the altar; but they are enjoined to sustain their holiness by obedience to all God's commandments. It is not enough for priests to be ritually holy; they must prove themselves worthy of their special privileges by ethical behavior away from the altar that does not diminish their stewardship of the gift they have been given (on the priestly responsibilities, see further 21:1–22:16). Second, the gift of holiness is not limited to priests. Laypersons *consecrate themselves*, as do priests, by keeping all God's statutes and ordinances. As Milgrom notes, the Holiness Code "democratizes" the understanding of holiness. In his words, "Holiness is no longer a priestly prerogative. It is available to and attainable by everyone" (*Leviticus 17–22*, p. 1741).

The closing exhortation in 20:22–26 provides further definition for how priests and laity are to consecrate themselves in holiness. They must exemplify holiness not only by tuning their devotion to God's nature—"You shall be . . . because I am"—but also by conforming their lives to the way God acts. Leviticus 20:24–26 links the latter task to God's primordial decision to create the optimum conditions for life by dividing between order and chaos. Four times in Genesis 1, God performs acts of "separation" or "division" that summon forth and sustain the basic elements of the created order (vv. 4, 7, 14, 18). Encoded in God's acts is a complementary mandate for creation itself to engage in reciprocal acts of division. As God divides the light from the darkness (Gen. 1:4), God also commissions the lights in the sky to divide between day and night (vv. 14, 18). As God divides the waters above the firmament from those below (v. 7), the firmament mirrors God's act with its endowed capacity to sustain what God has accomplished (v. 6). Leviticus 20 returns to this creational design with a fourfold repetition of the word *divide* (vv. 24, 25 [two times], 26). The first and fourth occurrences define God's holiness as the act of separating Israel from other nations (vv. 24, 26). The third occurrence ties Israel's separation from the nations to God's decision to divide between clean and unclean foods (v. 25b). Framed by these three, the second occurrence enjoins Israel to honor God's decision by observing the dietary laws (v. 25a). In sum, when Israel consecrates itself to God, by devotion and by deed, it does so not only for its own sake but also for the sake of the world. For the wholeness that God intends, creation itself requires a people who aspire to be holy as God is holy.

Framing Prohibitions (18:6–23; 20:2–21, 27)

The framing prohibitions in chapters 18 and 20 contain a number of linguistic and stylistic connections that suggest the two lists, while perhaps composed independently, are intended to complement one another. The following connections may be singled out (for a full discussion, see Milgrom, *Leviticus 17–22*, pp. 1765–68).

- Both lists deal with the same two general issues, sexual transgressions and sacrifices to Molech, although the order of presentation is reversed. Chapter 18 begins with sexual offenses (vv. 6–20, 22–23), in the midst of which it devotes one verse to Molech (v. 21). Chapter 20 begins with a longer unit on Molech (vv. 2–5), which is followed by sexual transgressions (vv. 9–21).
- The sexual prohibitions in chapter 18 build on the phrase "to uncover nakedness" (v. 6), a euphemism for sexual intercourse, and proceed to list forbidden relationships, arranged in descending order from the closest family relationships to more distant nonfamily relationships: *family*—with a mother (v. 7), with a

155

father's wife (v. 8), with a sister (v. 9), with a grand-daughter (v. 10), with a stepsister (v. 11), with a paternal aunt (v. 12), with a maternal aunt (v. 13), with an aunt who is wife of a father's brother (v. 14), with a daughter-in-law (v. 15), with a brother's wife (v. 16), with a mother and a daughter (v. 17a); *nonfamily*— with a woman and her granddaughter (vv. 17b–18), with a wife's sister (v. 18), with a menstruating woman (v. 19), with a neighbor's wife (v. 20), male with male (v. 22), with animals (v. 23). Chapter 19 also uses the key phrase "uncover nakedness" (vv. 11, 17, 18, 19, 20, 21), along with other terms—*marry* (vv. 14, 17, 21), *lie* (vv. 11, 12, 13, 15)—to proscribe sexual behaviors. The forbidden relationships are not identical to those in chapter 18, but the list addresses essentially the same concerns: adultery with a neighbor's wife (v. 10), sex with a father's wife (v. 11), sex with a daughter-in-law (v. 12), male homosexuality (v. 13), marriage to a woman and her mother (v. 14), bestiality (vv. 15–16), marriage to a sister (v. 17), sex with a menstruating woman (v. 18), sex with a paternal or maternal aunt (v. 19), sex with an uncle's wife (v. 20), marriage to a sister-in-law (v. 21).

• The language condemning proscribed behaviors is similar in the two lists, but the consequent penalties are different. Molech worship "profanes the name" of God (18:21; 20:3). Forbidden sexual practices are a "perversion" (18:23; 20:12), a "depravity" (18:17; 20:14), and an "abomination" (18:22; 20:13). All of the proscribed behaviors are violations of God's "statutes" and "ordinances" (18:4, 26; 20:22). Both lists stipulate that the penalty for transgression is exile—the land will "vomit out" the offenders (18:25, 28; 20:22)—but the correlating penalties differ. Both lists use the general phrase "cut off" (18:29; 20:17, 18) to describe the complete banishment of offenders from the community and the extermination of their lineage, but chapter 20 goes further by providing a sliding scale of penalties pegged to the seriousness of the violation: death (vv. 10–16); being "cut off" (vv. 17, 18), and childlessness (vv. 20–21). The variation in sanctions suggests the two lists address different audiences. Chapter 18 addresses family relations from the perspective of the father, who, as the head of the "house" (the "father's house"), has primary responsibility for the nuclear family (father, mother, children) and their extended blood relations (e.g., aunts, uncles, daughters- and sons-in-law, grandparents, grandchildren). Within this family structure, the father executes the punishment (excision from the family), which, significantly, provides no license for putting offenders to death. Chapter 20 addresses family relations from the perspective of the authorized judicial leaders, who are charged with the responsibility for fairly adjudicating offenses that impact on the welfare of the entire community, especially those that may justify the death penalty.

- Both lists condemn Molech worship because it profanes God's name (18:21; 20:2–5), but the contexts for the condemnation appear to be different. Chapter 18 devotes but one verse to Molech, and it is rather awkwardly inserted within a long list of sexual violations. One possible explanation is that sacrificing children to Molech threatens family relationships in a manner comparable to incest or other illicit sexual behaviors (cf. Hartley, p. 336). Chapter 20, which provides a more extensive discussion, condemns Molech worship as profaning not only God's name but also God's sanctuary (v. 3). Within the same pericope, God condemns those who "prostitute" (v. 5) themselves to Molech, which is metaphorical language typically used to describe chasing after other gods (Exod. 34:15–16; Num. 15:39; Deut. 31:16; and frequently in the prophets, e.g., Jer. 3:1–2, 6–9; Ezek. 16:16–17; Hos. 1:2; 4:10, 12, 15). Leviticus 20:6 uses the same metaphor to condemn the practice of consulting "mediums and wizards" (cf. 20:27 and 17:7), which suggests that in this chapter the prohibitions concerning Molech have more to do with idolatry than with sexual practices that destroy family relationships.

157

The structural and rhetorical connections between chapters 18 and 20 indicate that these chapters should be read as an intentional frame for Leviticus 19. That this is so, however, raises two related theological questions. What do sexual practices have to do with the summons to holiness? How do the condemnations of Molech sacrifice, which clearly have to do with Israel's relationship to God, contribute to the sexual prohibitions that dominate these two lists?

It is apparent that prohibitions of certain sexual practices promote healthy family units, which are essential for the covenant community that bears witness to God's presence in the world (Hartley, pp. 298–302; Kaiser, p. 1128; Gerstenberger, pp. 257–58). One clue concerning the threat of sexual misconduct to the stability of the family occurs in 18:18. In the context of the injunction against marrying two sisters, the text warns against relationships that produce "rivalry." The Hebrew root, which means "show hostility toward, vex," may be paradigmatic for the dissension in the family that is implicit in all these prohibitions: Whenever the bonds of love are conflicted by illicit sexual practices, the family is threatened by strife and hostility.

Milgrom acknowledges the importance of this clue but pushes beyond it to posit a still more basic rationale (*Leviticus 17–22*, pp. 1530–31). The fundamental issue behind all these prohibitions, he suggests, is the concern to honor God's procreational commission to "be fruitful and multiply" (Gen. 1:28). In the Priestly account of creation, this command, which constitutes God's first words to human beings who are created in God's image, concerns their sexual relationship. By God's directive, men and women are given the responsibility to produce seed that fills the earth with progeny and sustains God's hopes and expectations for a human embodiment of the divine image. The commission to exercise creaturely "dominion" (Gen. 1:26, 28) over the world's resources further defines the divine image God entrusts to the human community. The language of dominion conveys the idea of royal power, specifically the king's power to create and secure the conditions necessary for the safety and welfare of every citizen in his charge. By analogy, God commissions humans to be fruitful and multiply in ways that advance and secure the welfare of the human community. Sexual behavior that produces seed destructive of family relationships—adultery, incestuous marriages—and sexual behavior that produces no seed—intercourse with a menstruating woman, male homosexuality, sodomy—violates God's procreational commission and diminishes the human community's capacity to reproduce and sustain itself in God's image.

It is prudent to add a word about the prohibitions in Lev. 18:22 and 20:13, for these texts are regularly championed as a biblical mandate for the condemnation of homosexuality. The issue of homosexuality has long vexed the religious conscience and moral scruples of the human community. The prohibitions in Leviticus 18 and 20 must certainly be a part of our struggle with this issue, but it is wise to remember that they are only a part; a wide range of other considerations—social, biological, and political—must also be factored into the positions we take. Even so, it is incumbent upon all who strive to tune their decisions to the witness of Scripture that these particular texts be interpreted within the context of their setting in Israel's priestly tradition.

The following points deserve careful reflection: (1) The ban on homosexuality is but one of more than a dozen behaviors proscribed in Leviticus 18 and 20. It is accorded no more importance than other prohibitions, many of which seem not to have made much impact on the community of faith. Except perhaps among the most fundamentalist religious communities, we do not measure obedience to God by killing children who curse their parents (20:9) or men who commit adultery with another's wife (20:10). (2) All the prohibitions in chapters 18 and 20 assume a patriarchal structure for society. As such, they are addressed primarily to males, not females. It may be noted in this regard that the homosexual ban addresses only sexual acts between men; there is no proscription against lesbianism. (3) The latter part of the phrase "lie with a male *as with a woman,*" which occurs in both 18:22 and 20:13, is an idiom used only for homosexual acts performed by heterosexuals (Milgrom, *Leviticus 17–22*, p. 1786; Douglas, *Leviticus as Literature*, p. 238; Levine, p. 123). The text does not address homosexuality in terms of permanent sexual orientation. Moreover, the text does not proscribe all acts of male homosexuality. It focuses instead on heterosexual males performing homosexual acts with other males in the family unit, for example, nephew with uncle, grandson with grandfather (Milgrom, *Leviticus 17–22*, p. 1786). (4) Finally, however we may decide to appropriate these prohibitions, we should remember that the rationale behind all of them, including those dealing with male homosexuality, is the overriding concern to honor God's procreational commission. Their intent is to promote relationships that image the compassion of God; they do not endorse discrimination and abuse that destroys people by labeling them as enemies of God.

To return to the second of the two theological questions posed above, what does sacrifice to Molech have to do with the sexual prohibitions that dominate Leviticus 18 and 20? The name Molech occurs fewer than a dozen times in Hebrew Scriptures, five of which are in these chapters (Lev. 18:21; 20:2, 3, 4, 5; 2 Kgs. 11:7; 23:10; Jer. 32:35; three additional references are less certain: Isa. 30:33; 57:9; Zeph. 1:5). The evidence is open to multiple interpretations, but it appears that Molech is a figure of the underworld, perhaps identified with Canaanite gods

159

known variously as Melqart and Malik (Day, pp. 46–55; for a full discussion of the issues, see Hartley, pp. 334–37). The worship offered Molech is equally elusive, but it seems clear that Leviticus presumes it to have involved the sacrifice of children. Given such an understanding, the inclusion of a warning concerning Molech is not as unrelated to the sexual prohibitions as it may appear. The sacrifice of a child would certainly have threatened a family's stability in ways comparable to the sexual practices forbidden in these chapters.

There may be another clue, however, in the metaphor that is used to describe Molech worship in 20:5. To "prostitute" oneself to Molech, as noted above, is a sexual term appropriated to refer to chasing or "whoring after" other gods. The imagery suggests forming an illicit union with another god. From this perspective, the warning concerns idolatry, worshiping a god other than YHWH. That sexual language and imagery are used in all the prohibitions of Leviticus 18 and 20, including those concerning Molech, may justify a further discernment. Yielding to selfish and destructive passions is idolatrous. It exemplifies the worship of one's own desires, which subverts the family, diminishes the community, and violates God's creational designs in ways that are just as condemnable as bowing down before another god.

The Central Summons to Holiness (19:1–36)

Framed by these intensely pragmatic concerns about human conduct, Leviticus 19 begins with the theological rationale they assume—"You shall be holy, for I the Lord your God am holy" (v. 2)—and then explicates this rationale in terms of both religious (vv. 3–8) and ethical responsibilities (vv. 9–18). A third collection of miscellaneous instructions addresses a mixture of religious and ethical responsibilities (vv. 19–37). There is some slippage in judging whether individual responsibilities are religious, ethical, or both at the same time, but the list as a whole makes it clear that here, as in the framing chapters, the summons to holiness can be fulfilled only when fidelity to God is embodied with equal passion by both ethical and religious commitments. While most of the prohibitions are couched negatively, as behavior that must be avoided, a significant number are stated positively, thereby reiterating the assertion in chapters 18 and 20 that holiness must be manifest in lives that say both yes to what God requires and no to what God forbids. One without the other will never be sufficient to obey God's commandments. The strategic placement of two positive exhortations to keep all God's statutes and ordinances (vv. 19, 37), both echoing the framing exhortations in chapters 18 and 20, underscores the assertion that holiness must always be exemplified by *active engagement* with the world, never only by *passive withdrawal*.

Two important structural features of Leviticus 19 merit careful attention: First, two rhetorical markers—an inclusio in vv. 2b and 36b and the chiasm in vv. 3–4 and 30—emphasize that all the instructions in this chapter function as commentary on the Decalogue given at Sinai (see the comments above on "The God of Sinai"). The inclusio in vv. 2b and 36b repeats the preamble to the Decalogue (Exod. 20:2). Verse 2b, the trailer for the summons to holiness, ends with the first words of the first sentence in Exod. 20:2: "I am the Lord your God." Verse 36b picks up the last words of the first sentence in the Exodus verse: "who brought you out of the land of Egypt." The rhetorical effect is to suggest that all the instructions in between these two framing phrases have the same claim on Israel's obedience as the Ten Commandments.

Commentators often suggest, in fact, that each of the Commandments is referenced in these instructions. The parallels suggested by Kaiser are representative (Kaiser, p. 1131):

Ten Commandments	*Leviticus 19*
1 and 2	v. 4
3	v. 12
4 and 5	v. 3
6	v. 16
7	v. 29
8 and 9	vv. 11, 16
10	v. 18

On close inspection, however, more than half these parallels are inexact at best. The only Commandments clearly echoed are numbers one, two, four, and five, and these are referenced in the theologically instructive chiasm of Leviticus 19:3–4 and 19:30 (see Figure 3). This chiasm reverses the order of the Commandments in the Decalogue, elevating Commandment Five, reverence for father and mother, to the position of first importance. It then places Commandments Four, One, and Two, each of which deals with reverence for God, in the second position. This inversion of the Commandments conveys the radical perspective of the Holiness Code: The importance of how one lives in relationships with others in the human community is equal to, if not even greater than, the requirement of fidelity to God. In the Priestly perspective, ethical behavior is *not merely the necessary consequence* of love for God; it is the *fundamental prerequisite* that establishes the authenticity of that love.

161

Figure 3

Leviticus 19:3–4 (Commandments 5, 4)

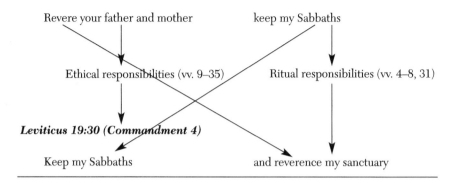

Revere your father and mother   keep my Sabbaths

Ethical responsibilities (vv. 9–35)   Ritual responsibilities (vv. 4–8, 31)

Leviticus 19:30 (Commandment 4)

Keep my Sabbaths   and reverence my sanctuary

This chiasm, in turn, provides the hermeneutical clue for reading the remainder of the instructions in Leviticus 19. The lead commandment to revere father and mother (v. 3a), who represent the most intimate union in the family structure, is amplified with further commandments (vv. 9–35) that extend the requirement for ethical relationships to the broader "community" of all God's creation. The land must be harvested with a compassion that does not ignore the needs of the poor (vv. 9–10; see also vv. 23–25), and plants and animals must be protected against mixed breeding that weakens the species God has created (v. 19). The welfare of the human community must not be jeopardized by dishonesty (vv. 11–12), oppression (vv. 13–14), economic injustice (vv. 15–16, 35–36), hate and vengeance (vv. 17–18), abusive sexual practices (vv. 20–22, 29), or disrespect for elders or aliens (vv. 32–33). The integrity of the human body must not be violated by anything one consumes internally (v. 26) or "wears" externally (the cutting of hair, lacerations, or other marks; vv. 27–28). The closing words of the chiasm in v. 30, which rhetorically link each of the above commandments with reverence for God's sanctuary, provide a further clue to the distinctiveness of this presentation. The sanctuary in which holiness must be exemplified is not defined only by the physical space of a tent or a temple; the sanctuary that would mirror God's holiness must extend to all aspects of everyday life (cf. Milgrom, *Leviticus 17–22*, p. 1598).

Figure 4

"Speak to the people of Israel and say to them: I am YHWH your God" (Lev. 18:2)

> "I am YHWH your God" (18:4)
> "I am YHWH" (18:5)
> "I am YHWH" (18:21)
> "I am YHWH your God" (18:30)

"You shall be holy, for I YHWH your God am holy" (Lev. 19:2)

> "I am YHWH your God" (19:3)
> "I am YHWH your God" (19:4)
> "I am YHWH your God" (19:10)
> "I am YHWH" (19:12)
> "I am YHWH" (19:14)
> "I am YHWH" (19:16)
> "I am YHWH" (19:18)
> "I am YHWH" (19:25)
> "I am YHWH" (19:28)
> "I am YHWH" (19:30)
> "I am YHWH" (19:31)
> "I am YHWH" (19:32)
> "I am YHWH" (19:34)
> "I am YHWH" (19:36)
> "I am YHWH" (19:37)
> "I am YHWH your God" (20:7)
> "I am YHWH" (20:8)
> "I am YHWH your God" (20:24)

"You shall be holy to me, for I YHWH am holy" (Lev. 20:26)

In a similar manner, the commandment in 19:3b to keep the Sabbath is followed in vv. 4–8 (see also v. 31) with commandments that continue its focus on honoring the things of God. To keep the Sabbath means to abstain from all forms of idolatry, whether worshiping gods manufactured by hand (v. 4) or seeking revelation from gods associated with the spirits of the dead (v. 31). It also means to pay heed to the sacrificial regulations concerning the well-being offering (vv. 5–8). Of all

163

the sacrifices to God, this one is perhaps most vulnerable to abuse, because its ritual procedure permits offerings designated as holy to God to be shared by laypersons. To underscore the instructions already provided (see 3:1–17; 7:11–21), the Holiness Code reiterates the stipulation that donors must eat their portion of the sacrifice within two days; after that, the portion becomes unclean. In Exodus, the Fourth Commandment, to keep the Sabbath holy, is the bridge between the commandments to love God exclusively (Commandments One through Three; Exod. 20:3–7) and the commandments to live with one another in ways that concretize that commitment in ethical behavior (Commandments Five through Ten; Exod. 20:12–17; see further Balentine, pp. 121–36). In Leviticus 19, loving God absolutely is the end product of the catalytic requirement to love each other with the same devotion that joins a mother and father.

A second structural marker in Leviticus 19 is the repetition of the formulaic phrase "I am YHWH (the Lord)/I am YHWH (the Lord) your God" (see Figure 4). With its clear parallels to the preamble to the Decalogue (Exod. 20:2; Deut. 5:6), this phrase suggests that, from the Priestly perspective, the summons to holiness originates in the moral authority of the God who covenanted with Israel at Sinai. The sixteen occurrences of this phrase in Leviticus 19, coupled with additional occurrences in chapters 18 and 20, emphasize that obedience to God's commands must include more than religious devotion; it requires that affirmation be matched by action, that words of commitment to God in heaven be bodied forth on earth in deeds of justice and righteousness.

It is all the more instructive, therefore, to note that embedded in these commands to be holy is the clarion charge to model obedience to God through love for others: "You shall love your neighbor as yourself; I am the Lord" (19:18). Although this verse is typically isolated from its context, its full force can be discerned only when it is read in conjunction with v. 17. Together, these verses comprise a single unit with parallel prohibitions, instructions, and rationales. Milgrom clearly lays out the parallels as follows (*Leviticus 17–22*, p. 1646; cf. Levine, pp. 129–30):

	Lev. 19:17	*Lev. 19:18*
Prohibition	You shall not hate in your heart anyone of your kin;	You shall not take vengeance or bear a grudge against any of your people,
Instruction	you shall reprove your neighbor,	but you shall love your neighbor as yourself:
Rationale	or you will incur guilt yourself	I am YHWH

Hating someone in one's heart, where emotions may fester into strategized deeds of angry retribution, is forbidden by God. According to the biblical witness, the responsibility for vengeance resides with God alone (Jer. 15:15; Nah. 1:2; Ps. 94:1), unless God explicitly delegates the task to human beings (Num. 31:2–3; Milgrom, *Leviticus 17–22*, p. 1652). Nursing a grudge against someone permits anger to seethe until it explodes in uncontrollable rage. Vengeance and rage wound the human spirit and fray the fabric of society. The sin (19:17; NRSV: "guilt") that results when people yield to these temptations infects not only those who are attacked; it extends with equally negative results to those who execute their destruction in the name of punishment.

The solution proposed is twofold. First, one should reprove openly those who have erred, which in this context implies seeking legal relief from the court, where justice is shaped by clear statutes and reasoned arguments. Second, one should love one's neighbor as oneself. The meaning of this latter charge, enshrined in public consciousness since the eighteenth century as the motivation behind the Golden Rule, rests on three discernments: (1) The word *love* implies both attitude and act; one must not only feel love but also act in ways that translate love into concrete deeds. Just as one expresses love for God through active obedience to God's commandments, so one must demonstrate love for others by reaching out to them with tangible deeds of compassion and concern. It is not without reason, therefore, that when instructing the disciples on the matter of judging others, Jesus frames his admonition positively: "*Do* to others as you would have them *do* to you" (Matt. 7:12; Luke 6:31). (2) The word *neighbor* refers to a wide range of persons with whom Israel would have had relationships. The list of ethical admonitions in Lev. 19:9–18 uses no fewer than eight words to describe the persons Israel is obligated to care for: "poor" (v. 10), "alien" (v. 10), "neighbor" (v. 13), "laborer" (v. 13), the "deaf" (v. 14), the "blind" (v. 14), "poor" (v. 15), "fellow citizen" (vv. 15, 17; NRSV: "neighbor/people"). The inclusiveness of this list indicates that the "neighbor" is not limited to the peer with whom one shares a certain social status. It is also the disadvantaged person shunted to the edges of society, especially those persons the community may be tempted to ignore, perhaps even abuse, for economic, political, or physical reasons (see further Balentine, pp. 169–71). (3) The phrase "as yourself" is open to different interpretations, perhaps the most illuminating of which can be found in a rabbinic discourse cited by Milgrom. In response to Rabbi Akiba's claim that Lev. 19:18 constitutes the fundamental law in the Torah, Ben Azzai says, "When God created man, he made him in the likeness of God (Gen. 5:1), so that you should not say: 'Since I despise myself, let my fellow be

165

despised with me; since I am cursed, let my fellow be cursed with me'" (*Sipra Qedoshim* 4:12; cited in Milgrom, *Leviticus 17-22*, p. 1656). Ben Azzai's comment turns on the recognition of a creational foundation for loving one's neighbor as oneself. Because every human being bears "the likeness of God," the failure to love others is equivalent to saying that neither they nor we have value in the eyes of God. It may be likened to saying that in the decision to invest human beings with the divine image, God has made a terrible mistake.

If the summons to holiness in 19:2 constitutes the keynote message of Leviticus, the command to love and not hate each other in 19:17–18 brings us to the epicenter of the book. The abiding claim of this charge, which Jesus elevates as the second of the two greatest commandments (Matt. 22:39–40; Mark 12:31; Luke 10:27), serves notice that when God says, "I am," what necessarily follows in the divine vocabulary are the words "You shall be." As the author of James puts it, after having appealed to the command in Lev. 19:18 (James 2:8): "What good is it, my brothers and sisters, if you say you have faith but do not have works?" (2:14; cf. 1 John 3:11–18).

Even so, the summons to aspire to God's holiness, and especially the summons to love as God loves, is fraught with difficulties. Holiness is constantly under assault by defilement that assumes seemingly endless disguises; the command to love one's neighbor, not to mention one's enemies, seems increasingly banal and vacant. As I write these words, the events of September 11, 2001, hang heavy in the air. Although it is always risky to link theological interpretation to any single contemporary event, it is a reasonable assumption that the bombings of the World Trade Center in New York City and the Pentagon in Washington, D.C., have fundamentally changed the perspective of virtually every human being on the globe. As far as the eye can see, the impulse that will drive our politics, and perhaps our religion, for the foreseeable future is the yearning for revenge, coded as "justice," against those who perpetrated such unconscionable acts of mass murder. In such a climate, the community of faith is hard pressed to know what to make of an ancient biblical admonition not to "take vengeance or bear a grudge." In the wake of the deaths of thousands of innocent people, how can any community that yearns for and deserves justice be obedient to the command to love, not hate, its enemies? Easy answers will not suffice for vexed and complicated issues. What is required is a full immersion in the texts that shape our faith commitments and in the world that defines the arena in which we must enact them. As the community of faith ponders the stirrings for retribution, whatever the catalyst may be, the words of W. H. Auden provide an important touchstone for reflection on the command to "love your neighbor as yourself": "Violence is never just, though Justice may sometimes require it: tyrants are persons to whom requisite evil is fun" (Auden, p. 859).

To summarize, Leviticus 18–20 is a literary and theological unit composed of a frame and a center. The frame, chapters 18 and 20, insists that the journey toward holiness goes through the ethics of human relationships. The center, Leviticus 19, insists that how humans relate to one another is the measure of their fidelity to God. Neither the frame nor the center can stand alone without the meaning of the whole being diminished. Without the frame, the summons to holiness too easily slides into theological abstraction, "faith without works" as James puts it. Without the center, the summons to ethical relationships in the human community is cut loose from the anchor that provides its moral authority. "Let us love one another," the author of 1 John says, "because love is from God" (4:7). This tensive connection between the frame and the center recalls the elegiac concern of William Butler Yeats: if "the centre cannot hold," then "things fall apart" ("The Second Coming," *Collected Poems of William Butler Yeats*, ed. R. J. Finneran, pp. 184–87).

Leviticus 21:1–22:23
You Shall Be Holy . . .
because I YHWH Am Making You Holy

Chapters 21–22 continue the summons to be holy that begins in chapters 18–20. Whereas the first two chapters are addressed to the laity (18:2; 19:2; 20:2), the following two address primarily the priests (21:1, 16; 22:2). Priests, in fact, carry still heavier responsibilities than the laity, for their ordination charges them to be faithful stewards of the rites and rituals that sustain the connection between a holy God and a world all too vulnerable to sin and defilement. Perhaps because their responsibilities to be holy are at once so heavy and so important, God twice reminds Moses that these priestly instructions must be delivered in the presence of "all the people of Israel" (21:24; 22:17). The implication appears to be that the laity have a responsibility both to help the priests faithfully discharge their duties and to hold them accountable when they do not.

The instructions may be grouped into six sections: instructions to all priests concerning mourning and marriage (21:1–9); instructions to the high priest concerning mourning and marriage (21:10–15); instructions concerning disqualifying blemishes (21:16–24); instructions to the

167

priests concerning eating sacred food (22:1–9); instructions concerning who may and may not eat sacred food (22:10–16); and instructions concerning blemished sacrificial animals, followed by a summary exhortation (22:17–33). Two interrelated structural markers repeat in all six sections and link them thematically to the larger unit of chapters 18–22. The self-introduction formula "I am the Lord (YHWH)," which occurs twenty-six times in chapters 18–20, repeats here in 21:8, 15, 23; 22:9, 16, and 32. To this phrase these verses now add the words "I (YHWH) sanctify you/him/them" (see also 20:8). Encoded in this verb is an important theological girder that bears the entire weight of chapters 18–22. For all their considerable emphasis on the command to *be holy*, these chapters affirm that the One who issues the command is the same One who empowers its recipients to obey it. "You *shall be holy* . . . I YHWH *am holy* . . . and *I will make you holy*." Without the last promise, the command would be heavy indeed. From the human perspective— perhaps from God's as well—and given Israel's history, the command would likely buckle under the weight of its own futility.

Instructions to Priests concerning Mourning and Marriage (21:1–9 and 21:10–16)

Priests must observe special restrictions concerning mourning and marriage, for both areas potentially involve impurities that defile and so disqualify them from service. Mourning the dead involves association with corpses, which defile anyone who comes into contact with them. To counter this threat, a graduated scale of instructions applies. Laypersons may become impure, when necessary, by mourning their dead, whereupon they must cleanse themselves through appropriate ritual procedures (see Num. 19:11–22). Ordinary priests are given special dispensation to come into the presence of corpses when mourning, but only in the case of their "nearest of kin," here specified as mother, father, son, daughter, brother, and virgin sister (21:2). Even in these cases, however, there are restrictions to be observed: They must not shave their heads, cut their beards, or make gashes in their flesh (21:5), all mourning practices that are identified in other cultures with the worship of the dead. The high priest must observe still more stringent precautions. He must not dishevel his hair, rend his holy vestments, or enter into any place where there is a dead body, not even to mourn the death of his father or mother (21:10–11). Because he bears the singular responsibility of representing all Israel by entering into the Holy of Holies, the most sacred zone of the sanctuary, the high priest must not risk defilement by any means.

168

Marriage for priests presents potentially similar concerns, for the union between a priest and a woman has serious implications for the purity of the priestly lineage. Ordinary priests must not marry a woman who is promiscuous or "defiled" (perhaps the meaning is "raped"; cf. Milgrom, *Leviticus 17–22*, p. 1807) or divorced (21:7). Once again, the restrictions are tighter for the high priest. He must not marry a widow, a divorced woman, or a woman who has been "defiled" (21:14). He may only marry "a virgin of his own kin" (21:14; cf. v. 13), which likely means a daughter of a priest. The transparent concern is with the purity of the priestly line, for the offspring of this union could be a future high priest.

Instructions concerning Disqualifying Blemishes (21:16–24)

Ancient cultures, including Israel, required that priests be free of physical blemish. In Israel's priestly system the concern for the wholeness and integrity of the physical body is an extension of the understanding that God's holiness is perfect and complete. Holy and unblemished persons (and sacrifices) are external expressions of the requirement to be holy as God is holy. Ancient Israel's concerns that physical deformity can impair a priest's capacity to serve are of course expressed in different terms than we would use today, but there is good reason to believe that we view the requirements for our own leaders in much the same way. One has only to recall the great care that was taken to hide President Franklin D. Roosevelt's paralyzed legs from public view, presumably on the assumption they might have signaled a physical weakness that was politically damaging (Milgrom, *Leviticus 17–22*, p. 1842).

Twelve disqualifying blemishes are listed. Several of the terms are imprecise, thus the translations are only approximate: blindness, lameness, disfigurement (perhaps a facial abnormality), deformity (perhaps a limb that is too short or too long), a broken leg, a broken arm, a hunchback, a dwarf, a discoloration of the eye, a festering sore, a skin disease, a crushed testicle (vv. 18–21). Priests who have one of these blemishes are restricted from officiating at the altar, although a concession is made allowing them to eat their requisite portions of the holy offerings (vv. 22–23).

Each of the listed afflictions comes under the umbrella term *blemish*, used primarily for physical and (mostly) externally visible defects. The focus on *physical* as opposed to *moral* blemishes raises the question whether priests attached more importance to physical characteristics than to moral character. Two considerations argue against such a conclusion. First, chapters 18–20 have already stipulated that the requirements

169

for holiness in the presence of God clearly include ethical obedience (e.g., 19:9–18). Those requirements for moral and ethical behavior are assumed here; they are neither displaced nor relegated to secondary importance. Second, following Milgrom, we may note that the list of twelve blemishes for the priests was likely compiled to match the list of twelve blemishes that disqualify sacrificial animals (22:22–24; see below). Because animals have only physical blemishes, not moral ones, it appears the structural parallel between animals and humans is the major factor here. Theological judgments about the priests' characters are not the governing concern (Milgrom, *Leviticus 17–22*, pp. 1821–22, 1836–40).

Instructions concerning Eating Sacred Food (22:1–9 and 22:10–16)

After the concession that blemished priests may eat the sacred portions of the sacrifices (21:22), two sets of instructions qualify the concession. The first (22:1–9) stipulates that priests may not eat their designated portions when they are in a state of ritual impurity, for to do so profanes YHWH's holy name. The list of impurities (vv. 4–9) essentially reprises the skin diseases (chaps. 13–14), discharges (chap. 15), and contamination from dead corpses (11:39) that have been previously addressed. If a priest deliberately eats of the sacred portions while impure, he will be "cut off" and his priestly lineage will be terminated (22:3). If a priest inadvertently violates these proscriptions, he must abstain from eating until evening and bathe his body before he can resume his normal privileges (vv. 6–7).

The second set of instructions (22:10–16) concerns laypersons who may and may not partake of the holy offerings. Those who may not eat are the priest's non-Israelite hired servants and the daughter of the priest if she has married a layperson. Those who may eat are the priest's slaves (and their children) who live with him as resident aliens and the widowed or divorced daughter (without children) of a priest who returns to her father's house to live "as in her youth" (v. 12). The underlying principle for these restrictions is that persons who are neither servants nor family members of the priest may not eat the sacred food. Should any one of these persons inadvertently violate the proscription, that person must restore to the priest what he or she has taken and add a 20 percent penalty payment.

Instructions concerning Blemished Sacrificial Animals (22:17–33)

This section is addressed to "Aaron and his sons and all the people of Israel," thus indicating that priests and laity alike must assume the responsibility for bringing only unblemished sacrificial animals to the altar. The sacrifices in view are the voluntary offerings—votive and freewill, the latter of which may be presented as either burnt offerings or well-being offerings. These offerings are of special concern because they are vulnerable in part to the discretion of the donors, who may be guilty of being less rigorous than they should have been in selecting their presentations. The offerings required for expiation of sin—purification and reparation—are not mentioned, presumably because in these cases the requirement of unblemished animals is not discretionary.

Milgrom has helpfully noted that the blemishes listed for sacrificial animals (vv. 22–24) correspond in kind and number with those listed for the priests (21:18–20; cf. Milgrom, *Leviticus 17–22*, pp. 1875–82). Five of the twelve blemishes are the same: blindness, limbs too long, broken bones, sores, and scabs. The remaining blemishes are close but not exact matches with those listed for the priests, which may be explained by the biological differences between animals and humans. The comparison between the two lists helps to explain the reference in 21:20 to "crushed testicles," which seems odd in its context, if only because it is the only nonexternal, nonvisible defect mentioned. While it may be argued that the reference is to be associated with the stipulation that impaired testicles disqualify persons from belonging to Israel (cf. Deut. 23:2), it seems just as likely that it is included here to bring the priestly blemishes into structural conformity with the list of animal blemishes.

Verses 26–30 prescribe additional criteria for sacrificial animals. The animal must be no younger than eight days old (v. 27). The mother and her young must not be slaughtered on the same day (v. 28). The meat of the thanksgiving offering must be consumed on the same day in which it is presented (vv. 29–30). In sum, the list of proscribed blemishes for animal sacrifices, as well as the additional criteria defining their presentation and consumption, indicate that the requirement for holiness in the presence of God extends not only to priests and laity but also to everything that is presented at the altar.

The closing exhortation (vv. 31–33), which corresponds to the exhortations in 18:1–5, 24–30; 19:37; 20:7–8, 22–26, serves to tie chapters 18–22 together as a thematic unit. The common denominator throughout is the command to all Israel, priests and laity alike, to image God by being holy in every sphere of life—ritual, ethical, social, and moral. The rhetoric of vv. 31–33 now fine-tunes this command with a theological precision. At the beginning and end, the self-introduction formula "I am the Lord (YHWH)" (vv. 31, 33) establishes the moral authority of the One who issues the command to be holy. In between these two revelatory declarations and the unyielding expectations for

171

obedience they set in motion, the phrase "I sanctify you" (v. 32) provides the coupling that promises God will not ultimately allow the call for a holy people to fail. As the seventh of seven occurrences (20:8; 21:8, 15; 21:23; 22:9, 16, 32), the words "I sanctify you" bring into full view God's inviolable commitment to be at work in Israel's midst, sanctifying them in their obedience, forgiving them their failures, and restoring them to new possibilities for attaining the holiness God requires.

Leviticus 23:1–44
The Holy Calendar

The word *holy* occurs for the first time in Hebrew Scripture in Gen. 2:3, which reports that "God blessed the seventh day and *hallowed* it." In priestly theology, this primordial blessing places a divine imprimatur on the distinction between ordinary time and sacred time. This distinction reflects the priestly understanding that the regular passing of "days and years" (Gen. 1:14) must be punctuated by holy times that keep creation tuned to God's hopes and expectations. Toward that end, Leviticus 23 turns to instructions concerning the seventh day, which is "a sabbath to the Lord" (v. 3), and builds on its model a calendar that marks the holy days that Israel must observe.

The general contours of this calendar are relatively clear, as is the sabbatical principle that gives it definition. The year is divided into two halves: the spring, which begins with the first month of the year (mid-March; v. 5), and the fall, which begins with the seventh month (September–October; v. 24). The two halves of the year are in turn punctuated by six festivals, three in the spring—Passover and Unleavened Bread, a seven-day festival (vv. 4–8); First Fruits (vv. 9–14); and Weeks (vv. 15–22)—and three in the fall, all in the seventh month—Trumpets (vv. 23–25); the Day of Purification (vv. 26–32); and Booths, which, like its counterpart in the spring, is also a seven-day festival (vv. 33–36, 39–43). Scattered throughout the year and interwoven with its festivals are seven "holy convocation" days that are marked by solemn rest: the first and seventh days of Unleavened Bread (vv. 7–8), the day the Festival of Weeks is celebrated (v. 21), the first day of the seventh month (v. 24), the Day of Purification (v. 27), and the first and last days of Booths (vv. 35–36). The calendar as a whole is framed by an introduction (vv. 1–2), in which God commands Moses to deliver these instructions to the Israelites, and a conclusion (v. 44), which reports that

Moses did what God commanded. The strategic repetition of the formula "I am the Lord your God" at the end of the instructions concerning the spring festivals (v. 22) and again at the end of those concerning the fall festivals (v. 43) links the entire chapter to chapters 18–22 and to the God of Sinai, whose covenant with Israel requires that it exemplify holiness in all aspects of its life (see the commentary on chapters 18–20 and 21–22).

This rather straightforward presentation of the chapter's outline, however, belies its complexity. Calendrical matters are presented in various and often conflicting ways in Hebrew Scripture, as may be discerned from the five calendar texts in the Pentateuch (Exod. 23:12–19; 34:17–26; Deut. 16:1–17; Leviticus 23; Numbers 28–29). There is considerable debate concerning the relationship between Leviticus 23 and Numbers 28–29, which are the only two calendars that list all the major holy days. The majority of scholars has argued that Numbers 28–29 is the later of the two calendars. Milgrom, following Knohl, has convincingly countered that Leviticus 23 is the product of the Holiness School, which produced an inner-priestly redaction of an earlier version of the calendar in Numbers 28–29 (Milgrom, *Leviticus 23–27*, pp. 2054–56; Knohl, pp. 8–45). Moreover, there are clear indications that Leviticus 23 has itself gone through several layers of redaction. The most obvious is the expansion concerning the Festival of Booths in vv. 39–43, which adds several details not found in vv. 33–36. However these issues may be resolved, it is clear that the instructions in Leviticus 23 are addressed primarily to the laity. As such, the emphasis is not on the details of the sacrifices to be offered on the various holy festivals, as in Numbers 28–29, but instead on the summons to remember and observe the sabbatical principle that orders the liturgical year.

Introduction: The Sabbath (23:1–3)

The instructions concerning "holy convocations" are addressed not to the priests, as in the previous pericope (21:1, 16: 22:2), but to the laity (v. 2). It is they who are charged with responsibility for sustaining the fixed times of public worship that will keep the community focused on God's abiding summons to live as holy people. Clearly, the priests are also indispensable for this worship, but ultimately only the people can translate worship into faithful living. The general parameters for the "fixed times" that become occasions for worship are encoded in God's design for creation's harmony. According to Gen. 1:14, they are grounded in the rhythmic movement of the sun, the moon, and the stars that mark the "seasons" and measure the "days and years."

173

That the first command concerns the observance of the Sabbath (v. 3) is instructive on several counts. The seventh day differs from the six festivals described in the succeeding verses. Whereas they are annual occasions whose place on the calendar Israel determines by calculating the shifting phases of the moon, the seventh day is a weekly occurrence that falls where it does because God has so decreed it. The Sabbath is therefore not a time that Israel must fix on the calendar; it is a day God has already established and commanded Israel to observe. For this and other reasons, many commentators regard the Sabbath instructions to be an interpolation (e.g., Milgrom, *Leviticus 23–27*, pp. 1952–56).

From another perspective, however, the placement of Sabbath instructions at the beginning of the list of holy days is quite appropriate, for it effectively provides the theological model upon which the rest of the calendar is built (see below, "Further Reflections on Sacred Time"). The Sabbath is the only day whose observance is commanded in the Decalogue, and this command is, in turn, the only one that is grounded in creation theology (Milgrom, *Leviticus 23–27*, p. 1960):

> Remember the sabbath day, and *keep it holy*. Six days you shall labor and do all your work. But the seventh day is a sabbath to the LORD your God; you shall not do any work. . . . For in six days the LORD made heaven and earth, the sea, and all that is in them, but rested on the seventh day; therefore the LORD blessed the seventh day and *consecrated it*. (Exod. 20:8–10a, 11)

Two points deriving from this theological grounding for Sabbath observance deserve reflection. First, the command to keep the Sabbath day holy, that is, to sanctify the day by setting it apart from the other six days, engages the people in an act of imaging God. The subject of the verb "keep holy" in Exod. 20:8 is Israel; in v. 11 the subject of the verb "make holy/consecrate" is God. While God bestows upon the day its foundational quality of holiness, Israel is summoned to complementary acts of sanctification that sustain God's primordial work. The explicit rationale for doing so is that Israel's *work* and *rest* should image God's work and rest in creating and sustaining a world that always yearns to realize its capacity to be "very good" (cf. Gen. 1:31). T. Fretheim's observation makes the point nicely: "Sabbath-keeping is creation-keeping. To keep the sabbath is to participate in God's intention for the rhythm of creation" (Fretheim, *Exodus*, p. 230).

Second, observing the Sabbath prepares Israel for a working-resting-working rhythm that sustains and extends what God "finished" at creation with ongoing acts of creaturely creativity. Leviticus 23:3 describes the seventh day as a day of "complete rest" (cf. 23:24, 32, 39).

While the rest envisioned is total and involves a complete cessation of work, it is also a rest in anticipation of the return to work. In other words, the Sabbath is an uncoupling from work that enables and energizes a resumption of work, now freshly charged with the memory of ultimate objectives: to uphold and nurture the very good world God has entrusted to the human community.

We may get our bearings on this matter by placing Lev. 23:3 alongside Gen. 2:3b: "God rested from all the work that he had done in creation." The words "that he had done in creation" translate two verbs in Hebrew: *bārāʾ* ("create") and *ʿāśâ* ("make"). The first verb, which in Hebrew always occurs with God as the subject of the action, is reserved for the wondrous works that only God can bring into existence. The second verb is the common word for human creativity. In Gen. 2:3, for the first time, the two verbs are used as virtual synonyms, a suggestive hint that God's unique creative capacities actually include, model, and invite a complementary human creativity. One implication of this suggestive rhetoric is that when God rests from divine creativity that models human creativity on the seventh day, it is not for the purpose of retiring from the world. It is rather a rest that awaits and expects subsequent acts of human creativity that will bring forth new and future creations. Ibn Ezra captures this sabbatical symmetry between God's creation and humankind's re-creation by stating that God rested from all the work that God created in order "[for man] to [continue to] do [thenceforth]" (cited in Sarna, p. 15). In the liturgical calendar that Leviticus 23 now commissions, what "man continues to do thenceforth" is envisioned as a rhythm of work and "sabbatical rest" that honors creation and sustains God's best hopes for its wholeness and prosperity (see further Balentine, pp. 94–95).

The Spring Festivals (23:4–22)

The liturgical calendar is tuned to the agricultural year, and as such it punctuates the regular work cycles of planting and harvesting with intentional stops for recentering reflection on God's design for the world. The year is divided into two halves, the first six months of spring and summer, and the second six months of fall and winter. Three festivals occur in the first six months: Passover and Unleavened Bread, First Fruits, and Weeks.

Passover and Unleavened Bread (vv. 5–8). The details of these two festivals are found in Exod. 12:1–20 and Num. 28:17–25, respectively. Leviticus 23 presumes both texts and does little more than offer a brief summary of the information they provide. Passover and Unleavened Bread were originally distinct festivals. The former is usually

175

associated with the spring rituals of the presettlement period, when shepherds sought to secure the successful movement of their flocks to summer pasture. The latter likely has its origins in the rituals of farmers as they sought to secure the fertility of their flocks and crops after the settlement in Canaan. When and how the two festivals came to be celebrated as one is a matter of considerable debate, although it is clear that the combination had taken place at least by the time of Deuteronomy (see Deut. 16:1–7). No doubt the combination was influenced by the memory of the exodus experience, which reports that on the night God passed over the houses of the Israelites enslaved in Egypt, they ate the paschal lamb along with unleavened bread and bitter herbs, in preparation for the ensuing journey to freedom (Exod. 12:8).

Leviticus 23 stipulates simply that Passover is to be observed at twilight on the fourteenth day of the first month (v. 5), which places it during the first full month after the spring equinox. The next day marks the beginning of a seven-day Festival of Unleavened Bread, so called because during this period Israel was to eat no leavened bread. The ritual reenacts the memory of the exodus, when the Israelites, prepared to flee Egypt when the time was right, had no time for baking bread with a leavening ingredient. The Festival of Unleavened Bread is described as a *ḥāg*, which indicates that it involved a "pilgrimage," either to a local, nearby altar or, especially in later times, to the central sanctuary in Jerusalem. The one prohibition cited is that Israel should refrain from any activity requiring physical labor on the first and seventh days of Unleavened Bread. The Hebrew phrase that NRSV renders with the one word "work" (vv. 7, 8) occurs eleven times in conjunction with what is forbidden during festival days (Lev. 23:7, 8, 21, 35, 36; Num. 28:18, 25, 26; 29:1, 12, 35). The prohibition is similar to that which applies to the Sabbath day (v. 3) and the Day of Atonement (v. 28; cf. v. 32). In these cases, however, the Hebrew term "any work" is more restrictive, implying that apart from these two days when "complete rest" is required, the Israelites are permitted to continue with their normal activities during the festival days (Milgrom, *Leviticus 23–27*; pp. 1977–78).

First Fruits (vv. 9–14). "On the day after the sabbath" (v. 11), presumably the eighth day after the seven days of the Unleavened Bread, Israel is to bring an offering of first fruits of the harvest to the priest. The offering consists of the first sheaf of barley, the first grain to ripen in the spring, plus a burnt offering of an unblemished year-old lamb, a grain offering of two-tenths of an ephah mixed with oil, and a drink offering of one-fourth of a hin of wine. The grain offering is twice the normal amount (Num. 28:13), which may signify the hope that God will bless the forthcoming harvest abundantly. The requirement of the libation of wine along with the burnt offering and the grain offering is absent from the sacrificial laws in Leviticus 1–7, but it is present in Numbers 28–29 (e.g., 28:7, 14; 29:6, 11), which provides additional evidence that Leviticus 23 was composed with this earlier version of the calendar in mind.

The priest raises the sheaf of barley "before the Lord" (v. 11), a ritual act that sanctifies the offering for its special use. The objective of the offering is twofold: to give thanks for the present harvest and to ask God's blessings on the harvests to come. Until thanksgivings are offered for the first fruits, none of the new harvest may be eaten.

Weeks (vv. 15–22). The Festival of Weeks (so named in Num. 28:26; cf. Exod. 34:22; Deut. 16:10) occurs seven weeks after Passover and Unleavened Bread, that is, fifty days, counting from the "the day after the sabbath," on which first fruits are offered, until the day after the seventh sabbath. The Greek name for the festival is Pentecost ("fiftieth"), which the New Testament associates with the fiftieth day after Jesus' resurrection, when the Holy Spirit descended on the apostles in Jerusalem (Acts 2). The Jewish festival is conventionally associated with the end of the harvest period. Milgrom has called attention to rabbinic discussions that suggest it more likely marks the beginning of the wheat harvest. In this view, Weeks parallels First Fruits, which marks the beginning of the barley harvest, and as such serves the similar purpose of thanking God for the abundance of what has been received and expressing the hope that God will also bless future harvests (Milgrom, *Leviticus 23–27*, pp. 1991–92).

The offering for this one-day festival consists of two loaves of leavened bread baked from the new wheat crop, which are elevated to God in a ritual of sanctification (cf. v. 11). People must also present seven one-year-old unblemished lambs, one bull, and two rams for a burnt offering, along with their cereal offering and libations as gifts that give pleasure to God (v. 18). In addition, a goat is presented as a "purification" offering and two one-year-old male lambs as a "well-being" offering. The primary motivation behind all the offerings is joy: As the harvest season draws to a close and the crops are gathered, Israel has good reason to be mindful once again of the abundance of God's blessings.

Indeed, when the three festivals of the first half of year are considered in sequence, each contributes a verse to a common hymn of thanksgiving. That thanksgiving is anchored in Israel's peculiar and palpable realization of creation's bounty. Given the gift of freedom and a land of their own to inhabit, the memory of which Israel rekindles each year with the rituals of Passover and Unleavened Bread, offering thanks for the first fruits of barley and wheat this land bestows on them is but a logical, we may even suppose spontaneous, response to the God who continues to bless and prosper Israel so faithfully. In this context, then, it should not be surprising that the last words of the final observance of the first half of the year remind Israel that with great blessing there always comes great responsibility. Returning to a command that has already been given (19:9–10), v. 22 reiterates that Israelites must mirror God's compassion for them by extending a like compassion for the more vulnerable persons in their world. When they harvest the bounty of their fields, they must leave some grain for the poor. The self-identification formula that concludes this command, "I am the Lord your God," grounds Israel's ethical responsibility once again in the overarching commission that ultimately governs every aspect of its life: "*I am*," therefore, "*you shall be*" (see the commentary on Leviticus 18–20).

The Fall Festivals (23:23–43)

The seventh month is the most sacred month in the liturgical calendar. The three festivals that occur during this month—Trumpets, the Day of Purification, and Booths—total ten days; hence one-third of the month is marked for special observance. The significance of the seventh month, which is the annual analogue to the weekly Sabbath day, is inextricably tied to priestly creation theology. The ordering of the Decalogue (Exod. 20:1–17; cf. Deut. 5:6–21) positions the command to observe the Sabbath day (Commandment Four) between the mandate to love God with unqualified religious devotion (Commandments One through Three) and the mandate to live ethically in community with others in ways that reflect one's love for God (Commandments Five through Ten). This structure for the commandments suggests that keeping the Sabbath day holy is the primary ritual by which Israel calibrates its obedience to God's ultimate design for its life. To profess love for God without the corresponding deeds that manifest this love to others will not constitute the obedience God requires; neither will it sustain the "very good" world God has created (see the commentary above on vv. 1–3). In a similar fashion, the seventh month, which falls at the critical intersection between the end of the harvest season and the beginning of the rainy season, marks a pivotal moment when Israel recenters itself with rituals that refresh its commitment to be good stewards of the world God has entrusted to its care. Whereas the rituals in the first half of the year invite Israel's affirmation of the bounty God has faithfully provided, the rituals of the seventh month invite

Israel's commitment to continue living in such a way that God will honor its fidelity by providing the rains for the next harvest.

Trumpets (vv. 23–25). The first day of the seventh month is commemorated with a loud blast of the trumpet. The ram's horn, or shofar, is most likely the instrument used, although the text does not give details. Trumpet blasts serve a variety of purposes in ancient Israel, but the most important one for understanding the use in this context is the summons to Israel to break camp and embark on a mission (often described in military terms; see Num. 10:9; Jer. 4:19; Amos 1:14) that responds to God's call and requires God's presence for success. It is instructive, but probably not determinative, for understanding the original meaning of this festival that it later came to be associated with Rosh Hashanah and thus with the New Year's Day, which cultures throughout the ancient Near East understood to be the time when the gods determined their destinies for the coming year.

Beyond the general requirement of rest and the presentation of "offerings" (for the list, see Num. 29:1–6), the most important detail provided about Trumpets is that it is a "reminder" (v. 24; NAB; cf. REB: "a day of remembrance"). It is likely that the term conveys two related ideas. On the one hand, the observance of this day clearly constitutes a *reminder to Israel* of God's care and provision. On the other, Priestly texts also use the term to refer to things that invite *God to remember* divine commitments to Israel. The day functions, therefore, much like the stones set into the priest's ephod (Exod. 28:12) or the names of the twelve tribes inscribed on the priest's breastplate (Exod. 28:29), both of which are reminders that keep before God the divine promise to be ever present in Israel's life. What is most striking about such a rite of divine reminder is that it is God who commands that it be observed. God gives to Israel the very means by which it may keep God tuned to its needs. In sum, the sound of the trumpet blast arouses Israel and God to reciprocal fidelity.

The Day of Purification (vv. 26–32). The Day of Purification falls on the tenth day of the seventh month. The general contours of this day are described in Leviticus 16. To that text may be added Num. 29:7–11, which further elaborates on the "offering by fire" that is merely summarized here (Lev. 23:27). Such details are assumed in the present text, which now supplements them with a threefold repetition of the command to fast and abstain from work (vv. 28–32). Such a requirement emphasizes that it is not only the sanctuary that must be purified from the effects of Israel's sin. The people themselves also need cleansing. By refraining from food and work, they enact a ritual pause in the

179

midst of the routine of everyday life that invites them to recognize where they have erred and to seek God's forgiveness. When they have done so, the Day of Purification invites the people to embark on a new beginning, with the refurbished hope that they may now live in ways that more faithfully honor the holiness of the God in whose sanctuary they profess their commitments.

The failure to comply with these requirements is stated with a stark severity. Those who do not fast will be "cut off" (v. 29). Those who do not abstain from work will be punished by God directly (v. 30). As the only case in the priestly instructions where God is described as *causing* an offender to perish, this latter penalty dramatically underscores the importance that God attaches to this auspicious day. In God's judgment, the failure to cease from human labor in recognition of the rest that joins the community to God's rhythm of working and resting is a capital offense. It puts the community, and indeed the world, at risk in a way that is no less serious than taking another's life.

The Festival of Booths (vv. 33–36, 39–43). The Festival of Booths (also called Tabernacles or Ingathering) begins on the fifteenth day of the seventh month and lasts for seven days. The first day and the eighth day, the day after the festival ends, are "holy convocation" days on which no labor is to be done. Sacrifices are to be offered on each of the seven days. Only the general term "offerings by fire" is used here (v. 36); the text assumes the details provided in Num. 29:12–34.

The addendum in vv. 39–43 embellishes this brief description with two points. First, it associates this festival with the memory of the time when Israel lived in "booths" during its wilderness journey from Egypt to Canaan (vv. 42–43). Second, it remembers and now ritually reenacts this time as an occasion of great joy in the midst of very precarious circumstances (v. 40). Toward this end, the ritual calls for Israel to take the branches of "majestic trees"—perhaps palm, myrtle, and poplar trees— and "rejoice before the Lord for seven days." The precise meaning of this ritual is difficult to determine, but each of the trees cited, even though the names are open to debate, seems to be associated with the bounty of the promised land, not the barrenness of the wilderness. In terms of creation theology, the bounty of the earth that surpasses barrenness, like the divine order that exceeds primordial chaos, is reason to praise God.

Further Reflections on Sacred Time

180

The notion of a calendar that marks only sacred days—and not a single ordinary day—may strike the average reader as quite strange. In the ongoing press to be good "time managers," we learn, almost in self-defense, to *schedule our work* in the hope there may be some *time left over for our rest*. It is the work that gives us definition and security in the world, and it seems only prudent that it take precedence. Thus, when we open our calendars to mark the appointments around which we schedule our lives, we instinctively look for Monday–Friday, typically 9 A.M.–5 P.M., although both boundaries for the workweek are constantly eroding. To be sure, religious institutions will keep us at least somewhat mindful that the calendar also includes holy days, but their effect on our lives too often seems minimal, and our observance of them is sporadic. If we are present in a congregation on Passover or Easter, we will join in the liturgy; if we are not, the days may come and go without our knowing it, even though the sales at the malls may keep us vaguely apprised of seasonal shifts that are cleverly pegged to propitious times for splicing a buying spree into our busy schedules. The thought that we are *commanded* to observe holy days is not, in most cases, the first imperative we consider when we mark our calendars. Practically speaking, we tune our lives to ordinary time, not sacred time.

The priestly calendar in Leviticus 23 envisions time differently. It centers on holy days, not ordinary days, and insists that they provide the compass for navigating every minute that falls in between. It makes the daring claim that holy days are not the leftovers in the calendar; they are instead the core that gives definition and purpose to everything else. Practically speaking, this calendar commands us to tune our lives to sacred time, failing which there can be no order to anything else we may do. On first, and perhaps even second and third inspection, it seems an odd perspective. It is likely that we will consider such a command little more than a further intrusion into schedules that are already overcrowded, an imposition that only makes life more difficult, not less, to manage. To invite reflection on this matter, I offer two contemporary perspectives that may provide a framework for reevaluating our priorities. Not coincidentally, both are grounded in the Jewish tradition.

The first comes from Leon Wieseltier, literary editor of the *New Republic* (see also "Further Reflections on Voluntary Offerings" at the end of Leviticus 3). Wieseltier begins his book *Kaddish* with these words:

> On March 24, 1996, which was Nisan 5, 5756, my father died. In the year that followed I said the prayer known as the mourner's kaddish three times daily, during the morning service, the afternoon service, and the evening service. In a synagogue in Washington and, when I was away from home, in synagogues elsewhere. It was my duty to say it, for reasons that will become clear in this book.

181

> I was struck almost immediately by the poverty of my knowledge about the ritual that I was performing with such fidelity. And it was not long before I understood that I would not succeed in insulating the rest of my existence from the impact of this obscure and arduous practice. The symbols were seeping into everything. A season of sorrow became a season of soul-renovation, for which I was not at all prepared. (Wieseltier, p. vii)

In the course of the journey through the ritual times of this year, Wieseltier kept a journal of his thoughts. From the entries he records, one gathers that when the year began, he was not an observant Jew. He was going through the motions of saying the ritual of kaddish, because this is what his father would have wanted. He merely recited the words, although he did not understand them and had little reason to think that he would believe them even if he did. But something unexpected happened to him during the year of marking sacred time. The more he said the words, the more he wanted to understand what they meant. The more he understood, the more he wanted to know. And the more he learned, the more he wanted to do the ritual. His journal traces the slow and steady trek toward what he calls his year of "soul-renovation."

After a short while, he enters these words into the diary:

> I have begun to notice that my prayers are refreshing my life with language. Three times a day, Hebrew music. (p. 62)

Then a few pages later: "Ritual is the conversion of essences into act" (p. 68). A few pages further on: "I study the old texts because I hope to be infected by their dimensions, to attain the size of what I read" (p. 75). About a third of the way through the year, he adds these words:

> A lovely morning, a heavy heart. A few months ago I worried that my mourner's life would interfere with the rest of my life. Now I worry that the rest of my life will interfere with my mourner's life. The temptation is growing to surrender to the drill and to the sadness. (p. 131)

By year's end the immersion into the ritual has taken hold, and Wieseltier can no more imagine life uncoupled from sacred time than living without breathing. Two entries from the last day chronicle the transformation:

> On my walk back to work I pause at the little plaza with the statue of Longfellow. It is no more than an island in the traffic, but an island in the traffic is what I want. The old poet sits sternly above me. His right hand has drooped over the side of his chair, and he holds a book. He is considering what he has just read, or forgetting it. I sit under a

> naked tree, on a wooden bench that shows its winters, and I watch the pigeons. My head empties out. I am beyond reasons. I am aware only that I am aware. I know only that there is something rather than nothing. This is the rustle of being. It passes quickly and I return to work. (p. 573)

> Then I said the kaddish. I stood in the ashes of fury and spoke the sentences of praise. Was that my voice? It was no longer the effusion of woe. Magnified, I said. Sanctified, I said. I looked above me, I looked below me, I looked around me. With my own eyes I saw magnificence. (p. 585)

Perhaps Wieseltier's journey is paradigmatic for those who measure their busied lives by the celebrations of sacred times. Perhaps the more we observe the sacred moments that keep us tuned to God's hopes and expectations for us and our world, the more the ordinary times are enlarged, transformed, ennobled by a *chronos* that ticks to an inviolable vision. As Wieseltier discovered, much to his surprise, the small but repetitive punctuations of life's calendar by sacred time gradually grow into sentences, the sentences into paragraphs, then chapters, until finally a life's story has taken on a new shape. Israel's calendar is punctuated by "holy convocations" that keep it mindful that God always intends life to be more about "something" than "nothing." Its response to this realization is to "rejoice before the Lord" (23:40). Wieseltier's observance of kaddish generated a similar awakening and an equal exuberance: "With my own eyes, I saw magnificence." Neither the holy time he honored nor the response that it invoked from him is mentioned in Leviticus 23, but both may be said to have their roots there.

The second discernment about sacred time, specifically Sabbath time, comes from Abraham Heschel, one of the foremost Jewish scholars of the twentieth century. In *The Sabbath: Its Meaning for Modern Man*, Heschel relates the following legend:

> At the time when God was giving the Torah to Israel, He said to them: My children! If you accept the Torah and observe my mitzvot, I will give you for all eternity a thing most precious that I have in my possession.

> —And what, asked Israel, is that precious thing which Thou wilt give us if we obey Thy Torah?

> —The world to come.

> —Show us in this world an example of the world to come.

> —The Sabbath is an example of the world to come. (p. 73)

183

The liturgical calendar in Leviticus 23 is modeled on the Sabbath day (v. 3), which, as Heschel's legend makes clear, is among the most precious gifts God bestows on Israel. As suggested in the commentary above, the Torah's command to observe the Sabbath is itself but an extension of the claim in Genesis 1–2 that a sabbatical principle undergirds God's primordial design for the world. This principle takes embryonic shape in the seventh day, which God sanctifies with a divine rest that invites all of creation to celebrate the wonder of what God has wrought, even as it prepares to contribute to this wonder with ongoing acts of creaturely creativity. The principle extends to the liturgy of covenant making at Sinai (Exodus 19–24), which portrays Sabbath observance (the Fourth Commandment) as the linchpin that holds together the Decalogue's twin imperatives to love God absolutely (the First through Third Commandments) and to live in the world with absolute fidelity to God's purposes (the Fifth through Tenth Commandments). The sabbatical principle extends still further to the tabernacle and its rituals. Exodus 25–31 and 35–40 depict the building of the sanctuary as the completion of the work God began at creation (see the commentary on Lev. 1:1–2). Leviticus presents itself as the continuation of the liturgy at Sinai, only now in the more intimate form of God's direct address from the tabernacle, which from this point forward becomes the only place in all creation that is said to be filled with the "glory of God" (Exod. 40:35). From this tabernacle, Leviticus suggests, God himself extends the sabbatical principle by using *seven* divine speeches to convey instructions for sacrifice (Leviticus 1–7), commanding *seven* consecrated steps through which the priests are ordained (Leviticus 8), and setting forth a liturgical calendar in which the *seventh* day, the *seventh* month, and the *seven* "holy convocation" days sprinkled throughout the whole reverberate with the memory of creation's first Sabbath day.

The Torah's long trajectory of sabbatical imagery informs the legend Heschel invites us to ponder. I am particularly struck by the fact that he turned to this legend about Sabbath in the aftermath of the calamitous experiences of World War II. His book was published in 1948, just three years after the world had been broken and emptied of both revelation and reason by the killing of six million Jews. In a fractured world, where as far as the human eye could see all that is sacred about life had forever buckled under the weight of ordinary time's murderous tyranny, this Jewish scholar found the scriptural claim about Sabbath to be both comforting and redemptive. Sabbath is the sign and the summons to believe that by God's decree, the immediate will never be sufficiently empowered to defeat the eternal. By calling all human-

184

ity, not Jews alone, to remember and share in that which is eternal in time, the Sabbath invites us to participate in the holiness of the special day that empowers the sanctification of all time. In Heschel's words, Sabbath prepares us to turn "from the world of creation to the creation of the world" (Heschel, *The Sabbath*, p. 10; see further Balentine, pp. 236–38, 242–44).

Finally, we may note that the New Testament embraces and commends the celebration of holy seasons that transform ordinary time with sacred possibilities. Three of the festivals commanded in Leviticus 23 are associated with the most significant acts in Christ's ministry: Passover, with Jesus' death on the cross; Unleavened Bread, with his Easter resurrection; and Weeks or Pentecost, with the postresurrection gift of the Holy Spirit. The Festival of Booths or Tabernacles is the backdrop for the Gospel of John's presentation of Jesus' promise of abundant life: "On the last day of the festival, the great day, while Jesus was standing there, he cried out, 'Let anyone who is thirsty come to me, and let the one who believes in me drink. As the scripture has said, "Out of the believer's heart shall flow rivers of living water"'" (John 7:37–38).

The Sabbath, too, though frequently a topic of contention between Jesus and Jewish authorities, remains nevertheless central for his life and the model of worship he commends to his followers. As the Gospels report, Jesus began his ministry by going to synagogue on the Sabbath "as was his custom" (Luke 4:16; cf. Matt. 13:53–58; Mark 6:1–6). In keeping with Jesus' model, the epistle to the Hebrews understands the Sabbath rest to remain an open invitation to all who would participate with God in the creational promise that exists from "the foundation of the world" (Heb. 4:3). We may, of course, choose to neglect this promise; but as this writer makes clear, it is Jesus' abiding hope that none will do so: "So then, a sabbath rest still remains for the people of God; for those who enter God's rest also cease from their labors as God did from his. Let us therefore make every effort to enter that rest, so that no one fall through such disobedience as theirs" (Heb. 4:9–11; cf. v. 1).

In the words of the poet George Herbert, Sundays (and Sabbaths) are the pillars "On which heav'n's palace arched lies: / The other days fill up the spare / And hollow room with vanities." When we give ourselves to their abiding promise, we receive "blessings more plentiful than hope":

> The Sundays of man's life
> Threaded together on time's string,
> Make bracelets to adorn the wife

Of the eternal glorious King.
On Sunday heaven's gate stands ope:
Blessings are plentiful and rife,
    More plentiful than hope.
                (Herbert, "Sunday,"
            Complete English Poems,
                ed. J. Tobin, p. 69)

Leviticus 24:1–23
Oil, Bread, and Blasphemy

Chapter 24 comprises two distinct units. The first, vv. 1–9, provides instructions concerning the oil for the tabernacle lamps (vv. 2–4) and the bread for the tabernacle table (vv. 5–9). The second, vv. 10–23, is a narrative about a case of blasphemy. The relationship between these two units has long been a challenge for interpreters. Verses 1–9 fit well with what has preceded, for they may be viewed as a continuation of instructions in chapter 23 concerning the laity's responsibility for maintaining the public cult. When the harvest season is completed, the people must bring a portion of the vintage, which will be used for the oil that lights the lamp in the tabernacle, and a portion of the grain, which will be used for the bread placed on the tabernacle table. The narrative about blasphemy seems at first oddly disconnected from such concerns, and commentators frequently bracket it as a separate unit, having little or nothing to do with what precedes or follows (e.g., Hartley, pp. 403–13; Noth, pp. 178–81; Wenham, pp. 307–13).

Others have sought a solution in the thematic and structural relationships between this narrative and the longer one in 10:1–20, both of which pose intriguing issues concerning the juxtaposition of law and narrative in Priestly literature (see especially Douglas, *Leviticus as Literature*, pp. 195–217, and "Forbidden Animals in Leviticus"). One suggestive clue that contributes to this discussion is the sevenfold repetition of the name YHWH ("Lord") in vv. 1–9. The emphasis on the purity of the presentations of the oil and the bread to YHWH provides a marked and possibly intentional echo of the condemnation of the blasphemy of the divine name in 24:10–23. The *laity's defilement* of God's holy name *by word* provides in turn an evocative parallel with the *priests' defilement* of God's holy sanctuary *by an unacceptable ritual act* in chapter 10. These and other possible connections are explored further in the commentary below.

The Oil and the Bread (24:1–9)

The instructions concerning the oil for the lamp fulfill the command in Exod. 27:20–21. Moses commands the people to bring "pure oil of beaten olives" (Lev. 24:2) for lighting the lamp. The details indicate that the olives are to be beaten by hand, then strained to remove any impurities. Aaron is to set up the lamp on the south (or left) side of the inner sanctum, facing the "curtain of the covenant," that is, just before the veil that marks the entrance to the Holy of Holies, which contains the ark of the covenant. It is unclear whether the text refers to the traditional seven-branched menorah (Exod. 25:31–40; 37:17–24) or perhaps to an earlier, simpler form of the lamp (cf. Meyers). The one detail emphasized is that the lamp is to burn "regularly" (*tāmîd*; vv. 2, 3, 4). It is to be lit every evening, then rekindled before it dies out each morning. The rationale for the ritual is not provided. Given the tabernacle's extension of creational imagery, it is reasonable to suppose that the perpetually burning light sustains the memory of God's abiding promise to create light out of darkness (see the discussion of "The Tamid" at 6:8–7:38). As Gerstenberger puts it, "God forfeits none of his power, even as the sun 'goes down.' He asserts himself daily against the powers of chaos, and dispatches the sun on its heroic course" (Gerstenberger, p. 336).

The people are also charged to supply the grain for the bread placed on the table that sits on the north (or right) side of the tabernacle, opposite the lamp (vv. 5–9; cf. Exod. 25:23–30; 37:10–16). The bread goes by various names in other texts: "bread of presence" (Exod. 25:30; 35:13; 39:36); "regular bread" (Num. 4:7); "rows of bread" (Neh. 10:33; 1 Chron. 9:32; 33:29). From the people's gifts Moses bakes twelve loaves, each made of two-tenths of an ephah of fine flour. The loaves are to be arranged (or piled) on the table every Sabbath day in two rows of six, along with "pure frankincense," which provides a "token offering" (see the commentary on 2:1–3). When new loaves are supplied each week, the priests consume the old bread in a holy place. It is assigned as their priestly portion (see 6:14–18).

As with the oil, the rationale for the ritual of the bread is not explained. Perhaps the ritual is informed by the common practice in the ancient Near East of supplying bread as a food offering for the gods. Whatever distant linkage there may be to this understanding, however, it is evident that Israel's priests have shaped this ritual in accordance with their distinctive theological perspectives. The most important clue is the designation of the ritual as a "covenant forever" (v. 8). This phrase occurs for the first time in Priestly literature in Gen. 9:16, which reports

187

God's postflood promise to establish an "everlasting covenant" with a still sinful but redeemable world. Subsequent Priestly texts apply the same phrase with still more precision to Israel, suggesting that God's cosmic promises will be uniquely realized in the peculiar covenant relationship with this people. God establishes an "everlasting covenant" with Abraham (Gen. 17:7, 13, 19), institutes Sabbath observance as a "sign" that keeps this "everlasting covenant" forever tied to God's creational design (Exod. 31:17), and establishes a "covenant of perpetual priesthood" with Aaron's descendants, who provide the ritual leadership to sustain God's intentions (Num. 25:13). Within this trajectory of thought, Lev. 24:8 suggests that the twelve loaves of tabernacle bread, which call to mind the twelve tribes of Israel, are an essential reminder of the "everlasting covenant" that keeps both God and Israel focused on their commitments to each other (cf. Joosten, pp. 119–20).

A Case of Blasphemy (24:10–23)

The case of blasphemy described in these verses follows a pattern—crime (vv. 10–11), imprisonment (v. 12), oracular decisions (vv. 13–22), and resolution (v. 23)—that is found in three other cases in Hebrew Scripture (Num. 9:1–14; 15:32–36; 27:1–11). As M. Fishbane has shown, each case is set in the wilderness period when Moses was confronted with a controversy that could not be decided by any established legal precedent. In each incident, the Israelites first bring the problem to Moses, who in turn seeks a resolution from God (Fishbane, *Biblical Interpretation*, pp. 98–102). The case in Leviticus 24 involves a man of mixed parentage—his mother was an Israelite, his father an Egyptian—who fights with an Israelite and in the course of that fight blasphemes the name of God. That a violation has occurred is clear: Cursing God is forbidden (Exod. 22:27; cf. Exod. 20:7; Deut. 5:11). The questions the violation presents to Moses are, does the law apply to a half-Israelite, and if so, what is the appropriate penalty?

The narrative places its emphasis on the oracular decisions that address these questions (vv. 13–22). God's instructions are that the offender should be taken outside the camp. All those who heard the blasphemy are to lay their hands on the offender's head. The rite conveys the community's understanding that they have all been adversely affected by the sin of this one. The whole community is then instructed to participate in the punishment: death by stoning (vv. 13–14).

The crime and the punishment God decrees are then set within the framework of seven laws that provide a context for understanding (vv. 15–22). At the beginning (v. 16b) and end (v. 22a), God decrees that the

188

laws apply equally to resident aliens and native Israelites. The first two laws concern blaspheming the name of God. The remaining five address violations of human beings and animals, at the center of which is placed the *lex talionis* principle that undergirds the whole. The structure may be illustrated as follows:

Aliens as well as citizens (v. 16b)

1. Anyone who curses God shall bear the sin (v. 15)
2. One who blasphemes the name of the Lord shall be put to death (v. 16a)
3. Anyone who kills a human being shall be put to death (v. 17)
4. Anyone who kills an animal shall make restitution for it (v. 18)
    5. Anyone who maims another shall suffer the same punishment in return (v. 19a)
        fracture for fracture, eye for eye, tooth for tooth (v. 20a)
        the injury inflicted is the injury to be suffered (v. 20b)
6. One who kills an animal shall make restitution for it (v. 21a)
7. One who kills a human being shall be put to death (v. 21b)

You shall have one law for the alien and for the citizen (v. 22)

The arrangement of these laws invites two observations. First, it correlates blasphemy against God (laws 1 and 2) with the taking of life (laws 3–7). Both are treated as capital crimes punishable by death. This correlation, in turn, provides a key to understanding the seriousness of the blasphemy incident Moses must adjudicate. When any person, native Israelite or resident alien, curses God by saying something like "may God be damned," that person has made a rhetorical assault that theoretically seeks to take God's life. Underlying this judgment is the presumption that words no less than deeds have the power both to enhance life and to curtail it. Inasmuch as one may bless God with words of praise that honor and enlarge God's capacity to be God, so one may speak curses that dishonor and minimize the ways in which God desires to be present in the world. The analogue with the human taking or injuring of life is instructive here. To kill another person is to eliminate one who has been created in the image of God (Gen. 1:27; 9:6), which in turn reduces God's capacity to be "bodied forth" in the world. By the same measure, to "maim" persons is to disfigure them in such a way that they can no longer realize their full potential as human beings. The word *maim* (v. 19) is highly suggestive, for it recalls the same term used for the physical blemishes of priests and sacrificial animals that disqualify them from their roles in mediating God's presence

189

in the world (see 21:16–24; 22:22–25; Douglas, "Forbidden Animals in Leviticus," pp. 18–20; Milgrom, *Leviticus 23–27*, p. 2131). In short, the one who blasphemes God has inflicted a malicious wound that diminishes God's life in irrevocable ways.

Second, the principle defining the punishment of the blasphemer is tied to the law of retribution known in Roman jurisprudence as *lex talionis*. The principle has its origin in Mesopotamian law, specifically the laws of Hammurabi, which prescribed proportional punishment for physical injury. Leviticus 24:20a is a variation of the classic formulation of this principle in biblical law: "life for life, eye for eye, tooth for tooth, hand for hand, foot for foot, burn for burn, wound for wound, stripe for stripe" (Exod. 21:23–25; cf. Deut. 19:21).

It is not immediately clear why the case of blasphemy should be tied to the principle of *lex talionis*, but two observations deserve consideration. First, in keeping with Hammurabi's innovative elevation of injuries against persons from civil offenses to capital crime, Leviticus treats blasphemy as a grievous assault against God that is the equivalent of murder. Douglas explicates the proportional punishment required as follows: "The blasphemer has hurled insults at the name of God, let him die by stones hurled at him" (Douglas, *Leviticus as Literature*, p. 202). Second, *lex talionis* in Mesopotamian law was an advance beyond older legal constructs that allowed the rich to make monetary compensation to those they had wrongly injured. Legal statutes that mandated penalties commensurate with the damage done effectively erased the inequalities between the rich and the poor, the person of rank and the commoner, thus enabling a more egalitarian judicial system. Those with wealth could not pay their way out of punishment by compensating their victims; those without could not claim special exemption simply because they could not make a monetary restitution for their offense. The author of Leviticus 24 may have seized on this egalitarian legal principle to buttress the theological conviction that the same law must apply to the native Israelite and the resident alien. In this connection, Milgrom has persuasively argued that one of the principal concerns of the Holiness Code is to extend the requirements of holiness beyond the sanctuary to the promised land on which both Israelites and resident aliens live. The rationale behind this concern is that everyday life, not only the rituals of religious life, must reflect the holiness of God. While resident aliens would not be required to worship Israel's God, they would be expected to honor the prohibitions against cursing God that are incumbent on every Israelite (Milgrom, *Leviticus 23–27*, pp. 2131–32).

One question remains: Why this rather odd departure from the litany of instructions concerning holiness in 17:1–23:9 to a seemingly "intrusive" narrative concerning blasphemy? One solution is to concede that the narrative has little or no connection to the priestly instructions that precede and follow it. Alternatively, we may follow the lead of both legal theorists and biblical scholars who have argued that law and narrative are by nature inextricably intertwined. Legal prescriptions respond to and are necessitated by real-life stories (cf. Cover, Watts). The most inviting hypothesis is proposed by Mary Douglas, who suggests that the two narratives in Lev. 10:1–20 and 24:10–23 have been strategically inserted into the laws as structural markers that provide a hermeneutical clue for reading the entire book (*Leviticus as Literature*, pp. 194–217).

Douglas argues that the "architecture" of the book of Leviticus intentionally corresponds with the architecture of the tabernacle. Addressed to an audience for whom the tabernacle at Sinai was but a distant memory, Leviticus presents itself as a guidebook for a spiritual journey around and into the sacred place that defines Israel's relationship to God and its role in the world God has created. The journey through the book projects the journey through the three zones of the tabernacle.

The journey begins in the outer court with Leviticus 1–7, which provides instructions for sacrifices, and thus brings the readers to the entrance to the inner sanctum. At just this juncture, however, when the promise of moving a step closer to God lies just ahead, chapters 8–10 create a literary pause. The journey requires priests who will faithfully administer the rituals inside the shrine, but as the narrative in 10:1–20 makes clear, the priests' first efforts in this regard end tragically. The narrative of their violation, and the punishment that follows in its wake, corresponds with the first screen that now blocks their entry into the inner sanctum. They and the people they serve must proceed around the tabernacle for further instructions on what is required if they are to distinguish faithfully between the holy and the common, the clean and the unclean (cf. 10:10). Those instructions come in chapters 11–15, following which the rituals for the Day of Purification (chapter 16) offer cleansing that enables the journey to return to its beginning with new possibilities. Chapter 17, the introduction to the Holiness Code, begins where chapter 1 began, with further instructions, now addressed to all Israelites, concerning the gifts of sacrifice that enable proximity to a holy God.

The journey now continues past the first screen and into the inner sanctum. A series of instructions (18:1–24:9) makes clear that holiness requires of the entire community not only ritual purity inside the sanctuary but also ethical fidelity in the everyday affairs outside it. When the

191

instructions concerning the preparation of the lamp and the table in the inner sanctum are completed (24:1–9), the third zone in the tabernacle, the Holy of Holies, would now seem open and available for entry. At just this point, however, Leviticus once again creates a literary pause that brings the journey to a standstill. The narrative about blasphemy in 24:10–23 provides a critical reminder that the holiness of God may be violated by word as well by deed, by everyday life that minimizes God's work in the world as well by ritual acts that defile the devotion offered to God in the sanctuary. The second narrative provides a literary projection of the second tabernacle screen, the veil, through which Israel may not pass until the penalty for disobedience has been paid. When the punishment for blasphemy has been enacted, the spiritual journey into the innermost sanctum of God's earthly presence may continue. The instructions in chapters 25–27 complete the journey with a resounding jubilee promise of the liberty and justice that await all who faithfully commit themselves to God's statutes and ordinances.

The details of Douglas's proposal must surely be scrutinized. Nevertheless, she has shown that the two narratives in 10:1–20 and 24:10–23 may be read as integral parts of the priestly laws that surround them. The former keeps Israel mindful that for all the attention to ritual purity, the sanctity of ritual may be defiled, and especially so by the priests, who bear special responsibilities for the community's religious life. The latter keeps Israel mindful that for all the fidelity to the rites and rituals performed inside the sanctuary, all persons may give the lie to this fidelity by the blasphemies they speak and enact in their everyday life. Taken together, the two narratives bring into view the two major ways of approaching God that Israel has been given: ritual act and spoken word (cf. Milgrom, *Leviticus 23–27*, p. 2141). The *rituals* of the sacrificial system are the priests' responsibility. When they are faithfully enacted, they enable Israel to offer gifts to God that symbolize their devotion and sustain it with concrete deeds. When they are not, the ritual system becomes an empty relic. It neither pleases God nor sustains Israel. The *words* are available to everyone at any time and in any place. When they take the form of honest prayers, they enable every person, irrespective of title or social standing, to approach God in ways that maximize God's capacity to be present in people's lives. When those words are blasphemous, they profane God's name and subvert God's hopes for communion.

The emphasis of 24:10–23, like its counterpart in 10:1–20, is not on the potential for Israel's disobedience, ever-present as this is. It is instead on the ritual acts and the spoken words that provide second chances to change course and rejoin the journey that promises intimacy with God's demanding presence. On the other side of chapter 24, to return to Douglas's suggestive imagery, the entrance to the Holy of Holies beckons. In the rhetorical strategy of Leviticus, the invitation to take the next step comes, as it has since the opening chapter, in the continuing word from God, spoken as if the journey from Sinai toward the promised land were still in progress: "The Lord spoke to Moses on Mount Sinai, saying: Speak to the people of Israel and say to them: When you enter . . ." (25:1).

> It's a long way off but inside it
> There are quite different things going on:
> Festivals at which the poor man
> Is king and the consumptive is
> Healed; mirrors in which the blind look
> At themselves and love looks at them
> Back; and industry is for mending
> The bent bones and the minds fractured
> By life. It's a long way, but to get
> There takes no time and admission
> Is free, if you will purge yourself
> Of desire, and present yourself with
> Your need only and the simple offering
> Of your faith, green as a leaf.
> (Thomas, "The Kingdom,"
> *Poems of R. S. Thomas*, p. 82)

Leviticus 25:1–26:46
Sabbatical Year, Jubilee, and Blessings and Curses

R. S Thomas's poem above portrays the kingdom of God as a journey in faith toward a way of living in this world that promises justice for all. In his apt description, the kingdom is "a long way off but inside it / There are quite different things going on." Leviticus 25–26 envisions a similar journey: from promises spoken by God "on Mount Sinai" to the actualization of these promises in Canaan, where, in the proleptic words of 26:6, God has already seeded a land with the possibilities for such peace that "no one shall make you afraid."

In their present form, these two chapters comprise a thematic unit. The inclusio that frames the unit—"on Mount Sinai" (25:1; 26:46; see also 7:38 and 27:34)—provides a geographical reference point that effectively locates what follows as an integral part of the instructions that undergird God's covenantal relationship with Israel. These instructions

193

have to do with observance of the sabbatical year (25:2–7) and the jubilee year (25:8–17), both of which are foundational for "the redemption of the land" from injustices that mar its potential for peace and prosperity (25:18–24). Toward this end, chapter 25 concludes with a survey of cases in which persons may become destitute and therefore require God's intervention to redeem their land should they fall into insurmountable debt (25:25–55). On the heels of this survey, chapter 26 reiterates God's command to observe the Sabbath (vv. 1–2), to which it adds the promise of blessings on the land for obedience (vv. 3–13), curses for disobedience (vv. 14–39), and provisions for restoration of the covenantal promises when Israel confesses its sin (vv. 40–46).

The present arrangement of these chapters reflects a compositional unity that masks its redactional complexity. On the one hand, the concern in Leviticus 25 with sabbatical years must be compared with Exod. 23:10–11 and Deut. 15:1–6, both of which deal with the same issue, although with notable differences. On the other, the blessings and curses of chapter 26 must be compared with Deuteronomy 28 and various texts in Ezekiel (e.g., Ezek. 34:25–28; 36:28; 37:24–27). In each instance, the question that must be addressed is whether Leviticus is earlier or later than the texts with which it shares common themes. The answer to this question is understandably difficult, and readers may consult other commentaries for an assessment of the strengths and weaknesses of different positions. The commentary that follows will focus on the thematic and theological unity of chapters 25–26. Although such an approach will not do justice to some important details, it has the advantage of keeping the focus on theological issues that remain critical to this day for the appropriation of these texts (see below, "The Sabbatical Vision of Liberty and Justice for All").

Sabbatical Cycles and Provision for the "Redemption of the Land" (25:1–24)

God's instructions begin with a mandate to extend the principle of a weekly Sabbath rest to the land itself (vv. 1–7). Every seventh year "the land shall observe a sabbath for the Lord." During this time there is to be neither sowing nor pruning, for the land, like God and God's creatures, must be returned to the freedom from toil that it enjoyed on creation's first Sabbath. Whatever the land yields naturally may be consumed as food, and its abundance is envisioned as more than sufficient to sustain life during the fallow year. The list of the seven recipients of its bounty—"you, your male and female slaves, your hired and your bound laborers . . . your livestock . . . the wild animals" (vv. 6–7)—

indicates that none need fear diminishment by observance of the land's sabbatical year.

The sabbatical year extends to seven seven-year cycles, which culminate in the fiftieth year with the celebration of jubilee (vv. 8–22). The year of jubilee is announced on the tenth day of the seventh month, on the Day of Purification, by the blowing of the shofar horn, which proclaims liberty throughout the land. The liberty is envisioned as the promise of returning home. Israelites who have been forced to mortgage their land because of economic distress are allowed to reclaim their holdings and resume their lives as free and unindentured persons who may work toward the promise of providing for themselves and their families. The redemption of lost property must take place in a way that is fair and equitable for both the seller and the buyer. The price for redemption is calculated according to the number of years between the time the land was relinquished and the next jubilee year. Sellers must not unfairly profit by selling the land for more than the estimated value of the harvest years that may be lost. Buyers must not demand a price that is less than the value of the harvests that they stand to gain from the repurchase. The transaction clearly involves matters of economic justice, but the rationale for obedience is couched in decisively theological terms. Persons are not to "cheat one another," because to do so dishonors their relationship with God (v. 17). This is followed by a still more basic reason for obedience: The land belongs not to buyers and sellers. In truth, both are but "aliens" and "tenants" on the land; they are custodians of a title that only God can give. "The land is mine" (v. 23), God announces, and as the stewards of its promise of liberty and freedom for all, Israel must take care to provide for its redemption (v. 24).

The Jubilee's Guarantee of Redemption (25:25–55)

The remainder of the chapter deals with three principal cases in which the jubilee laws of redemption apply. Each case begins with a situation of destitution ("If anyone becomes impoverished"; vv. 23, 35, 39) that results from an owner having been forced to sell property.

> - If an Israelite farmer falls on difficult times and is forced to sell his land to cover his debts, he may reclaim it when he has sufficient funds to do so. The price of redemption must be set as the original sale price, minus the value of the crops harvested since it was sold. If the farmer is unable to redeem his land, his nearest of kin must do so, and he must hold it on

195

his behalf until the jubilee year, at which time the land automatically reverts to its original owner (vv. 25–28). Verses 29–34 make exceptions for the sale of houses in walled cities, which must be redeemed within one year, after which they become the purchaser's property, and for Levitical houses in cities, which "shall forever have the right of redemption," because these houses, along with the land surrounding them, are, by God's decree, part of the priestly inheritance (cf. Num. 35:1–8; Joshua 21).

- Israelites who experience crop failure may be forced to default on a loan, thus becoming in effect tenants on their own land while they work off their debt. In such cases, their creditors must amortize the loan (without interest), allow them to work the land, and produce what they need to live. All Israelites know what it means to be forced into slave labor that creates capital for an economic system in which they have no voice. It is this memory, and especially the memory of the God who redeemed them from such exploitation in Egypt, that must motivate their compassion for those in need (vv. 35–38).

- The third set of instructions, which builds on the previous two, deals with the issue of slavery (vv. 39–55). If an Israelite falls into such debt that he cannot work off what he owes, he must forfeit to the creditor not only his land but also its harvests. He becomes, in effect, vulnerably dependent on his creditor. Such a person is, however, not to be treated as a slave but as a hired laborer whose wages may be used to pay off his debt. In any case, his time of dependency is not unlimited. Whatever the status of his debt, his time of servitude ends in the jubilee year, when he and his family are freed to return to their land and resume their lives as before (vv. 40–41). The jubilee laws do not abolish all forms of slavery—Israelites may have slaves from other nations (vv. 44–46)—but they resolutely prohibit the enslavement of fellow Israelites, for they are "slaves" (NRSV: "servants"; v. 42) only to God. Based on the experience of their gracious redemption from slavery in Egypt, Israelites are forbidden to treat each other with the pharonic "harshness" from which God has delivered them (vv. 43, 46; cf. Exod. 1:13–14). There is here no explicit prohibition against harsh treatment of non-Israelite slaves. Elsewhere, however, Scripture addresses the rights of slaves (e.g., Deut. 5:14; 15:12–18; 23:15–16), stipulates legal penalties if they are abused (Exod. 21:20–21, 26–27), and insists that because all human beings have the same Creator, any abuse of other persons, whatever their social status, is unacceptable to God (e.g., Job 31:13–15; Prov. 14:31; 22:2).

A final set of instructions deals with Israelites who may fall into a vulnerable dependency upon non-Israelite creditors (vv. 47–55). In such cases, the indentured person retains the right to purchase his redemption, failing which his relatives are obligated to redeem him themselves. The price of the redemption is set according to the same principle that defines the redemption of the land (cf. vv. 15–16, 27), the major difference being the calculation in terms of labor rather than crops. In any case, the Israelite must be released in the jubilee year. Once again, the instructions offer a two-pronged rationale: Israelites must not be treated harshly; they are servants to God alone and owe ultimate allegiance to no other power (vv. 53, 55).

"Keep My Sabbaths" (26:1–2)

Chapter 26 reiterates God's command that Israel obey all of the covenant "commandments" and "statutes" (vv. 3, 14, 15, 43). The same terms are used elsewhere with reference to the instructions in the Holiness Code (e.g., 18:4–5, 26; 19:37; 20:22; 22:31). The addition of the all-inclusive word "laws" (*tôrôt*) in v. 46 suggests, however, that what this chapter envisions is a summons to obey all of the ritual and ethical commandments that Leviticus advances. Given the comprehensive sweep of its concerns, it is all the more instructive to note that chapter 26 begins by focusing on two specific commandments from the Decalogue that may be understood to encapsulate the essence of the whole law. The first is the Second Commandment (v. 1; cf. Exod. 20:4–6; Deut. 5:8–10), which prohibits all forms of idolatry: "idols," "carved images," "pillars," and "figured stones" (perhaps stones engraved with images of a deity). In sum, Israel is to worship God and God alone. The second is the Fourth Commandment (v. 2; cf. Exod. 20:8–11; Deut. 5:12–15), which summons Israel to keep the Sabbaths and reverence the sanctuary.

Milgrom has persuasively argued that these twin concerns—idolatry and Sabbath observance—betray the exilic provenance of vv. 1–2. In his judgment, an exilic priestly redactor added them (along with vv. 43–45) to the Holiness Code, after it had assumed its present form, to make the point that just as Sabbath observance holds the key for Israel's redemption of the land, so neglect of the Sabbath thwarts its promise of liberty and justice and leads to Israel's exile from the land (Milgrom, *Leviticus 23–27*, pp. 2275–79). However we may judge the compositional history of the text, the present form of chapters 25–26 makes a clear and important theological claim: The survival of Israel's "covenant" with God (note the repetition of "covenant" in vv. 9, 15, 25, 42 [three times], 44, 45), and with it Israel's survival on the land the covenant promises, depends on faithful observance of the Sabbath.

The elevation of the Sabbath to a position of such singular importance means that Leviticus places it at the center of God's decisions concerning Israel's future. The stakes are indeed high, as the following litany of blessings (vv. 3–13) and curses (vv. 14–39) makes clear. Given the candid concessions in Leviticus that both priests and laity are ever vulnerable to failure, both inside (10:1–20) and outside (24:10–23) the sanctuary, we might well read chapter 26 as a recipe for disaster. That it is not becomes clear in vv. 40–46, which introduce God's radical fidelity to the covenant with Israel with the words "But if they confess . . ."

Blessings and Curses (26:3–39)

Blessings and curses frequently occur at the conclusion of covenants and legal treaties both in the ancient Near East (e.g., the Code of Hammurabi) and in Israel (Exod. 23:20–33; Deuteronomy 28; Josh. 24:20). Their efficacy derives from the authority of the one who speaks them, that is, the one who has the power to reward obedience and punishment disobedience. Blessings and curses in the Old Testament, including those in Lev. 26:3–39, rest on two cardinal theological convictions: (1) Obedience to God's will, as expressed in the commands of the covenant, results in blessing; disobedience brings divine wrath and punishment; and (2) those who enter into covenant relationship with God must choose whether to obey or disobey God's will; the choice is theirs and the consequences are clear (cf. Levine, p. 182).

The blessings and curses in Leviticus may be grouped into two sets of five (Milgrom, *Leviticus 23–27*, pp. 2287–88). The blessings are framed by a chiasm that introduces a condition—"If you will walk (NRSV: 'follow') in my statutes" (v. 3)—and concludes with a corresponding promise—"I will walk among you" (v. 12). Within this frame, three of the blessings begin with the words "(then) I will give" (vv. 4, 6,

11); two convey promises that are structured somewhat differently (vv. 7–8, 9–10). The curses begin with the statement "If you will not obey me" (vv. 14, 18, 21, 23, 27), which is followed by a description of punishments that gradually increase in severity, conveyed in part by the repetition of the words "sevenfold for your sins" in the last four cases (vv. 18, 21, 24, 28). The fifth and final curse (vv. 27–39) announces a complete reversal of the fifth blessing (vv. 11–12): The promise of God's presence in return for obedience now becomes a warning that if Israel disobeys, God will abandon the holy places in Israel. The outline below provides a general overview of the structure and content.

Blessings (vv. 3–13)	*Curses (vv. 14–39)*
"If you follow my statutes and keep my commandments" (v. 3)	"But if you will not obey me, and do not observe all these commandments" (v. 14)
1. Rain and fertility (vv. 4–5)	1. Famine and defeat (vv. 14–16)
2. Peace in the land (v. 6)	2. Drought and poor harvests (vv. 18–20)
3. Victory over enemies (vv. 7–8)	3. Wild animals that kill children and livestock (vv. 21–22)
4. Prosperity beyond measure (vv. 9–10)	4. War, pestilence, famine (vv. 23–26)
5. God's presence (vv. 11–13)	5. God's abandonment of Israel to exile (vv. 27–39)
"I will walk among you . . . I have broken the bars of your yoke and made you walk erect" (vv. 12, 13)	"You shall have no power to stand against your enemies" (v. 37)

The collection of blessings and curses invites three observations. First, the blessings and curses are for the most part (see below) structured to show a symmetry between obedience-reward and disobedience-punishment (Levine, p. 276). God promises that if Israel is obedient, the land will be fertile (vv. 4–5, 10), but if it is disobedient, the land will become unproductive (vv. 16, 19–20, 26). Similarly, God will look with favor on Israel (v. 9) or turn away from Israel, leaving it vulnerable to its enemies (v. 17). Israel will repel its enemies (v. 8) or be delivered into their hands (vv. 17, 25). Wild beasts will be removed from the land (v. 6), or they will be let loose on the land to devour the people and their livestock

199

(v. 22). God will permit no sword to pass through the land (v. 6), or God will bring an avenging sword to destroy the land (v. 25). Israel's obedience will result in secure settlement on the land (v. 5), or its disobedience will lead to exile from the land (v. 33a). Israel will remain free from slavery and walk erect in the land (v. 15), or it will languish with no power to stand against its enemies (vv. 37–38). In effect, God's way of dealing with Israel exemplifies the *lex talionis* principle that God has previously instructed Israel to apply in the case of the blasphemer (see 24:20). In matters of reward and punishment, the blessings and curses assure Israel that the justice God requires will be commensurate with the justice God dispenses (cf. Douglas, "Poetic Structure in Leviticus," p. 252).

Second, the blessings and curses are especially focused on the repercussions to be realized by the land. The word *land* occurs seventeen times in vv. 3–39 (vv. 4, 5, 6 [three times], 13, 19, 20 [two times], 32, 33, 34 [three times], 36, 38, 39), and even when it is not explicitly mentioned, it is apparent that the land will either prosper from Israel's fidelity to God or be diminished by its disobedience. A crucial part of the rhetoric that conveys the land's destiny, and hence Israel's future as its inhabitants, is the sevenfold recurrence of the word *eat*, two times in the blessings (vv. 5, 10), five times in the curses (vv. 16, 26, 29 [two times], 38). If Israel obeys God's statutes and ordinances, God will bless the land with rain, and Israel will eat from the abundance of its produce without anxiety (vv. 5, 10). If Israel disobeys it will sow seed in vain (v. 16). There will be so little grain that all the loaves can be baked in one oven; when the bread is rationed out, people will eat and hunger for more (v. 26). If Israel continues to disobey, the hunger will drive it to cannibalize its own children (v. 29). But even this desperate act will not enable the people to survive, for in the end they will lose their land to enemies. In the graphic words of v. 38, the land itself will "devour" them. In view of what is at stake, the blessings and curses that fall on the land make the reiteration of God's command to observe the Sabbath (26:1–2) all the more important. If Israel's obedience to the sabbatical and jubilee years enables it to redeem the land's promise of liberty and justice for all, its violation of God's sabbatical commands has the potential to condemn the land and all those who depend on its nourishment to certain destruction. Neither Israel nor the land can survive the neglect of the sabbatical rest that allows them to replenish their energies, renew their capacities, and fulfill their God-given destinies.

Third, the rather careful measure-for-measure correlation between disobedience and punishment that governs the first four curses is missing in the fifth and climactic curse (vv. 27–39). The divine punishments of cannibalism, destruction of the cult places, desolation of the land, exile, and the utter demoralization of the people exceed in severity any violation with which Israel could reasonably be charged. Moreover, as if to make a difficult warning still more unsettling, the text seems to go out of the way to stress God's personal responsibility. Whereas in previous curses God sends the agents of destruction—wild beasts, plagues, enemies—now God executes the punishment: "I will devastate the land, I myself" (v. 32; cf. Milgrom, *Leviticus 23–27*, p. 2315). God's intent to punish seems now to have passed beyond the pale of recall. There will be no further discussion, no more delays, no more second chances. Gerstenberger comments as follows:

> Yahweh's intention . . . is to requite Israel "in fury" and "full of anger" (v. 28a). This is the intensification that makes the person of antiquity genuinely quake. "Do not rebuke me in your anger, or discipline me in your wrath," pleads the psalmist (cf. Pss. 6:2 [1 E]; 38:2 [1 E]). What they do not want is to be subjected to impulsively imposed—albeit justified—punishment; rather, they would prefer to wait. All this is conceived in a very human fashion until God has calmed down and is able to allow his milder disposition to reign. In this text however, God's full wrath is turned loose. (Gerstenberger, p. 420)

The result of Israel's disobedience will be counted in the piles of corpses scattered about, and those "fortunate" enough to number the dead will themselves be rotting away on the inside, Dorian Gray–like, because of the sins they have committed (v. 39).

When the blessings and curses conclude, there would appear to be no escape clause for those who violate God's commandments. God commands Israel to apply a *lex talionis* principle for judging the wrongs of others. God seems committed to model this principle in the adjudication of divine punishment for human sin. But, when the final curse is announced, Israel must have good reason to fear that God will not always be bound by God's own principles of justice.

"But if They Confess Their Iniquity" (26:40–46)

After the list of curses, the final section of chapter 26 announces a new and perhaps unexpected word from God. Despite Israel's propensity for disobedience, and despite the repeated warnings that God will punish, and punish it severely, in ways that seem to erase every possible avenue for escape, God now announces that Israel's future remains open, not closed, to new possibilities. If Israel confesses its sins (v. 40), allows its heart to be changed (NRSV: "humbled"), and accepts its punishment for violating God's commands (v. 41), then God will remember both the covenant with the ancestors and the land (v. 42). The rhetoric

201

of the announcement employs an important combination of active and passive verbal forms. Israel must take responsibility for the confession of sin; the rest of the activity it need only accept as the work God does on its behalf. God will effect the change of heart, and God will enact the punishment the people must receive.

Such an announcement anchors a unique and innovative approach in Israel's understanding of the atonement for sin. Forgiveness may be found, God's favor may be restored, and the possibilities for covenantal partnership may be reopened by repentance alone. It is most instructive that in the midst of a Priestly text so focused on the importance of sacrifice as a means of expiating sin, there is here no requirement of sacrifice at all. As Milgrom has discerned, the significance of this concession should not be underestimated. "It approximates, and *perhaps influences*, the prophetic doctrine of repentance, which not only suspends the sacrificial requirement, but eliminates it entirely" (Milgrom, *Leviticus 23–27*, p. 2330; emphasis added). The Priestly endorsement of repentance for sin provides an important corrective to a long-standing caricature of the respective legacies of Israel's priests and prophets. To be sure, the prophets were often critical of the abuses in Israel's sacrificial system and of the priests who administered it (e.g., Isa. 1:10–17; Jer. 7:1–15; Hos. 4:4–5:7; Amos 2:6–16; Mic. 3:9–12). The Holiness Code, however, invites the consideration that Israel's prophets came to their distinctive summons to repentance *as a result of* their immersion in the very ritual system they felt compelled not only to critique but also to preserve.

For all its promise of God's redemptive work on Israel's behalf, the Priestly understanding of repentance does not, however, remove the burden of making restitution for sin. Israel's sins violate not only God's commands but also the land's potential to provide liberty and justice for its people. If Israel violates God's commands by depriving the land of its sabbatical rest, the land will reclaim what it is due during the fallow years when Israel languishes in exile (vv. 43–45; cf. vv. 34–35). If these verses derive from an exilic priestly redactor of the Holiness Code, as Milgrom has argued (*Leviticus 23–27*, pp. 2363–65), they serve as yet another indication of the critical importance that came to be attached to the sabbatical theme. In the wake of the destruction of Jerusalem and the exile to Babylon in 586, the priests understood that Israel's restoration would not take place until the land had been compensated for its neglected sabbaticals.

How, then, does one account for the "justice" God displays toward Israel? If God's curses demonstrate that divine punishment can exceed the measure-for-measure principle that Israel may expect (vv. 27–39), the possibility of restoration conditioned on Israel's repentance seems

202

at odds with the fear of a God who will judge "in fury" and "full of anger." The key to understanding lies in the eight references to "covenant" that are scattered throughout chapter 26, five of which are located in vv. 40–45 (vv. 9, 15, 25, 42 [three times], 44, 45). God will "maintain" the covenant (v. 9) with Israel's ancestors, the very covenant that in the future (from the canonical perspective of the text) Israel will promise but fail to obey. For its part, Israel may break the covenant (v. 15) by disobeying God's commandments. But for all its disobedience, God never "breaks" the covenant with Israel (v. 44; cf. Judg. 2:1; Jer. 14:21). God's promise to uphold the covenant is unilateral; it will not be subverted, not even by God's own commitment to the talionic principle for judgment. Even when Israel languishes in exile, convinced that its sins have effectively canceled every conceivable divine incentive for mercy, God will not abandon the covenant that begins with an inviolable divine promise—"I am the Lord your God" (v. 1)—and ends with an equally inviolable divine hope—"You shall be my people" (v. 12). When the final word of chapter 26 is spoken, the gift of "the statutes and ordinances and laws" at Sinai (v. 46) should summon Israel to celebrate, not fear, God's promise not to be bound by God's own principles of justice.

The Sabbatical Vision of Liberty and Justice for All

A sabbatical year when the land lies fallow, but no one goes hungry? A jubilee year when all debts are canceled, slaves are set free, and everything lost is returned and restored? The laws in chapter 25 paint a wonderful picture of worship in the service of social justice. But are they realistic? Were they ever observed in ancient Israel? And even if they were, what, if any, is their claim on the contemporary community of faith? A basic and perhaps abiding wonderment about the feasibility of God's instructions seems to be encoded in the text itself. To the promise that God will provide for Israel's security and prosperity if it lives in accordance with the sabbatical vision comes a freighted question: "What shall we eat in the seventh year, if we may not sow or gather in our crop?" (25:20). God's answer is "I will order my blessing for you in the sixth year" (25:21). Then, as now, the answer would seem only to beg another question: Will God's promised blessing be enough to evoke and sustain our obedience?

Concerning the question whether sabbatical and jubilee years were actually observed in Israel, the evidence is inconclusive. Extrabiblical parallels suggest that seven-year cycles in which societies joined religious belief with agricultural practices were a common practice. There

203

is, however, nothing directly comparable in other cultures to Israel's Sabbath day. There are also ancient Near Eastern parallels for the periodic remission of debts and the release from slavery, which provide a likely historical antecedent to Israel's jubilee year, but they typically refer to the prerogatives of a human sovereign, who may make such proclamations upon succession to the throne as a sign of personal benevolence. There are no clear parallels, however, to the biblical notion of a jubilee that is ordained by God as a fixed and irrevocable basis for a society's economic practices.

If we limit the discussion to biblical texts, the picture is not much clearer. Despite the legislation in Exod. 23:10–11, Lev. 25:2–7, and Deut. 15:1–2, there is no firm textual evidence that the sabbatical year was observed in preexilic times. That it was observed in the Second Temple period (e.g., Neh. 10:32; 1 Macc. 6:49, 53; Josephus's *Antiquities* 12.234; 14.202–6) may tilt the balance in favor of the argument that it was a long-standing practice in Israel, but such a conclusion is more supposition than fact. There is no evidence that the jubilee year was ever observed. Although there are some rather famous cases that seem to assume that jubilee laws existed in Israel (e.g., Jer. 32:1–15), the evidence suggests that if such laws existed, they were often ignored (e.g., 1 Kings 21; Ruth 4:1–6; for further discussion, see Milgrom, *Leviticus 23-27*, pp. 2245–48, 2257–70).

Given the uncertainty of the historical data and the ambiguity of the textual evidence, it would be reasonable to suppose that with the passage of time the notion of sabbatical principles for redemption of the land and its owners would have faded from memory. It did not. Israel's prophetic tradition turned to the lingering memory of jubilee's promise as a way of believing against all odds that "the year of the Lord's favor" was an ever-present possibility. With the ashes of Jerusalem still smoldering, the voice of one who proclaimed "liberty to the captives, and release to the prisoners" continued to summon those who would remain open to God's vision for the future (Isa. 61:1–3). That vision gives way to an abiding hope that in due course all of creation will join with the blind, the deaf, the lame, and the mute in a doxology of praise to the One whose promise of restoration makes all things possible (Isa. 35:1–2, 5–6, 9–10).

Even as the hard realities of life seek to thwart it, the hope for that time when people and nature may be redeemed by the sabbatical promises of justice ekes out a place to survive in Israel's memory. Through the lens of apocalyptic thought, Daniel envisions an eschatological jubilee ("seventy weeks" of years, or 490 years), when the worship of God in a "most holy place" will put an end to sin and bring about an "everlasting righteousness" that will transform the world (Dan. 9:24–27). Ezekiel contributes to a similar vision with the promise of the coming of a "prince" of God who will make a gift of land to his sons out of his own inheritance, so that none shall ever be displaced again (Ezek. 46:16–18). The book of *Jubilees* (second century B.C.E.) extends the vision still further by framing God's revelation "from the first creation until my sanctuary is built in their midst forever and ever" (1:27) as a recurring cycle of seven "weeks of years," or forty-nine jubilee years. In that final day, the jubilee of all jubilees, a new era will begin. What was unimaginable before will become real and permanent. Israel will then be

> purified from all the sin of fornication, and defilement, and unclean-ness, and sin and error. And they will dwell in confidence in all the land. And then it will not have any Satan or any evil (one). And the land will be purified from that time and forever. (50:5)

The hope for the coming of the "year of the Lord's favor" is dra-matically embodied in the life and ministry of Jesus. Luke reports that Jesus began his public ministry in Galilee by going into the synagogue on the Sabbath day and reading from Isaiah's vision of a grand jubilee:

> The Spirit of the Lord is upon me,
>   because he has anointed me to bring good news to the poor.
> He has sent me to proclaim release to the captives
>   and recovery of sight to the blind, to let the oppressed go free,
> to proclaim the year of the Lord's favor.
>
> (Luke 4:18–19)

When Jesus finished reading, Luke reports that he closed the scroll, sat down, and began to teach the crowd what he meant: "Today this scrip-ture has been fulfilled in your hearing" (4:21). What had long been promised had now arrived. From this moment on, his hearers were to live as if the gap between promise and fulfillment had been closed. And then, with a report that signals our fervently brittle journey from that day to this, Luke says that "all were amazed at the gracious words that came from his mouth" (4:22), and then they "drove him out of the town" (4:29).

The last Greek word in Luke's account of Jesus' teaching in Galilee is *eporeuto*, "he was going on" (4:30). The verbal form indicates con-tinuous action and implies that Jesus would move forward to new destinations and other peoples, bearing witness in his teachings that God's promise would not be thwarted, not even by the scandal of dis-belief. That the promise still lives and beckons can be measured by the

205

witness of those who have been grasped by its vision. The lingering hope for jubilee's redemption echoes in Lord Byron's nineteenth-century *Sardanapalus*, written while the poet was in shamed exile from his beloved England: "All hearts are happy, and all voices bless / The king of peace, who holds a world in jubilee" (3.1.17–18). It lingers among the thirty-two representatives from third-world countries who attended the "Jewish-Christian Symposium on the Jubilee," sponsored by the World Council of Churches, in 1996 in Bossey, Switzerland. When they unfurled the flag of the jubilee at their meeting, they bore testimony to their hope and belief that God's promised jubilee will not exempt the 80 percent of the world's population who scratch for survival on but 17 percent of the world's resources (Milgrom, *Leviticus 23–27*, pp. 2270–71). It lingers in the hope that led Pope John Paul II to proclaim the year 2000 as the jubilee year in which, perhaps, the community of faith might enact God's summons to redress the sad imbalance in the global economy that continues to threaten so much of the world's population (North, pp. 115–27).

Words that linger. "When you enter the land that I am giving you, the land shall observe a sabbath for the Lord" (25:2). "And I will grant peace in the land, and you shall lie down, and no one shall make you afraid" (26:6). In another context and on a different subject, W. Brueggemann has referred to the Old Testament as a collection of "texts that linger" in treasured tradition, then surprisingly erupt into new and daring usage when religious communities experience them afresh (Brueggemann). It is an apt description of the texts envisioning a sabbatical redemption that brings liberty and justice to all. The original audience for Leviticus 25–26 has passed on, as have those who first gladly heard Jesus in the synagogue, then drove him out of the city. Byron died in exile, never returning home to the "world of jubilee" he yearned for but could not attain. Whether the jubilee flag still flies in Bossey, Switzerland, I cannot say, but it is abundantly clear that the new millennium has brought too little difference to the poorest of the world's poor, despite the pope's hopeful declaration in the year 2000. And yet . . . and yet. These ancient texts linger, endlessly mesmerizing us with promises ungraspable but true. In this country, the inscription on the Liberty Bell from Lev. 25:10—"proclaim liberty throughout the land"—may symbolize more than first meets the eye. The bell is cracked, but the promise has been preserved.

Perhaps, as T. S. Eliot discerns, we now live in a world of "hollow valleys" and "lost kingdoms," where a huge shadow darkens every bridge over the chasm between our best hopes and our worst fears ("The Hollow Men," *T. S. Eliot: Collected Poems 1909–1962*, p. 81).

Still, for all its brutal power to annul, history has not been able to eliminate from our consciousness the sabbatical vision of liberty and justice for all. Perhaps this lingering hope is the true measure of a text whose promise is not yet overcome. When and if we yield to its claim on us, perhaps that will be the true measure of what we often too glibly call our religious commitments.

> Every living and healthy religion has a marked idiosyncrasy. Its power consists in its special and surprising message and in the bias which that revelation gives to life. The vistas it opens and the mysteries it propounds are another world to live in; and another world to live in— whether we expect to pass into it or no—is what we mean by religion. (G. Santayana, *Reason in Religion*, cited in Geertz, "Religion as a Cultural System," p. 87)

Leviticus 27:1–34
Vows, Consecrations, and Other "Gifts" to God

The structure of this closing chapter is relatively clear. Its purpose—the discussion of which is suspended until its contents are examined—is, however, more difficult to assess. Framed by an introduction (v. 1) and a summary statement (v. 34), God's concluding instructions address the making of vows (vv. 2–13), the consecration of houses and fields (vv. 14–25), and certain restrictions that apply to what Israel may bring as gifts to God, specifically firstborn, anything that falls under the law of *hērem* ("devoted to destruction"), and tithes (vv. 26–33). The first two sections are clearly delineated by the introductory formula "If/When a person" (vv. 2, 14); subsidiary cases are introduced by "and if" (vv. 4, 5, 6, 7, 8, 9, 11, 13, 16, 17, 18, 20, 22). The third section (vv. 26–33), which comprises a list of exceptions that deserve special attention, is introduced by the restrictive particle "however" (v. 26).

Vows of Persons and Animals (27:1–13)

The frequent mention of vows in the Old Testament indicates that they played a significant role in Israelite life (e.g., Gen. 28:20–22; Num. 21:2; Deut. 23:22–24; Judg. 11:30–31; 1 Sam. 1:11; Pss. 22:25; 50:14; 61:5, 8; 116:14, 18; Isa. 19:21; Jonah 1:16; Mal. 1:14). Perhaps because the instinct to make promises to God is so natural, biblical texts also frequently warn against making impulsive vows that one either cannot or will not fulfill. Unfulfilled vows not only call into question the integrity of the one who makes the promise; they also insult and anger God, whose name has been invoked without thinking. The sage's admonition in Eccl. 5:4–6 makes the point clearly:

> When you make a vow to God, do not delay fulfilling it; for he has no pleasure in fools. Fulfill what you vow. It is better that you should not vow than that you should vow and not fulfill it. Do not let your mouth lead you into sin, and do not say before the messenger that it was a mistake; why should God be angry at your words, and destroy the work of your hands? (cf. Deut. 23:21; Prov. 20:25; Sir. 18:22)

The instructions in 27:1–13 are part of a similar trajectory of concerns about the vows one may make to God. When persons vow that they or their children will be dedicated to the service of God, how should that vow be fulfilled? Hannah makes good on the vow concerning her son Samuel by giving him over to service in the sanctuary in Shiloh (1 Sam. 1:11, 21–28). The instructions in Lev. 27:2–8 recognize, however, that priestly duties at the sanctuary are the prerogatives of Aaron's descendants; thus they provide a way for persons to dedicate themselves to God's service by commuting their pledge into a predetermined payment to the sanctuary. The payments are set on the basis of a person's age and gender—not the person's intrinsic worth as a human being—presumably taking into account one's physical ability to do the manual work that would be involved:

Age	Male	Female
20–60 years of age	50 shekels	30 shekels
5–20 years of age	20 shekels	10 shekels
1 month to 5 years of age	5 shekels	3 shekels
60 years of age or older	15 shekels	10 shekels

Wenham notes that these monetary assessments are very high, perhaps intentionally so to discourage people from making such vows without careful deliberation. If workers earned on average only about one shekel per month, as he notes, then surely few could have risked the financial liabilities set out here (Wenham, p. 338).

As with the exceptions made for the poor in the sacrificial offerings (1:14–17; 5:1–13), here, too, the priestly instructions make exceptions for those who pledge themselves wholeheartedly but can afford to pay only minimally. For those with minimal resources, the priest will make an assessment "according to what each one making a vow can afford" (v. 8).

208

Persons may also pledge their animals to God (vv. 9–13). Such gifts are holy to God; hence persons must not pledge one animal then decide later to exchange or substitute another of lesser value in its place, perhaps because they now see they cannot afford or no longer have the incentive to make good on their promise. If persons make such a substitution, the penalty is the forfeiture of both animals—the vowed one and the substitute—to the sanctuary (vv. 9–10). A subset of this case concerns the vowing of an unclean animal, perhaps an animal that an owner does not know will not be acceptable as sacrifice until the priest inspects it (vv. 11–13). If the priest determines that the animal is unclean, he will assess its value. It may then be sold and the profits presumably contributed to the sanctuary. Alternatively, owners may redeem the animals for their own use by paying their assessed value plus 20 percent.

Consecrations of Houses and Fields (27:14–25)

Vows typically concern the dedication of animate things, as in the preceding instructions about persons and animals. Consecrations are a form of dedication typically applied to inanimate things, as in these verses dealing with houses and lands. Both vows and consecrations are voluntary. The primary distinction between them is that vows are conditional and will be fulfilled at some future time; consecrations become effective the moment they are spoken (for further discussion, see Milgrom, *Leviticus 23–27*, pp. 2409–12).

Persons may consecrate for God's use a house, a portion of their ancestral land, or a purchased field. In each case, provisions are made for a monetary redemption of what has been promised, based on the sanctuary shekel (v. 25). If a person consecrates a house to God (vv. 14–15)—presumably a house in a walled city that is not subject to the laws of jubilee (cf. 25:29–30)—the house becomes the property of the sanctuary. If a person wishes to redeem the house, the priest will assess its value, to which the original owner must add 20 percent. The redemption will be paid into the sanctuary treasury. If a person consecrates a portion of ancestral land to God (vv. 16–21), the priest shall assess its value based on the amount of seed required to sow the field; one homer of barley seed is valued at fifty shekels. The assessment takes into consideration the standing provisions for the redemption of the land in the jubilee year. If the field is consecrated in the jubilee year, the initial assessment of the priest stands. If the land is consecrated before the jubilee year, the assessment will be reduced according to the number of years the land may be sown until the next jubilee.

209

The original owner may redeem the land by paying its assessed value plus 20 percent. If the person does not redeem the land before the jubilee year or chooses to sell it to someone else, then the land reverts to the sanctuary in the jubilee year and becomes "holy to the Lord as a devoted field" (v. 21). If a person consecrates purchased land, that is, land that is not part of an ancestral inheritance (vv. 22–24), the priest will assess its value according to the number of crop years before the jubilee year, and the one who purchased the land must pay the set price as a "sacred donation to the Lord" on the very day the assessment is made. It is unclear why the assessment must be paid immediately. Perhaps it is to discourage persons from dedicating to God land to which they do not have a permanent (or ancestral) claim; thus one may not offer purchased land as "collateral" for a pledge to God (cf. Levine, p. 197). Perhaps it is to protect the rights of the land's original owner to redeem the land whenever he is able to do so. In any event, in the jubilee year the land must be returned to its original owner.

Restrictions on Vows and Consecrations (27:26–34)

The final section addresses three restrictions that apply to vows and consecrations: "firstlings" (vv. 26–27), anything that is devoted to destruction (vv. 28–29), and tithes (vv. 30–33). The firstborn of clean animals—animals suitable for sacrifice—cannot be consecrated to God, because they already belong to God by birth (v. 26; cf. Exod. 13:2; 34:39). J. Hartley explains the rationale as follows: "A person may not use the ploy of paying a vow with a first-born animal, attempting to gain double spiritual benefit from the presentation of a single animal" (Hartley, p. 484). The firstlings of unclean animals, which are nonsacrificeable, may be vowed to God and redeemed by paying to the sanctuary their assessed value plus 20 percent (v. 27). There are a number of differences between 27:26–27 and legislation concerning the firstborn elsewhere in the Old Testament (cf. Exod. 13:1–2, 12–13; 34:19; Num. 18:16–18; Deut. 15:19–23), which is an indication of their historical development and the changing perspectives of priestly and nonpriestly legal specialists (cf. Milgrom, *Leviticus 23–27*, pp. 2415–17).

Anything placed under the law of *ḥērem*, that is, anything that is *ḥāram*, "set apart, restricted, or proscribed," whether a person, an animal, or property, is already devoted to God and cannot be redeemed (vv. 28–29). In the Old Testament, the laws of *ḥērem* apply almost exclusively to situations of military conflict, either Israel's wars against external enemies, typically on God's command, or against rebels and idolaters within its own citizenry. In such contexts, persons and animals

210

may fall under the death penalty, and property, the spoils of battle, becomes consecrated to God. A classic example is Joshua's *ḥērem* on Jericho, which resulted in the death of the city's inhabitants and the consecration of their precious metals to the sanctuary (Josh. 6:15–21; cf. Num. 31:1–50; Deut. 13:12–18; Josh. 8:1–29; Judg. 21:1–12). P. Stern has persuasively argued that the war *ḥērem* is best understood as part of a chaos-versus-order paradigm. As such, it is part of the same grand cosmogonic myth that informs the Old Testament creation accounts, in which the objective of Israel's fight for the land is to create a "sacred space . . . consecrated by the presence of God" (Stern, p. 226). Milgrom helpfully extends Stern's insight as follows: "*Ḥērem* involves acting like the Deity does: it is an act of creation, bringing order out of chaos" (Milgrom, *Leviticus 23–27*, p. 2417).

The *ḥērem* instructions in vv. 28–29 represent an interesting and evocative variation on the texts mentioned above. They appear to envision a context of peace, not war. Although the idea of punishment for violators remains very much to the fore—hence the warning not to use things already devoted to God in fulfillment of vows—the instructions also hold the promise that observing their proscriptions is a consecratory act. The proper fulfillment of vows not only *sustains* but also *creates* the opportunities—in Stern's words, the "sacred space"—in which the union between God and Israel may be actualized.

The third restriction addresses the matter of tithes (vv. 30–33). The laws in the Old Testament concerning tithes indicate that the instructions underwent changes in the course of Israel's history. For example, the legislation in Num. 18:21–32 commands Israelites to pay a general tithe to the Levites in return for their service at the sanctuary. The Levites, in turn, must give one-tenth of the tithes they receive to the sanctuary; the remainder provides their wages. Deuteronomy 14:22–29 stipulates that a tithe of grain, wine, oil, and firstlings from the herd and flock be set aside each year for consumption in the holy place. If the distance to the sanctuary is too great to transport these items, the tithe may be commuted into money and spent on a meal that is to be consumed in the sanctuary. Every third year, the tithe must be left in the local settlement in order to provide for the Levites and the poor. Leviticus 27, which shares some but not all of these details, places its emphasis on the redemption of the tithes. All tithes from the produce of the land or from the herds and flocks belong already to God, hence they cannot be offered a second time in fulfillment of a vow. Persons may commute the crop tithe into currency by paying to the sanctuary the assessed value plus 20 percent. The animal tithe, however, may not be commuted. The procedure for the selection of the animals suggests that

211

when the animals are passed before the shepherd, every tenth one, irrespective of its condition, is marked as "holy to the Lord" (cf. Jer. 33:13; Ezek. 20:37). No substitution or exchange is permissible; should one make a substitution, both animals must be forfeited.

Final Words

"These are the commandments that the Lord gave to Moses for the people of Israel on Mount Sinai" (v. 34). This last verse clearly serves as a summary statement that invites concluding discernments of some kind, and yet, as commentators frequently notice, the substance of chapter 27 seems oddly anticlimactic when considered in light of what has preceded. It is almost as if readers reach the end of the book only to find there is still something more to be considered before the task of comprehension is complete. The following comments may provide a beginning point for those considerations.

There is general agreement that the blessings and curses of chapter 26 provide a logical conclusion to the book, and that chapter 27 therefore appears to be an appendix added by a later priestly redactor. This judgment, however, only invites a further question about why the chapter should be placed just here. A number of explanations have been proposed. It is often suggested that the redactor wanted to end the book on a more positive note than would have been the case if the last word had been the curses announced in chapter 26. The ending of Deuteronomy, which adds the blessings of chapters 30–34 to the curses in chapters 28–29, gives some support to this suggestion, as do the similar positive endings that appear to have been supplied to a number of other biblical books (e.g., Isaiah, Hosea, Amos, Ecclesiastes). Beyond this, Wenham has suggested that chapter 27 provides an intentional counterpart to chapter 26. Whereas the blessings and curses constitute, in a sense, *God's* vows to Israel, chapter 27, at least in part (vv. 2–13), treats *Israel's* vows to God (Wenham, p. 336). Others have pressed the connections between chapters 27 and 25–26 still further by suggesting that their common denominator is the theme of redemption. The two outer chapters, 25 and 27, emphasize Israel's responsibility to redeem land, people, and promises made to God. Chapter 26 rhetorically centers Israel's redemptive responsibilities in the model God provides by promising to redeem Israel in accordance with an irrevocable commitment to sustain the covenant (Douglas, *Leviticus as Literature*, p. 244; Milgrom, *Leviticus 23–27*, p. 2409).

212

It is also instructive to note that chapter 27 effectively returns the reader of the book of Leviticus to its beginnings. The sacrificial laws in chapters 1–7 begin with instructions concerning Israel's voluntary offerings, or "gifts" to God, specifically burnt offerings, cereal offerings, and well-being offerings (1:1–3:17). Chapter 27 returns to the topic of voluntary gifts, now addressed in terms of the personal vows, the dedication of animals and real estate, and the tithes and offerings that signal Israel's desire to consecrate everything at its disposal to the service of God (cf. Hartley, p. 479; Kaiser, p. 1186; Gerstenberger, p. 439). From a theological perspective, the beginning and ending of this book invite readers, both ancient and modern, to receive God's commandments from Sinai as a *gift*.

To be sure, this gift involves imperatives for obedience, failing which it cannot be actualized in the way God intends. Toward that end, Leviticus vigorously presses Israel to exemplify holiness, both in the rituals offered inside the sanctuary (chaps. 1–16) and in the ethics of everyday life outside it (chaps. 17–27), in a way that honors God's holiness. But in the end, Leviticus dares to hope and believe that both God's commands and Israel's opportunity for faithful response to them are a gift, not a burden. Such a gift becomes a summons to exuberant celebration, the ancient and abiding echo of which has been preserved in the words of the psalmist:

> I find my delight in your commandments,
> because I love them.
> I revere your commandments, which I love,
> and I will meditate on your statues. . . .
>
> Oh, how I love your law!
> (Ps. 119:47–48, 97a)

BIBLIOGRAPHY

For Further Study

Blenkinsopp, J. *Sage, Priest, and Prophet: Religious Leadership in Ancient Israel*. Library of Ancient Israel. Louisville, Ky.: Westminster John Knox Press, 1995.

Douglas, M. *Purity and Danger: An Analysis of the Concepts of Pollution and Taboo*. London: Routledge & Kegan Paul, 1966.

Gammie, J. G. *Holiness in Israel*. Overtures to Biblical Theology. Minneapolis: Fortress Press, 1989.

Gennup, A. *The Rites of Passage*. Chicago: University of Chicago Press, 1960.

Grabbe, L. *Leviticus*. Old Testament Guides. Sheffield: Sheffield Academic Press, 1993.

Jenson, P. P. *Graded Holiness: A Key to the Priestly Conception of the World*. Journal for the Study of the Old Testament, Supplement Series 106. Sheffield: JSOT Press, 1992.

Milgrom, J. *Leviticus 1–16*. Anchor Bible 3. New York: Doubleday, 1991.

———. *Leviticus 17–22*. Anchor Bible 3a. New York: Doubleday, 2000.

———. *Leviticus 23–27*. Anchor Bible 3b. New York: Doubleday, 2001.

Miller, P. D. *The Religion of Ancient Israel*. Library of Ancient Israel. Louisville, Ky.: Westminster John Knox Press, 2000.

Nelson, R. D. *Raising Up a Faithful Priest: Community and Priesthood in Biblical Theology*. Louisville, Ky.: Westminster/John Knox Press, 1993.

Olyan, S. M. *Rites and Rank: Hierarchy in Biblical Representations of Cult*. Princeton, N.J.: Princeton University Press, 2000.

Ringe, S. II. *Jesus, Liberation, and the Biblical Jubilee: Images for Ethics and Christology*. Overtures to Biblical Theology. Philadelphia: Fortress Press, 1985.

Wegner, J. R. "Leviticus." In *The Woman's Bible Commentary*, edited by C. A. Newsom and S. H. Ringe, pp. 36–44. Louisville, Ky.: Westminster/John Knox Press, 1992.

Literature Cited

Anderson, G. A. *Sacrifices and Offerings in Ancient Israel: Studies on Their Social and Political Importance*. Harvard Semitic Monographs 41. Atlanta: Scholars Press, 1987.

Auden, W. H. *W. H. Auden: Collected Poems*, edited by E. Mendelson. New York: Vintage International, 1991.

Balentine, S. E. *The Torah's Vision of Worship*. Overtures to Biblical Theology. Minneapolis: Fortress Press, 1999.

Blenkinsopp, J. "The Structure of P." *Catholic Biblical Quarterly* 38 (1976): 275–92.

———. *The Pentateuch: An Introduction to the First Five Books of the Bible*. New York: Doubleday, 1992.

Brueggemann, W. "Texts That Linger, Words That Explode." *Theology Today* 54 (1997): 180–99.

Carroll, M. P. "One More Time: Leviticus Revisited." In *Anthropological Approaches to the Old Testament*, edited by B. Lang, pp. 117–26. Philadelphia: Fortress Press, 1985.

Colenso, J. *Lectures on the Pentateuch and the Moabite Stone*. 2d ed. London: Longmans, Green & Co., 1873.

Cover, R. "Nomos and Narrative." *Harvard Law Review* 97 (1983): 4–68.

Craddock, F. "The Letter to the Hebrews: Introduction, Commentary and Reflections." In *The New Interpreter's Bible*, edited by L. Keck, et al., 12: 1–173. Nashville: Abingdon Press, 1998.

Damrosch, D. "Leviticus." In *The Literary Guide to the Bible*, edited by R. Alter and F. Kermode, 66–77. Cambridge, Mass.: Belknap Press, 1987.

Day, J. *Molech: A God of Human Sacrifice in the Old Testament*. Cambridge: Cambridge University Press, 1989.

Dickinson, E. *The Complete Poems of Emily Dickinson*, edited by T. Johnson. Boston: Little, Brown & Co., 1961.

Douglas, M. "The Forbidden Animals in Leviticus." *Journal for the Study of the Old Testament* 59 (1993): 3–23.

———. "Poetic Structure in Leviticus." In *Pomegranates and Bells. Festschrift Jacob Milgrom*, edited by D. P. Wright, et al., pp. 239–56. Winona Lake, Ind.: Eisenbrauns, 1995.

———. *Leviticus as Literature*. Oxford: Oxford University Press, 1999.

Elliger, K. *Leviticus*. Handbuch zum Alten Testament 4. Tübingen: J. C. B. Mohr (Paul Siebeck), 1966.

Eliot, T. S. *T. S. Eliot: Collected Poems 1909–1962*. New York: Harcourt, Brace & World, 1970.

Englander, N. *For the Relief of Unbearable Urges*. New York: Alfred A. Knopf, 1999.

Fishbane, M. "On Colphons, Textual Criticism and Legal Analogies." *Catholic Biblical Quarterly* 42 (1980): 438–49.

————. *Biblical Interpretation in Ancient Israel*. Oxford: Clarendon Press, 1985.

Fretheim, T. *Exodus*. Intrepretation. A Bible Commentary for Teaching and Preaching. Louisville, Ky.: John Knox Press, 1991.

————. "Creator, Creature, and Co-Creator in Genesis 1–2." *Word and World,* supplemental series 1 (1992): 11–20.

Friedman, R. E. *The Disappearance of God: A Divine Mystery*. Boston: Little, Brown & Co., 1995.

Frost, R. *The Poetry of Robert Frost: The Collected Poems, Complete and Unabridged*, edited by E. C. Lathem. New York: Henry Holt, 1975.

Geertz, C. "Anti Anti-Relativism." In *The Interpretation of Cultures: Selected Essays*. New York: Basic Books, 1973.

————. "Religion as a Cultural System." In *The Interpretation of Cultures: Selected Essays*, pp. 87–125. New York: Basic Books, 1973.

Gerstenberger, E. S. *Leviticus: A Commentary*. Old Testament Library. Louisville, Ky.: Westminster John Knox Press, 1996.

Godwin, G. *Father Melancholy's Daughter*. New York: Avon Books, 1991.

Gorman, F. H., Jr. *The Ideology of Ritual: Space, Time, and Status in the Priestly Theology*. Journal for the Study of the Old Testament, Supplement Series 91. Sheffield: JSOT Press, 1990.

————. "Ritual Studies and Biblical Studies: Assessment of the Past, Prospects for the Future." *Semeia* 67 (1994): 13–36.

————. *Divine Presence and Community: A Commentary on the Book of Leviticus*. International Theological Commentary. Grand Rapids: Wm. B. Eerdmans Publishing Co., 1997.

Grabbe, L. "The Scapegoat Tradition: A Study of Early Jewish Interpretation." *Journal for the Study of Judaism* 18 (1987): 152–67.

Grimes, R. L. *Deeply into the Bone: Re-Inventing Rites of Passage*. Berkeley: University of California Press, 2000.

Gruber, M. I. "Women in the Cult according to the Priestly Code." In *Judaic Perspectives on Ancient Israel*, edited by J. Neusner, et al., pp. 35–48. Philadelphia: Fortress Press, 1987.

Haran, M. *Temples and Temple-Service in Ancient Israel: An Inquiry into the Character of Cult Phenomena and the Historical Setting of the Priestly School*. Oxford: Clarendon Press, 1978.

Hartley, J. E. *Leviticus*. Word Biblical Commentary. Dallas: Word Books, 1992.

Herbert, G. *The Complete English Poems*, edited by J. Tobin. London: Penguin Books, 1991.

Heschel, A. *The Sabbath: Its Meaning for Modern Man.* New York: Farrar, Straus & Co., 1948.

———. *I Asked for Wonder: A Spiritual Anthology, Abraham Joshua Heschel,* edited by S. H. Dresner. New York: Crossroad, 1997.

Joosten, J. *The People and the Land.* Leiden: E. J. Brill, 1996.

Kaiser, W. C. "The Book of Leviticus." In *The New Interpreter's Bible,* edited by L. Keck et al., 4: 985–1191. Nashville: Abingdon Press, 1994.

Kazmierski, C. R. "Evangelist and Leper: A Socio-Cultural Study of Mark 1:40–45." *New Testament Studies* 38 (1992): 37–50.

Klostermann, A. *Der Pentateuch: Beiträge zu einem Verständis und seiner Enstehungsgeschichte.* Leipzig: U. Deichertsche Verlagsbuchhandlung, 1893.

Knierim, R. "The Composition of the Pentateuch." In *Society of Biblical Literature 1985 Seminar Papers,* edited by K. H. Richards, pp. 395–415. Atlanta: Society of Biblical Literature, 1985.

Knohl, I. *The Sanctuary of Silence: The Priestly Torah and the Holiness School.* Minneapolis: Fortress Press, 1995.

Lamb, C. "Jews, Quakers, Scotchmen and Other Imperfect Sympathies," *London Magazine,* 4, no. 20 (August 1821): 152–56.

Levine, B. *The JPS Torah Commentary: Leviticus.* Philadelphia: Jewish Publication Society, 1989.

Lundin, R. *Emily Dickinson and the Art of Belief.* Grand Rapids: Wm. B. Eerdmans Publishing Co., 1998.

Macht, D. I. "A Scientific Appreciation of Lev. 12:1–5." *Journal of Biblical Literature* 52 (1933): 253–60.

Mann, T. *The Book of the Torah: The Narrative Integrity of the Pentateuch.* Atlanta: John Knox Press, 1988.

Meier, S. "House Fungus: Mesopotamia and Israel (Lev. 14:33–53)." *Revue biblique* 96 (1989): 184–92.

Menninger, K. *Whatever Became of Sin?* New York: Hawthorn Books, 1973.

Meyers, C. *The Tabernacle Menorah.* Missoula, Mont.: Scholars Press, 1976.

Milgrom, J. *Cult and Conscience: The Asham and Priestly Doctrine of Repentance.* Studies in Judaism in Late Antiquity 18. Leiden: E. J. Brill, 1976.

———. *Leviticus 1–16.* Anchor Bible 3. New York: Doubleday, 1991.

———. *Leviticus 17–22.* Anchor Bible 3a. New York: Doubleday, 2000.

———. *Leviticus 23–27.* Anchor Bible 3b. New York: Doubleday, 2001.

Miller, P. D. *Deuteronomy*. Interpretation. A Bible Commentary for Teaching and Preaching. Louisville, Ky.: John Knox Press, 1990.

Murray, R. *The Cosmic Covenant*. Heythrop Monographs 7. London: Sheed & Ward, 1992.

Nelson, R. D. *Raising Up a Faithful Priest: Community and Priesthood in Biblical Theology*. Louisville, Ky.: Westminster/John Knox Press, 1993.

Norris, K. *The Cloister Walk*. New York: Riverhead Books, 1996.

North, R. *The Biblical Jubilee . . . after Fifty Years*. Analecta Biblica 145. Roma: Editrice Pontifico Istituto Biblico, 2000.

Noth, M. *Leviticus*. Old Testament Library. Philadelphia: Westminster Press, 1965.

Nouwen, H. *The Wounded Healer: Ministry in Contemporary Society*. Garden City, N.Y.: Image Books, 1979.

Plaskow, J. *Standing Again at Sinai: Judaism from a Feminist Perspective*. San Francisco: Harper & Row, 1990.

Putnam, R. *Bowling Alone: The Collapse and Revival of American Community*. New York: Simon & Schuster, 2000.

Pritchard, J. B. ed. *Ancient Near Eastern Texts Relating to the Old Testament*. 3d ed. Princeton, N.J.: Princeton University Press, 1969.

Rendtorff, R. *Text and Concept in Leviticus 1:1–9: A Case in Exegetical Method*. Forschung zum Alten Testament 2. Tübingen: J. C. B. Mohr (Paul Siebeck), 1992.

Rilke, R. "Just as the Winged Energy of Delight." In *The Rag and Bone Shop of the Heart*, edited by R. Bly et al. New York: Harper Perennial, 1993.

Sarna, N. *The JPS Torah Commentary: Genesis*. Philadelphia: Jewish Publication Society, 1989.

Schwartz, B. J. "The Prohibitions concerning the 'Eating' of Blood in Leviticus 17." In *Priesthood and Cult in Ancient Israel*, edited by G. Anderson and S. Olyan, pp. 34–66. Journal for the Study of the Old Testament, Supplement Series 125. Sheffield: JSOT Press, 1991.

Shaffer, P. *Amadeus*. New York: Signet, 1984.

Sontag, S. "The Aesthetics of Silence." In *A Susan Sontag Reader*, pp. 181–204. New York: Farrar, Straus & Giroux, 1989.

Steiner, G. *No Passion Spent: Essays 1978–1995*. New Haven, Conn., and London: Yale University Press, 1996.

Stern, P. *The Biblical Herem: A Window on Israel's Religious Experience*. Atlanta: Scholars Press, 1991.

Thomas, R. S. *Poems of R. S. Thomas*. Fayetteville: University of Arkansas Press, 1985.

Updike, J. "At War with My Skin." In *Self-Consciousness: Memoirs*, pp. 42–78. New York: Alfred A. Knopf, 1989.

Watts, J. W. "The Rhetorical Strategy in the Composition of the Pentateuch." *Journal for the Study of the Old Testament* 68 (1995): 3–22.

Wellhausen, J. *Prolegomena to the History of Ancient Israel*. 1878. Reprint, Gloucester: Peter Smith, 1973.

Wenham, G. J. *The Book of Leviticus*. New International Commentary on the Old Testament. Grand Rapids: Wm. B. Eerdmans Publishing Co., 1979.

Whitekettle, R. "Leviticus 15.18 Reconsidered: Chiasm, Spatial Structure and the Body." *Journal for the Study of the Old Testament* 49 (1991): 31–45.

Wieseltier, L. *Kaddish*. New York: Alfred A. Knopf, 1998.

Wood, J. *The Unbroken Estate: Essays on Literature and Belief*. New York: Random House, 1999.

Wright, D. P. *The Disposal of Impurity: Elimination Rites in the Bible and in Hittite and Mesopotamian Literature*. Society of Biblical Literature Dissertation Series 101. Atlanta: Scholars Press, 1987.

———. "Azazel." *Anchor Bible Dictionary, I*, edited by D. N. Friedman, et al., pp. 536–37. New York: Doubleday, 1992.

Yeats, W. B. *The Collected Poems of William Butler Yeats*, edited by R. J. Finneran. Rev. 2d ed. New York: Scribner Paperback Poetry, 1996.